ADVANCED RECOVERY

12 Keys *to* Long-Term Sobriety

Mark Denison, D.Min.

LUCIDBOOKS

TABLE OF CONTENTS

INTRODUCTION

I begin by looking back at a memorable moment in my recovery journey. This was no ordinary 12-Step meeting. The fellowship I have attended for the past nine years holds a special place in my personal recovery. Every week's meeting is special. But this particular week was *extra special*. Why? Because my good friend "Bob" received his ten-year chip at this meeting. I was honored to pass out the chips that night, so I was blessed to give Bob his chip, marking a decade of complete sexual sobriety.

What makes Bob's recovery especially noteworthy is not the length of his sobriety, but the depth of his sobriety. Early in recovery, I would have viewed anyone with ten years of sobriety as a unicorn from another planet. I couldn't imagine having one month of sobriety, let alone a year. *But ten years?* Impossible.

If you are early in your recovery, congratulations! You have already taken the most important step by getting started. Recovery is all about *direction*, not *destination*. (No one ever arrives.) And you are heading in the right direction by reading this book. Now, it is time to put some tools in your hands that will take you further, higher, and deeper. It's time to discover the way to advanced recovery.

Let's start with a question I get a lot: "At what length of sobriety do most people stay sober?" I'm a little apprehensive in answering this question because the length of sobriety is just one way of measuring recovery. Fortunately, some research (not a lot of research) has been done on this subject. Although we know of no such research specific to sexual addiction, for alcohol addiction, the sobriety target seems to be two years. Research indicates that among those who achieve one year of sobriety, just eighteen percent maintain their sobriety to year two. But among those who are sober for two years, sixty percent maintain their sobriety for the rest of their lives.[1]

What is it about two years? I have a theory. For the first year or so, we might be able to "white-knuckle" it or compartmentalize recovery. By that I mean we go to meetings, participate in therapy, and work the 12 Steps. We are committed to a *program*. But we are not yet committed to a *lifestyle*. It is one thing to check off the boxes, especially on the heels of having our addiction discovered by a loved one. We are desperate to keep our family together, to keep our job, and to keep our reputation. But we may not be committed to keeping our recovery. Initially, we are reacting to what has happened rather than being proactive with an eye on the future.

But to do something for two years requires a true lifestyle commitment. Dr. Milton Magness writes, "Recovery must be a lifestyle that permeates every part of life. Every decision a person makes should be with an awareness of its effect on recovery."[2] It often takes two or more years for the addict to arrive at this point in their recovery.

The first two years of sobriety are often referred to as the abstinence stage. It is during this time in early recovery that the addict is finding their footing in recovery. The addict is adopting the following practices:[3]

- Accepts that they have an addiction
- Practices honesty
- Develops coping skills to deal with their addiction
- Becomes active in self-help groups
- Practices self-care and learns to say no
- Understands the stages of relapse

All these practices are critical to advanced recovery. Obviously, the abstinence stage is a necessary part in one's journey to long-term sobriety. It is the launching pad for recovery. Without it, the rocket can't lift off.

We might think of advanced recovery as the stage in which the rocket achieves orbit. And that is the purpose of this book—to help you achieve orbit with your recovery. My prayer is that you will learn and practice tools that will serve you well for the rest of your life. But as you go into this process, do so with one eye on the tools and the other eye on the stories in the final chapter where you will find real-life advice from others who have been where you want to be. In the final chapter, you will meet brave friends who share their stories of what worked (and didn't work) in their recovery journeys.

Before we proceed, let me touch on two things:

- **What this book is not.** If you flip through the following chapters with the intent of learning a system that will never fail you, prepare to be disappointed. I will not be offering a one-size-fits-all approach to long-term recovery. Your recovery is *your* recovery. While certain principles are universal in successful recovery, the specifics of your plan will be unique to you, your triggers, past trauma, and dozens of other factors. Furthermore, none of us is static in our recovery, even if we want to be. Our circumstances evolve, our physiology changes, and our settings will inevitably alter from time to time. The specifics of my recovery plan cannot be yours. Develop your own plan, realizing that this book is only a guide.

  When I began offering my 90-Day Recovery Program several years ago, I designed a specific plan for each client, based on dozens of factors. I did this because I understood the uniqueness of each person and their struggles. Over time, it became impossible to create customized plans, so I wrote the *90-Day Recovery Guide* to enable people to create their own unique plans. Part of me wishes I could write a separate *90-Day Recovery Guide* for each person, because we are all different. One size does not fit all.

- **What this book is.** This book is intended to provide general guidelines that will foster sobriety beyond two years. If you use this book to learn a few principles that you find helpful, I will have met my goal. Each chapter offers valuable insights that you need to incorporate into your recovery program. But the greatest values this book offers are the personal insights and stories from people who have walked where you want to walk. Don't rush through the stories in the final chapter. In fact, you might want to start there.

Here are just a few of the subjects we tackle in the following pages:

- Relapse prevention
- Staying desperate
- Best habits
- The power of secrets
- Comparison trap
- Stages of recovery
- The silent assassin
- The man code
- Spiritual connection
- Helping others
- Five deadly signs
- Substitute addictions

Let's dive in. If you are ready for recovery that lasts, prepare for a great ride. The *rest* of your recovery will be the *best* of your recovery!

Chapter 1

RELAPSE PREVENTION

It seems that any discussion of advanced recovery should logically begin with a discussion of relapse prevention. If we don't avoid relapse, our recovery is no longer successful. That should be pretty obvious. But we need to start here because the day we take our sobriety for granted is the day we put it at risk. From Day 1, we need to focus on relapse prevention. Various studies indicate that addicts relapse at rates of sixty-five to seventy percent.[1] None of us should ever take our recovery for granted.

Let's begin with a simple definition. What, exactly, is relapse prevention? Drs. Alan Marlatt and William George, professors of psychology at the University of Washington, offer a helpful definition. "Relapse prevention is a self-control program designed to teach individuals who are trying to change their behavior."[2] They state the goal as one of anticipation, with a focus on recognition of potential relapse well before it happens, accompanied with a plan to avoid its clutches.

CAN YOU BE IN RECOVERY AND NOT BE SOBER?

We must understand the distinction between sobriety and recovery. In simple terms, to be sober means you are no longer engaging in addictive behaviors. You have stopped acting out. But recovery is more than that. Sobriety is about what you stop; recovery is about what you start. That leads to a question I hear a lot.

> *Can a person be sober and not be in recovery?*
> The short answer is yes. The long answer is yes. It's not complicated. As they say in AA, "Sober is not well." Giving up your addiction does not mean you are well. Sobriety is a great step, but it's only the first step. Quitting the addictive behavior is huge, but what you do next is epic. And that leads to a question I have begun asking men and women in the recovery community.

> *Can a person be in recovery and not be sober?*
> The apparent answer is no. If you lose your sobriety, you are no longer in recovery, right? I think that response is too simplistic. I would argue that one bad day (relapse) does not erase a good week, month, year, or decade. You can lose your sobriety in a moment—any of us can. But that does not negate the good recovery work you have done. Any relapse certainly exposes a hole in your recovery work, but it does not invalidate the solid progress you have made.

REMEMBER THE DITCH

One of the things I tell people in recovery all the time is that no matter how far you travel the road of recovery, the ditch is still there, on either side of the road. We never progress so far in our recovery that the enemy says, "Oh well! I'll leave them alone; they're beyond temptation!" In fact, the enemy has an even greater commitment to bringing you down if you have five or ten years of sobriety.

Let's unsettle the apple cart just a bit. I'm going to tell you the most controversial thing I ever say in recovery. It is a simple statement I make to my wife. And when I tell people this, angry emails and shock come from all corners. Here it is: "I'm not saying I'll never relapse, but I am saying it won't happen today."

I'm done with making pronouncements of what I will or won't do for the rest of my life. No more lifetime guarantees. And yet, I know this probably drives you nuts to read. Save your angry responses; I've already heard them.

"How can you say you might act out again?"
"Your wife deserves a lifetime guarantee."
"You're just giving yourself a pass to act out again."

No, actually, I'm giving myself a pass to focus on the only way any of us can stay sober:

One
Day
At
A
Time

I make no promises to others beyond the promises God has made to me. And he has not promised me another day beyond this one. I can only be sober today. I can't be sober tomorrow, because tomorrow never comes. When the next "today" comes, I'll do then what I did this morning. I will promise God and myself that I won't act out today.

If you are into making long-term guarantees, get over yourself! Before you ever got sober, how many times did you promise yourself, your God, your spouse, and your newspaper man, "I'm done! No more! I'll never act out again!" Raise your hand if the number is less than one million. We have all made that "never again" promise, only to break it. I have learned that life can only be lived one day at a time. Each morning, I remind myself that the ditch hasn't gone anywhere overnight. It is still just as close to Recovery Lane as it was the day I got sober.

GETTING OVER THE HUMP

Relapse is far too common. Dr. Thomas Brandon and his colleagues concluded that "most psychological disorders and problem behaviors are characterized by very high rates of post remittance relapse."[3] I will resist the temptation to cite statistics on relapse rates because research studies are all over the map, and much depends on the kind of addiction we are talking about. Within the two broad categories of addictions—substance and behavioral—there is a wide spectrum of relapse rates.

While it's true that the ditch is still just as close, no matter how far you go, something else is also true. Addicts with ten years of sobriety experience relapse far less often than those who are new to recovery. So, when do we "get over the hump"? By that, I am asking when can an addict know that they have reached a point in their recovery when relapse is unlikely? *My experience says one year.*

I have attended over 1,000 recovery meetings and led about as many through our ministry, There's Still Hope. While I have not taken notes on the subject, my personal observation is that once a person gets to about one year of total sobriety, they are less likely to experience relapse. Or said another way, half of all addicts I have observed who reached one year of sobriety stayed sober, while the other half suffered relapse. *My study says two years.*

Not much research has been conducted on relapse rates. If you find ten research projects on the subject, you will likely get ten different opinions and results. Again, much depends on the specific addiction, but the closest thing to a consensus that I can come up with is two years. The studies I have reviewed indicate that, on average, when a person reaches two years of sobriety, their odds of "making it" reach fifty percent.

PROCESS VERSUS EVENT

At most recovery meetings, you will hear a confession like this: "I relapsed two nights ago." Of course, that person is saying that two nights ago, they had a drink, viewed pornography, or indulged in some other addiction. But if I've learned anything about addiction, it is this: *Relapse is a process, not an event.*

My mentor, Dr. Milton Magness, writes, "Relapse is the end result of a gradual process that usually begins weeks or even months before you act out."[4] That is why so many addicts act out before making a call to a trusted friend in recovery. Their thinking is, "I'll call Charlie before it goes too far." But it has already gone too far. Missed meetings, missed calls, slow Step work, the wrong crowd, unguarded thoughts—these are all pieces in the relapse puzzle.

Would you think you could jump off a tall building and not get hurt? Well, that's exactly what you are doing when you dabble around the edges of relapse, thinking you won't get burned. Relapse is the predictable outcome of—I'll say it again—missed meetings, missed calls, slow Step work, the wrong crowd, and unguarded thoughts.

In their outstanding book, *Counseling for Relapse Prevention*, T. T. Gorski and M. Miller write, "The key to relapse prevention is to understand that relapse happens gradually. It begins weeks and sometimes months before an individual picks up a drink or drug."[5] Notice a trend in scholarship here? If you read about the process of relapse from multiple authors, you will find these words popping up over and over: "Relapse begins weeks, even months" before the act itself. Sadly, relapse is not relegated to those who simply attend 12-Step meetings or other meetings that are convenient and require little of the participant.

Relapse is also common among men and women who have attended in-house treatment centers. Dr. Thomas Brandon and his colleagues at the University of South Florida have provided extensive research on the prevalence of relapse among addicts who have successfully completed recovery programs, including those offered by in-house treatment centers. They cite two decades of studies, which led to "important advances in the conceptualization of relapse." They found that relapse is generally a long process and that it is a plague that exempts no treatment paradigm.[6]

This is an important lesson for long-term recovery. Rather than point to the event when we take our "drink," we must shift our focus to the little things early in the process. The slippery slope begins somewhere; it is critical to recognize that "somewhere." You need to identify the things that can creep into your recovery work, setting you up for a fall. That fall may not come today, this week, or even this month. But if you aren't diligent in your recovery work, it will come.

STAGES OF RELAPSE

Because relapse is a process and not an event, we need to recognize the stages of relapse. A model used by various recovery programs has become the standard most practitioners use. The process of relapse includes the following stages.[7]

Emotional Relapse

This initial stage of relapse refers to the potential emotions and behaviors that have influenced a past relapse. In this stage, the individual is not thinking about using, but they may be isolating themselves, may be avoiding meetings, may not be sharing during meetings, or may be focusing on themselves.

Mental Relapse

The second stage of relapse refers to the internal war that the individual faces. During this stage, the individual may start to think about using, begin to remember the people and places that were associated with past use, and may even begin to look for relapse opportunities.

Physical Relapse

The final stage of relapse occurs when someone acts out. At this stage, a single use of the drug or behavior may lead to a lasting slide away from sobriety if not dealt with immediately. Whether the addict has a momentary "slip" or dives into the depths of their addiction, they must begin to rebuild their sobriety at once.

WARNING SIGNS

Relapse doesn't just happen. It is the predictable outcome of something you've been doing or failing to do. When someone drops out of one of my meetings, I am seldom surprised. The warning signs are almost always evident. While we are all different, there are some common signs we need to look for—in ourselves and others. Here are just a few examples.

- Bottling up emotions
- Isolation
- Missed meetings
- Not sharing in meetings
- Focusing on the problems of others, not ourselves
- Poor eating habits
- Sleep disturbances
- Poor self-care
- Cravings
- Thinking about past acting out partners
- Daydreaming about our addiction

Do you see any of these signs in your own life right now? You will never work your recovery perfectly; no one does. But you need to recognize the signs of real trouble. I suggest that if three or more of the items listed above apply to you, you may be in real trouble.

CHANGE THINGS UP

I'm a systems person. And I am a planner. That means I want a once-and-forever program of recovery. I want to get in the same old car, drive the same old route to the same old meeting, where we read the same old stuff, sit in the same old chairs, and I have the same old sponsor. "Find the perfect plan; then stick to it!" we tell ourselves. That sounds great. There is just one problem: *What worked before no longer does.*

Let me say it like this: what it took to get you sober will not keep you sober. Otherwise, we would all need a fresh "discovery" by our husband or wife. I didn't choose recovery; recovery chose me. I didn't have a choice. If I wanted to stay married, if I wanted to keep my ministry, if I wanted to get off the crazy train, I had to get sober. Period.

So, I did that. I joined a certain 12-Step group. I saw a certain therapist. I read a certain book. And they all helped to get me sober. But I've moved on—about 1,000 miles, to be exact. I found a new group, a new therapist, and new books. I have changed groups from time to time. And counselors. And sponsors. Why? Because the things that *got* me sober no longer *keep* me sober. I have learned to adapt. I still have struggles, several years into sobriety, but not the same struggles that I had ten years ago.

On November 5, 2022, everything changed for me. At seven o'clock that evening, I suffered a heart attack. With blood cut off to the right side of my heart, I needed a stint. But things got worse. My doctors discovered that I had five major blockages in my arteries. We suddenly went from one stint to five heart bypasses. So, I went under the knife. My five-bypass open-heart surgery changed everything—the way I eat, exercise, and view life.

In the first days after surgery, my challenge was to get out of the hospital bed each day and take a few steps. Then the challenge was to go home and work with a therapist who came in several times a week. Then I progressed to a cardiac rehab center. Now, I work out on my own. As of this writing, I have walked a minimum of 10,000 steps every day—without a miss—since January 1, 2023.

Those 10,000 steps are like my daily recovery disciplines. There are certain things I do consistently. But the other things I have changed up in my exercise routine—e.g., weights, resistance bands, and so on—are like the various recovery tools I have added (or subtracted) to my regular routine. What got me sober won't keep me sober. The same is true for you.

THE 90-PERCENT PRINCIPLE

One of the great things about recovery is the clever statements you can find in 12-Step books and other literature. I'm sure you've heard these:

> *Take it one day at a time.*
> *The program works if you work it.*
> *It's about progress, not perfection.*
> *Let go and let God.*
> *You're as sick as your secrets.*
> *One is too many and a thousand is never enough.*

These are all powerful truisms. Any good recovery program will wear you out with such repetitious statements. Each is worthy of memorization, because they represent truth. But if I could preach one sermon on recovery, the title would be: "If You Are 90 Percent In, You are 100 Percent Out."

A failure to embrace this principle is at the root of virtually every relapse. Relapse is the predictable outcome of a series of bad decisions. And those bad decisions are the result of not working your recovery program to the full extent that it deserves. Let me be clear. Recovery cannot be a hobby; it must be a lifestyle.

The difference between winning and losing is not much. Let me illustrate the best way I know how—with a sports analogy. As of this writing, the world record holder for the one-mile run is Hicham El Guerrouj of Morocco, with a time of 3:43.13. He set that record on July 7, 1999.

For the sake of comparison, the current high school record holder for the mile run is Rheinhardt Harrison, from my home state of Florida, who ran the mile in 4:01.34 in 2020. The difference between the world record and the run of this high school student is about 18 seconds. That is a difference of less than ten percent.

Do you see where I'm going with this? A fifteen-year-old sophomore in high school can run ninety percent as fast as the fastest man in history. But he's not close to the world record. The same is true in recovery. If you are ninety percent sober, you aren't sober. If you give ninety percent effort, you don't have a chance. Of course, none of us does recovery perfectly. But to be successful, we must make recovery a lifestyle, not a hobby.

If you are 90 percent in, you are 100 percent out.

PAIN VERSUS PLEASURE

Every person I've ever known who did successful, lasting recovery work did so for one foundational reason. They will say they got into recovery because of a spiritual revelation or some moral awakening, but it always boils down to this: *The pain became greater than the pleasure.*

For most of us, this involved a discovery. Our husband or wife caught us "doing it," so we suddenly decided to seek help. Under the threat of divorce, losing our kids, or a health crisis, we turned to recovery. And that's okay. But it is important to remember that what it takes to get us into recovery is not enough to keep us there. Patrick Carnes writes, "A moment comes for every addict when the consequences are so great or the pain is so bad that the addict admits life is out of control because of his or her behavior."[8]

This has a practical application for those of us who are working with others in their recovery. Sometimes, we need to let them fall. God often allows what he hates (the fall) in order to accomplish what he loves (restoration). Said another way, whatever God allows, he redeems. He is more than willing to allow the pain that turns us back to him. This works in relapse prevention as well as initial recovery. I often hear someone say, "The thing keeping me sober is the fear of losing my wife." In some cases, the addict agrees to a series of clinical disclosures with polygraphs to prove that they are no longer acting out. The fear of a failed polygraph becomes greater than the pleasure of the addiction, so they don't do it.

SELF-MOTIVATED

I recently polled my Freedom Groups with this question: How many of you got into recovery without first being discovered by someone? Across my ten groups, only five percent raised their hands. Being discovered is what got most of us (including me) into recovery. We were caught by a spouse, son or daughter, boss, or friend. Recovery was not a choice, but a decree. We were faced with two options: get sober or hit the road.

Until the pain becomes greater than the pleasure, we generally choose the pleasure. We take what we want *now* over what we want *most*. But discovery catapults us into a whole new way of life. But most of us eventually hit a ceiling. Our recovery rises to a certain level, but no higher. Eventually, we stall out.

What happened? We learn that threats (divorce, job loss, health risks) are not enough to keep us on the right path. We learn that blaming our mother, father, brother, sister, priest, pastor, teacher, coach, society, church, and even God can only take us so far. We learn this important truth: *Until I take ownership for my addiction, I won't take responsibility for my recovery.*

At some point, the addict must own their recovery. In their work on relapse prevention, Marlatt and George address this head-on. "One important difference between initial treatment procedures and those designed to enhance maintenance effects over time is that the former techniques are usually administered to the client by the therapist, whereas maintenance procedures are often self-administered by the client."[9]

Marlatt and George contend that initial recovery work is heavily reliant on therapy and other professional guidance. But as we grow in our recovery, we must take full responsibility for our sobriety and progress. Factors such as the threat of losing it all and outside expertise only carry us so far. If we are not committed to sobriety for the sake of sobriety, it won't stick. And that motivation must come from within. That's why I preach, "Stay desperate!" to my clients and groups. In fact, I would argue that if you are only staying sober for someone else, you aren't really sober.

DIG DEEP

Any athlete understands this principle. There comes a time in any sport when you must find that extra level, dig deep, and unleash an unseen force from within. As Jesus taught, we learn to keep asking, keep knocking, and keep seeking (Matthew 7:7).

Marlatt and George contend that any successful relapse prevention effort must include "a psychoeducational program that combines behavioral training procedures with cognitive intervention techniques."[11] In other words, successful relapse prevention addresses both behavioral modification and underlying issues. This is the very definition of "digging deep." Recovery that works must be worked. It requires a shovel. We must be willing to do the hard work of self-analysis and then respond accordingly.

How does this work on a practical level? Digging deep often includes the following:

- Internal family systems therapy
- Intensive outpatient programs
- Family therapy
- Personal coaching
- Residential inpatient treatment
- Narrative exposure therapy
- PTSD treatment
- Psychotherapy
- 12-Step work
- EMDR therapy
- Personal retreat
- Cognitive behavioral therapy
- Comprehensive resource model

Until you understand the *why* of your addiction, you will struggle with the *how*. Understanding why you do what you do is critical to mapping a new course going forward. When you find yourself in quicksand, what you need is a rope. But you also need to figure out how you fell into the quicksand in the first place, in order to stay out in the future.

THREE TECHNIQUES THAT WORK

Sometimes, relapse prevention comes down to simply doing the next right thing. It's about learning the tools that will equip you to stay sober when faced with the greatest challenge to give in. Does it get easier to stay sober with every passing year? Generally speaking, yes. But remember, the ditch doesn't go away just because we have put together a period of lengthy sobriety. So, let's unpack some very simple strategies for staying sober in the moment.

The 20-Minute Miracle

This is my favorite tool. Research suggests that the dopamine rush that entices us to take the next hit will generally run its course in about twenty minutes. If your drug is alcohol, you will notice that when you see someone else take a drink, you will often experience a spike in your craving for alcohol. But if you get out of the bar, go to another room, or change the channel, this "rush" will pass in about twenty minutes. If you are a sex addict, you know what it is to experience moments of sexual fantasy. But this also passes in about twenty minutes. What do you do? For about twenty minutes, go for a walk, do some exercise, make a few calls, read a book, or engage in some other healthy activity until the urge passes.

The End Game

I learned this one from my sponsor several years ago. A strong temptation came upon me, and I really wanted to act on that temptation in the moment. So, I called my sponsor. He said something like this: "Go ahead. Act out. But before you do, think about the end game. Think about what it will be to act out, take your next polygraph, hurt your wife, reset your sobriety date, break years of trust, and step into shame. If you think it's really worth it, go for it!" Of course, I didn't. I have never met an addict who said, "I was tempted to act out, and I did. And I'm really glad I gave in to my addiction. It has really worked out well for me." Nope, that never happens. So, the next time you are tempted to do something stupid, remember the end game.

Thought Replacement

There is a cycle to our acting out. Without going into highly academic concepts and terminology, I would simply say that this is how the relapse cycle happens:

- I think it.
- I plan it.
- I do it.
- I hate it.
- I cover it.
- I do it again.

The key is to arrest the relapse process between "I think it" and "I plan it." There will be moments when you are triggered by an unwanted thought, image, or memory. When that happens, you may not have time or opportunity to call your sponsor, go for a walk, or get to a meeting. So, what do you do? Think about something else. I always have a plan for those times when my mind is bombarded with temptation. I immediately choose to concentrate on something else. I replace the addictive thoughts with productive thoughts.

A RELAPSE PLAN

I'm pretty sure you won't find this suggestion anywhere else: *create a relapse plan*. By that, I obviously don't mean to have a plan to relapse. What I mean is that you need a plan for how to handle your next relapse, should you have one.

Such a plan serves two purposes. First, it will help to keep you motivated to not have a relapse. Knowing that it will cost you something goes a long way toward keeping you in a good place. Second, this will give your spouse or accountability partner greater confidence in your sobriety.

This is my relapse plan. If I relapse, I will do the following:

- Tell my sponsor within twenty-four minutes.
- Tell my wife within twenty-four hours.

- See my therapist within forty-eight hours.
- Schedule a new polygraph so my wife can know she knows everything.
- Tell my 12-Step group.
- Tell my Freedom Groups.
- Back away from my ministry, at least temporarily.

A relapse plan is like an evacuation plan. I live in the state that has been hit by more hurricanes than any other state in America. In my nine years here, my area has been affected by three hurricanes. None of them hit us directly, but we are prepared for the unlikely event that a hurricane will happen one day. We know how to board up, when to leave, and where to go. We don't expect it to happen, but we'd be crazy to not be prepared, just in case.

You don't ever have to relapse. Let's pray that you don't. Putting together a simple relapse plan will go a long way toward securing your sobriety. Create your own plan today.

DISCUSSION QUESTIONS

1. When was your last relapse? How did it happen? What did you learn from that?

2. What is the difference between sobriety and recovery?

3. Can you be sober and not be in recovery? Can you be in recovery and not be sober?

4. If you have another relapse, how will it likely happen?

5. What is the best thing you can do to avoid a future relapse?

6. What are the main components of your recovery plan?

7. Do you have a relapse plan? If so, what does your plan include?

8. How do you stay self-motivated to maintain your sobriety?

Chapter 2

DELIVERANCE OR PERSEVERANCE?

" I am free!"

With those three words, my friend announced to our recovery group that he no longer had need for our services. God had healed him the night before, at a special service at his church. He had no need for further recovery work, therapy, Step work, recovery materials, groups—or us.

He was free! Praise God!

Fast-forward a few weeks, and my friend was back in group. Why? Because he had relapsed. "But I thought he was free," many of us said to ourselves. I mean, he had been prayed over, repented, and sought God with all his heart. God is in the healing business, isn't he? So how was relapse even possible? This is when I told my friend a very inconvenient truth: *Freedom is not a condition as much as it is a choice.*

I'm not saying God can't remove our addictions. I'm just saying it hasn't happened for me. And I'm so glad it hasn't! You see, I call my addiction "God's unwanted gift." Why? Because it keeps me grounded, surrendered, and connected. I can't imagine living life without it.

Don't misunderstand. I'm not saying God cannot remove the impulses. I'm not saying he *never* takes away the addiction. What I am saying is that he *rarely* takes away the addiction—even though he could, every time.

That's where persistence comes in. For those of us who are committed to a lifetime of recovery, there is no greater attribute than persistence. Dr. Philip Tate, with SMART Recovery, writes, "Persistence is the most important value in recovery."[1]

There is a simple reason we all need persistence: *we all fall from time to time.* Don't confuse *fall* with *failure.* Or *relapse.* Remember, recovery is all about progress, not perfection. Even those with ten or twenty years of unbroken sobriety stumble. Whether with our thought lives, random words we speak, or excessive time on social media, we all want a do-over from time to time. But we stay in the battle. We don't give up.

I have a friend who runs half marathons regularly. I asked him how he got started in this insane physical activity. He explained that he was recruited for the track team when he was in high school, even though he had never been a competitive runner. In his first race, he finished in last place. That day, he said to himself, "I'll never finish in last place again." And he never has.

That's how we do successful recovery. Endurance athlete turned science writer, Christopher Bergland says, "Perseverance separates the winners from the losers in life."[2] Bergland didn't say the difference was talent or athleticism. He said *perseverance.* I love the way Henry Ford said it: "Failure is only the opportunity to begin again, this time more intelligently." [3]

THEOLOGICAL PERSPECTIVE

Throughout the Gospels, we see Jesus healing multitudes of people in three basic ways. Sometimes, he heals immediately; other times, he heals gradually or eternally. The same is true with addiction. When we move into advanced recovery, our recovery simply shifts into another gear. The people I know who have done the best with long-term sobriety are the ones who know how to persevere.

Professor Angela Duckworth conducted an extensive survey of 300 achievers for her book, *Grit: The Power of Passion and Perseverance*. She discovered that every one of those 300 successful men and women cited perseverance as one of the primary keys to their success, above talent or intelligence.[4]

Perseverance is a gift from God. While most of us are praying for God to take away the disease, God is equipping us to live with the disease. Like Paul, I begged God to remove my "thorn in the flesh" repeatedly. My view was that if God would just remove the compulsions, I could live a free and victorious life. But I have learned that for me, that would have been the worst thing God could have done (or he would have done it). I surrender to my Higher Power, not *despite* my addiction, but *because* of it.

The Bible has a lot to say about perseverance.

Look to the LORD and his strength; seek his face always.
—1 Chronicles 16:11

Brothers and sisters, I do not consider myself yet to have taken hold of it. But one thing I do: Forgetting what is behind and straining toward what is ahead, I press on toward the goal to win the prize for which God has called me heavenward in Christ Jesus.
—Philippians 3:13–14

We have come to share in Christ, if indeed we hold our original conviction firmly to the very end.
—Hebrews 3:14

Fixing our eyes on Jesus, the pioneer and perfecter of faith. For the joy set before him he endured the cross, scorning its shame, and sat down at the right hand of the throne of God.
—Hebrews 12:2

You will be hated by everyone because of me, but the one who stands firm to the end will be saved.

—Matthew 10:22

Consider it pure joy, my brothers and sisters, whenever you face trials of many kinds.

—James 1:2

DAILY WORK

Perseverance is a gift. But it is also a choice. And the result of our daily habits. The key word is *daily*. It is what we do *daily* that pays the most dividends in long-term recovery. LifeRecoveryGroups.com suggests ten steps in perseverance. One of those is to take it one step at a time. They write:

> If you ask someone who is in recovery from an addiction what the secret to their success is, they might tell you it was to take it one day at a time. They focus on the present moment—not the past or the future. Sometimes, it is one minute at a time, which will eventually become your lifetime.[5]

Leah Marone, a psychotherapist and corporate wellness consultant, agrees. She writes, "People are not born with high levels of resilience. It is something they earn through practice and consistency."[6] Let that sink in for a minute. Perseverance is *earned*. The resilience that is necessary for lasting sobriety comes with effort. It is earned, an achievement reserved for those willing to put in the time and effort.

I would never put myself out there as the ultimate example for how to do recovery, but I have learned a few things over the years as I surrounded myself with the right people. Using what I gleaned from my mentors, sponsors, and fellow servants—and with much trial and error—my daily routine has evolved. And this matters, because the key to my sobriety today isn't what I did last year. It's what I did last night.

So let me share my recovery routine with you. Don't copy this; learn from this.

Daily Routine
- Serenity Prayer
- 3rd Step Prayer
- 7th Step Prayer
- ACTS Prayer
- Morning devotional
- One page of recovery reading
- Bible reading—one chapter of Scripture before bed

Weekly Routine
- 12-Step meeting
- Work with sponsees

Monthly Routine
- Recovery Day

Annual Routine
- Personal retreat

THE KEY IS PASSION

In every recovery meeting every week, a dear friend would close with these words: "Stay thirsty, my friends." What he understood was that without passion, we're toast. We don't have a chance. But it's hard to stay in desperation mode after several years of successful recovery. I learned a hard lesson several years ago: *recovery leaks.*

We will not maintain lasting sobriety apart from passion. Passion keeps us at the task because it overrides negative influences. We need to pray for passion. Strive for passion. Beg for passion. Or as my friend says, "Stay thirsty." You can't find passion in a bottle. Thomas Edison reminded those around him that genius was ten percent inspiration and ninety percent perspiration.

How do you find passion? Better yet, how do you maintain passion? Recovery expert James Haggerty has the answer. Writing for *Sober Living*, he cites several ways to maintain the passion that secures our freedom.[7]

- Start with things you already enjoy doing.
- Brainstorm to identify new areas of passion.
- Learn from the stories of others.
- Take it slowly.
- Practice your passion; don't quit too easily.

If you lack passion for your recovery, ask for that passion, seek that passion, strive for that passion. Do whatever it takes to get your passion back. As my friend would say, "Stay thirsty, my friends."

HOW TO RESIST

Sometimes, persevering in our recovery is simply a matter of resisting the urge to act out. The good news is that the longer you resist, the easier it gets. The trick is not to get long-term sobriety, but to get short-term sobriety day by day, week by week, and month by month. You can do this by resisting the temptation to give in. But how do you do that? Patrick Carnes offers eight strategies for resisting the temptation to return to our addictions.[8]

1. **Develop spiritual challenges.** All recovery is spiritual recovery. Seven of the 12 Steps refer to our Higher Power. To resist temptation, we must dig deeper into our spiritual connection. That is where we tap our power source.

2. **Decode your feelings.** By this, Carnes means that you should listen to your emotions. Let them speak to you. Ask yourself why you are feeling what you're feeling. Don't hesitate to access professional help in processing your feelings.

3. **Avoid triggers.** Don't go looking for trouble. Enough temptation will find you without you looking for it. Revisit your middle circle to make sure you are not engaging in those activities that set you up for trouble.

4. **Forgive yourself for slips.** Never forget the difference between guilt and shame. Guilt says you have done something wrong. Shame says you're just a bad person, beyond the reach of grace. When you understand that God has forgiven you, you can begin to forgive yourself.

5. **Work on nurturing yourself.** Self-care is one of the most forgotten aspects of recovery. God doesn't want you to live like a monk (unless he's called you to be a monk). I suggest you do a Recovery Day once a month, focusing on self-care and spiritual connection.

6. **Avoid secrets.** Addiction cripples, but secrets kill. Said another way, you are only as healthy as your secrets. You must bring your struggles to the light. That is the only place healing takes place.

7. **Find alternative passions.** Not all passions are bad. Find healthy activities that are fun. Do things that are healthy. Get a new hobby. The reason we get into trouble is that we don't get into anything else first.

8. **Acknowledge your choice.** No one ever made you act out. Every relapse is a choice you don't have to make. The Bible is clear. With every temptation, God provides a way to escape, if we really want to escape (1 Corinthians 10:13).

THE IMPORTANCE OF THERAPY

Everyone needs to be in therapy at some point. I suggest you have at least one therapist on file, who you see at least occasionally. In fact, I suggest you have two. Think of it like this. You probably have a general care doctor. You see him or her for annual physicals or whenever you are ill. But you don't expect that doctor to perform open-heart surgery. You go to a specialist for that. And the older you get, the more specialists you will have. At least that's been my experience!

The same should be true with therapy. For example, I have a licensed counselor I see when needed. I may go several years without seeking therapy. But I don't hesitate to reach out when necessary. I have recommended this therapist to a lot of friends. But I also have a specialist I see when needed. She has extensive training in addiction recovery. Beth and I first saw her in 2015, and have been back several times.

The importance of therapy is well-documented. "The effectiveness of cognitive therapy in relapse prevention has been confirmed in numerous studies."[9] Don't try to do this on your own. If your recovery is going to last, you will need the help of professionals from time to time. Just as you wouldn't try to do surgery on yourself, you shouldn't try to solve your addiction issues on your own. Today, we have so much training that is available to professions; we'd be crazy to not take advantage of their expertise.

SUPPORT FROM OTHERS

If you want to go fast, travel alone. But if you want to go far, travel with others.

I learned this from watching old westerns when I was young. How many times did we see a "bad guy" make a run for it? He'd steal a horse and gallop out of town as fast as he could, intent on escaping the law. When word of his escape came to the sheriff, the first thing he'd do was not to go after him. First, a wise sheriff assembled a posse. Then, as a group, they pursued the "bad guy."

The outlaw had a head start and created distance between himself and the posse. But eventually, something would go wrong, and the man in the black hat would run into trouble. The sheriff and his men would eventually catch up, and the "bad guy" would be returned to his jail.

The support of peers, family, and friends is an important factor in recovery. Studies on long-term recovery confirm this. Social support has several benefits that contribute to the recovery process over time. For example, social support has been found to buffer stress. Moreover, the support of recovery peers provides hope, coping strategies, and role models, giving strength in trying times.[10]

12-STEP GROUPS

Most people see a therapist for several weeks, perhaps months. They may seek treatment for their addiction with a visit to an in-house treatment center. Other tools include good podcasts, books, and webinars. What do all these things have in common? They are short-term solutions. While their benefits are lasting, the actual engagement with these tools is not.

On the other hand, 12-Step programs can be forever. Even if you aren't learning something new each time you attend a meeting, you reap the benefits. It's like good food. I don't return to my favorite restaurants because they have new items on their menu. I return because I like the same things I've liked for a really long time.

Recovery professionals generally agree on the effectiveness of consistent engagement in recovery groups. Humphreys notes that "12-Step groups often engage members more intensely and for longer periods than do professional treatment programs."[11] I have found that to be true with my own recovery. Over the past decade (as of this writing), I have attended four intensives, had a couple dozen therapy sessions, and attended over 1,000 groups. Yes, you read that right. And I am not alone. Show me a man or woman who perseveres in recovery, and I will show you someone who is in a group—and stays there.

NEGATIVE CONSEQUENCES

Now I'm going to say something that I know some will disagree with, including a few colleagues whose opinions I greatly respect. I suggest that one of the forces for staying at the hard work of recovery is the fear of negative consequences. Notice, I didn't say this is the *best reason* to stay sober, but it is *a reason.*

I'm in good company with this opinion. Writing for the *International Journal of Addictions*, R. M. Costello says, "Having something to lose if addictive behavior continues motivates change and is associated with positive outcomes."[12] I would argue that the fear of negative consequences is not enough to stay sober, but it is definitely one factor.

I don't know an addict who hasn't shared this experience. There were times when the only thing that kept them from acting out was the fear of negative consequences. I call it the "end game." Before you take the drink, pop the pill, grab the burger, enter the casino, or look at the porn, ask yourself, "How will this story end?" You know the answer. The trade-off isn't worth it. No one ever looks back after a slip or relapse and says, "That was a really good idea."

Negative consequences often include a breach of trust with our spouse, the loss of a job, health risks, loss of money, and ridiculous amounts of guilt and shame. Do the smart thing. Trade what you want *now* for what you want *most*.

FIVE KEYS TO PERSISTENCE

Long-term recovery is all about perseverance. Anyone can stay sober when it's easy. It's what we do when things get hard that counts. But perseverance doesn't come easily; otherwise, everyone would do it. Here are a few keys to successful persistence.

- Create a vision for recovery.
  The first key to persistence is to create for yourself a compelling vision for your recovery. Think about what you want to accomplish. If you aim at nothing, you will hit it every time. Give it some thought and come up with a vision worthy of your effort.

- Give it time.
  When you have a great vision for what you want from recovery, keep in mind that it may take a while. Remember that recovery is about progress, not perfection. You can lose long-term sobriety in a day, but you can't gain it in a day. It takes time.

- Create new habits.
  Don't pray for inspiration; pray for discipline. The key to lasting sobriety is found in your daily agenda. It's about doing the same thing day after day after day. The fact is, you will establish multiple

habits in your life. The question is whether they will be good habits or bad habits. Here are just a few habits that will serve you well: daily prayer, daily recovery readings, consistent calls, and weekly meetings. We'll talk more about habits in the next chapter.

- Set specific goals.
  Since there is no ending to recovery, it helps to have specific goals. These should support various aspects of recovery. Set goals for the length of your sobriety, but also for the depth of your sobriety. You might read a couple of recovery books each year, attend a conference, sponsor someone new. Make your own list of recovery goals.

- Accept bad days.
  After everything seems to go wrong, you might feel like you will never be able to sustain recovery. But remember that things are never as good as your best day, nor are they as bad as your worst day. One of the keys to persistence is to stay at it after a bad day.

THE BENEFIT OF HELPING OTHERS

When we are called upon to persevere, one of the best things we can do is to take our focus off ourselves. Anyone with a Christian worldview knows that this is a central theme of the Christian message. The greatest command is that we love God. The second greatest command is that we love others. Jesus stated his purpose succinctly: *"For even the Son of Man did not come to be served, but to serve, and to give his life as a ransom for many"* (Mark 10:45).

Several benefits come to the person who commits to serving others. The leaders of the Good Life Treatment Center identify four of those benefits:[13]

- Fostering a sense of purpose
- Building new relationships
- Improving your mental health
- Fostering personal growth

Let's focus on that last benefit. To attain advanced recovery is to help others attain beginner's recovery. You can do this in many ways. Perhaps the most obvious is by sponsoring someone who is new to recovery. You can do this at any 12-Step program. Or you can mentor someone. Or be their accountability partner. There are plenty of ways to give back. Recovery is the one thing that you get more of by giving it away.

POSITIVE REFRAMING

Nathaniel Lambert and his colleagues have done extensive research on the power of "positive reframing," which is a clinical description of the power of optimistic, positive emotions.[14] Lambert considered eight studies that tested the theory that gratitude results in fewer depressive symptoms. This is accomplished through positive reframing and positive emotions.

Study 1 found a direct path between gratitude and depressive symptoms. Studies 2–5 demonstrated that positive reframing mediated the relationship between gratitude and depressive symptoms. Studies 6–7 showed that positive emotion mediated the relationship between gratitude and depressive symptoms. Study 8 found that positive reframing and positive emotion simultaneously mediated the relationship between gratitude and depressive symptoms. In sum, these eight studies demonstrate that gratitude is related to fewer depressive symptoms, with positive reframing and positive emotion serving as mechanisms that account for this relationship.

What does this have to do with perseverance? Everything! One of the lessons any addict learns early on is that there will be tough days. As an old Baptist preacher once told me, "When you decide to follow Jesus, the enemy is comin' after you, because he wouldn't be much of an enemy if he didn't."

It is in those times of temptation, trials, and triggers that we need to simply persevere. Sometimes, it is as simple as that. "White-knuckling" gets a bad rap. But there are days when that's all we have. On the anniversary of a loved one's death, when laid off from a job, or while enduring some other setback, the allure of our addiction is greatest. Addiction is your most reliable friend—not best friend, but reliable friend. In moments of difficulty, we need to push on. One of the best ways to do that is with positive reframing.

TWELVE STRATEGIES FOR BUILDING RESILIENCE

Even during times when life feels like a stroll through blooming meadows, we regularly find ourselves battling against gusts and gales on our way to reaching our goals. We need a plan for persevering in our recovery. It won't just happen on its own. So, let's get specific, with twelve ways to build resilience.

1. Focus on the positive consequences of recovery.

    An extensive study was conducted on ways to stay at important tasks when the work becomes difficult or mundane. The most beneficial strategy cited was this one—focusing on positive outcomes.[15] This was the most popular and most frequently reported strategy from the study, and it can be applied in a variety of situations. For example, if you find yourself on a treadmill— exasperated and ready to give up—you could remind yourself of the good that you are doing for your physical and emotional well-being. Or if you are a student laboring over tedious reading material, you could think that studying now will likely help you pass your exams and achieve your academic goals. And in recovery, when the work becomes difficult or repetitious, remember the benefits of recovery—peace with God, restored relationships, serenity.

2. Regulate your emotions.

    There are many ways that people can regulate their emotional states to keep themselves in a good mood—even despite being in the middle of an otherwise unenjoyable task. For example, think of something that makes you happy—whether a memory of a sunny beach or your pet's joyful greeting when you come home. Regulating your emotions isn't the same thing as distraction, because distraction doesn't necessarily have the component of changing your mood for the better.

3. Monitor your goal progress.

   This strategy involves checking in with yourself and your progress to see how well you are doing on your task and how well you are doing on your goal. For example, if you are on a treadmill, you can monitor your progress by looking at the amount of time or distance that you have already put in. We do this mental evaluation of where we are compared with where we want to be often and naturally, and according to research, it can be a successful self-regulatory strategy to help us persevere at our tasks.

4. Look for a quick win.

   When you are getting close to completing your goal but feel the strain and effort of continuing, thinking of a short-term accomplishment might be another helpful strategy for reaching your goal. For example, if you had planned on running for thirty minutes, and you feel like you are about to give up after twenty-five minutes, thinking that you are nearly there can give you the extra boost of self-control you need to push through the last five minutes. In recovery, when tempted to give in, set a goal of getting home without a drink or going thirty minutes without a cigarette. Get a quick win; then watch these wins add up.

5. Find a sense of purpose.

   Finding a sense of purpose can help you find meaning in life's challenges. Instead of being discouraged by your problems, with a defined purpose, you'll be more motivated to learn from past experiences and keep going. Examples of purposes include:

   • Building a support system of loved ones
   • Giving a voice to a social movement
   • Leading a healthy lifestyle

- Learning about different cultures
- Making art or music
- Serving your community

In the face of emotional hardship—such as the death of a loved one or the end of a relationship, finding a sense of purpose can be especially important in your recovery. This might mean becoming involved in your community, cultivating your spirituality, or participating in activities that are meaningful to you.

6. Believe in your abilities.

   Author Kendra Cherry has identified this as one of the critical aspects to staying on task.[16] She emphasizes the importance of having confidence in our ability to cope with stress as a key component to resiliency. Becoming more confident in your own abilities, including your ability to respond to and deal with a crisis, is a great way to build resilience for the future. Listen for negative comments in your head. When you hear them, immediately replace them with positive ones, such as, "I can do this," "I'm a great friend/mother/partner," or "I'm good at my job." In recovery, with each trigger or temptation, remind yourself that while you may have failed several times in the past, you have succeeded hundreds of times. You can do it again.

7. Develop a strong social network.

   It's important to have people you can confide in. Having caring, supportive people around you acts as a protective factor during times of potential relapse. While simply talking about a situation with a friend or loved one won't make your triggers go away, it allows you to share your feelings, get support, receive positive feedback, and come up with possible solutions to your challenge. Never forget, even in advanced recovery, that this is a team sport.

8. Embrace change.

   Winston Churchill said, "Progress requires change. Great progress requires great change." Flexibility is an essential part of resilience. By learning how to be more adaptable, you'll be better equipped to respond when faced with a strong temptation to return to your addiction. To get to where you are you have used numerous tools that have served you well. But they can become stale. Embrace new groups, therapists, podcasts, and other resources, as needed.

9. Remain optimistic.

   Staying optimistic during challenging times can be difficult, but maintaining a hopeful outlook is an important part of resiliency. What you are dealing with may be difficult, but it's important to remain hopeful and positive about a brighter future. Positive thinking does not mean ignoring the problem to focus on positive outcomes. It means understanding that setbacks are temporary and that you have the skills and abilities to overcome the challenges you face.

10. Take care of yourself.

    When you are in a crisis, it can be all too easy to neglect your own needs. Losing your appetite, ignoring exercise, and not getting enough sleep are all common reactions to a challenging situation. Instead, focus on greater self-care. Make time for activities that you enjoy. By taking care of your own needs, you can boost your overall health and resilience and be fully ready to face life's challenges.

11. Develop problem-solving skills.

    For every problem, there is a solution. Finding a way out is what separates recovery from relapse. God has given you the gifts, intelligence, and network of friends to find a way out.

Never will you encounter a temptation that has no solution (1 Corinthians 10:13). But finding the path out of the forest may require a bit of effort. I try to start with this question: "What is the wise thing to do?" And when that doesn't give me a clear answer, I ask a trusted friend, "What do you think is the wise thing to do?" You may have to experiment with various strategies at times, but recovery is not a game of "hide and seek." The answers can be found.

12. Be proactive.

Persistence is a daily choice. Don't wait for the feeling to come. There will be times when you don't feel like staying sober, even if you have been in recovery for years. Always let your actions dictate your emotions, not the other way around. Like they say in 12-Step meetings, "Just bring the body." Show up to the next meeting, read the next book, do the next session. You didn't get sober without hard, intentional work. And what it took to get sober, it takes to stay sober.

DISCUSSION QUESTIONS

1. When was the last time you wanted to give up in your recovery?

2. When you feel like quitting, what keeps you in recovery?

3. What would be the consequences if you quit serious recovery work?

4. What are you doing to stay consistent in your recovery?

5. Who will you tell in the event of a relapse?

6. How does your spiritual connection keep you on track?

7. What is the hardest thing you do in recovery?

8. How long do you expect to continue attending recovery meetings?

9. Have you completed the 12 Steps? If not, why not?

Chapter 3

GOOD HABITS

The magic of successful recovery is found in the daily agenda. Show me two things, and I will tell you how your recovery is coming: your calendar and your checkbook. What you do with your time and treasure is everything. Let's focus on your time.

You have been given just enough time to do everything God wants you to accomplish. The problem isn't that you don't have enough time. It's what you do with that time that counts. There is a truism in organizational leadership that says you need to spend eighty percent of your time on the twenty percent of your tasks that produce eighty percent of your results. Apply that same principle to recovery. Cut out the things that don't work and add in the things that do.

Start with habits.

I have a friend who recently expressed his frustration with his lack of progress in recovery from sexual addiction. He wasn't looking at porn, and he wasn't looking for sex online, but he still battled massive temptation. When we dug down, I discovered the problem. My friend was spending six hours a day playing video games. *Six hours a day!* Can you say, "bad habit"?

Establishing good habits—in and out of recovery—is essential to establishing long-term recovery. Award-winning journalist John-Manuel Andriote writes:

> Your life depends on good habits. They are essentially your routines—such as going to work, fixing meals, and washing laundry. If you don't cultivate good habits like these, you face such negative consequences as being fired, going hungry, or wearing soiled clothing.[1]

Establishing *new* habits is easy. But establishing *good* habits is not. Let me explain. Suppose you wanted to establish a routine of working out every morning at five o'clock. That would be hard. But what if you decided to supplement your daily breakfast with a candy bar? That would be easy. The idea that it takes 21 days to establish new habits is a myth. I walk 10,000 steps a day. I haven't missed a single day in over a year, as of this writing. But it doesn't come easy. My Mountain Dew habit, on the other hand, was really easy to establish.

Over the next several pages, we will unpack specific ways to establish new habits that will keep your recovery on track. How does this work? The short version: "Breaking habits requires establishing a new behavioral pattern, a prepotent response, a new habit."[2]

FROM HABIT TO ADDICTION

Various authors have been credited with describing the progression from a thought to a destiny:

- Sow a thought, reap an action.
- Sow an action, reap a habit.
- Sow a habit, reap a lifestyle.
- Sow a lifestyle, reap a character.
- Sow a character, reap a destiny.

Now, substitute the word *addiction* for *lifestyle*. The leap from a habit to an addiction is not long. But how does this happen? Neuroscientist B. J. Everitt weighs in: "The 'must have' of the goal-directed behavior eventually develops into a habitual 'must do' response."[3] In other words, the behavior grows into a habit, and the unchecked habit grows into an addiction.

Habits and addictions look similar. Both are marked by repetitious behaviors, which often defy logic. So, what's the difference? "The most crucial distinction between habits and addiction is the role of choice."[4] With a habit, we have the willpower to say no. But with addiction, we become powerless. That's why Step 1 of the 12 Steps reminds us that we not only have a problem, but we are powerless to fix that problem. This is something non-addicts struggle to understand. Addiction takes away our ability to make wise choices.

RELAPSE PREVENTION

An obvious goal for advanced recovery is relapse prevention. The practice of establishing good habits is integral to avoiding setbacks. Authors G. A. Marlatt and W. H. George say it like this: "The main tools of relapse prevention are cognitive therapy and mind-body relaxation, which change negative thinking and develop healthy coping skills."[5]

In lay terms, Marlatt and George are saying that to reverse bad habits before they result in relapse, we must engage in a proactive program such as psychotherapy. To avoid relapse, we must avoid unhealthy habits, and that is hard to do apart from the expertise and counsel of those who are trained in this field.

Remember, no matter how far you go down the road of recovery, the ditch is still just as close on either side of the road. That means relapse is always a possibility. But it doesn't "just happen," especially for those with long-term recovery. It is the predictable result of a series of bad choices, which lead to bad habits, which lead to bad outcomes.

CYCLES OF HABITS

Dr. Judson Brewer, neuroscientist at Brown University, says that when we are triggered, "the prefrontal cortex of our brain goes offline."[6] This helps to explain the cycle we fall into when we relapse. When I work with clients one-on-one, I tell them that the cycle of addiction has six steps:

- You think it.
- You plan it.
- You do it.
- You hate it.
- You cover it.
- You do it again.

If you're old like me, you remember a certain sheriff's deputy on television named Barney Fife. When trouble loomed, his suggestion was, "Nip it in the bud." That's wise counsel. When you are triggered by a thought or temptation, you need to nip it in the bud. That means understanding the cycle that keeps you mired in habitual behaviors that bring negative consequences.

Dr. Diana Hill is a clinical psychologist and co-author of *ACT Daily Journal* and host of the podcast, "Your Life in Process." She helps us to understand habits in terms of cycles. Basically, she says we act out of our habits in three stages: trigger, behavior, results. She writes:

> Triggers are cues that spark our habits. We have triggers both outside of our skin (as when our phone pings a notification) and under our skin (anxiety, craving, stress). Behaviors are what we do when the triggers show up. Do you pick up your phone, eat the cookie, snap at your co-worker? Often, we don't even realize we're in a habit until we're already doing it. Results are what happens after you engage in the behavior. Whereas triggers spark your

habit, results are what fans the flame to keep it going. Our brain gives more preference to short-term rewards over long-term ones. And our most rewarding habits provide us with pleasure while distracting us from the discomfort of living.[7]

PRACTICES FOR RECOVERY

Let's get specific. If advanced recovery is dependent on establishing good habits, what are some of those habits? In his acclaimed workbook, *Facing the Shadows*, Patrick Carnes developed a profile of a typical recovering addict with long-term success.[8] Carnes found that successful recovering addicts typically established the following habits:

- They had a primary therapist.
- They were in some kind of therapy group.
- They attended 12-Step meetings every week.
- Secondary addictions were treated along with primary addictions.
- They worked to find clarity and resolution in their family-of-origin and childhood issues.
- The addicts' families were involved early in therapy.
- If they were in a primary relationship, the couple joined a 12-Step couples group.
- They developed a spiritual life.
- They actively worked to maintain regular exercise and good nutrition.

Of course, each addict must develop their own set of habits that bring intended results. I like what a friend said to another addict who was critical of my friend's recovery program. "I don't like the way you're doing it," said the critic. My friend responded, "Tell me about your recovery program." The critic said, "I don't really have a recovery program." My friend said, "Then I like my program more."

WHY WE DON'T BREAK BAD HABITS

We have established that behaviors lead to habits, which lead to addiction. Think about your own experience. One drink led to binge drinking, which led to alcoholism. One cigarette led to a pack a day, which led to nicotine addiction. One porn image led to hidden porn, which led to sex addiction. We could go on and on.

Part of my story was a sports autograph addiction. It started when a man in my church set me up to meet boxing heavyweight champion Evander Holyfield. I picked up some boxing gloves on the way, and he was glad to sign them. My favorite all-time baseball player was Willie Mays, so I bought a Willie Mays ball. Twenty years later, I had 300 autographed baseballs, dozens of signed NFL helmets, and autographed items from eleven sports.

Why don't we stop the habits before they become addictions? Steve Calechman, contributing editor for *Men's Health*, identifies the primary reason we don't change bad habits:

> We feel rewarded for certain habits. Good or bad habits are routines, and these make life easier. The brain doesn't have to work so hard. So, when we try to break a bad habit, we create dissonance, and the brain doesn't like that.[9]

Makes sense. The brain doesn't like change. Most of us prefer the problem we know over the solution we don't. So, we keep doing the same old stuff the same old way with the same old results—guilt, shame, and endless frustration.

CAUSES OF PROCRASTINATION

Just about everyone wants to quit their bad habit—later. My mom was a chain smoker. From my early childhood, I remember her smoking Lark cigarettes throughout each day. (Do they still make Lark cigarettes?) Just as consistent as her smoking habit were her lectures to my brother and me— "Don't start smoking!" It was a classic, "Do as I say, not as I do."

I never took up smoking, aside from one puff as a child, from which I nearly threw up my spleen. I asked my mom why she didn't stop smoking. Her answer never wavered. "I will—later." Later didn't come for another seventy years, when she was diagnosed with cancer for the second time. She finally quit at the age of eighty. But the damage was done. My brother and I held her funeral service a few weeks later.

The enemy doesn't tell us, "Don't quit your bad habit." He says, "Quit! By all means, quit! But do it later."

Dr. Tim Pychyl has conducted extensive research on the causes and solutions for procrastination, and he has found a powerful antidote. You ready for this? *To-do lists.*

Yes, that's what I said. Pychyl has identified four ways to overcome our bad habits through the power of making (and following) to-do lists.[10]

- Create to-do lists more often.
- Use to-do lists more consistently
- Have to-do lists that are more organized, structured, and detailed.
- Habitually create to-do lists as part of your daily workflow.

Whether you employ to-do lists or some other strategy, you need to overcome procrastination in order to break bad habits. As we say in 12-Step meetings, I wish there was a "softer, easier way." But there's not. You need to remove "later" from your vocabulary. To secure advanced recovery, take ownership for your disease. Only then will you take responsibility for your recovery.

STEPS TO CREATING NEW HABITS

Are you ready to develop a new habit—one that will carry your recovery forward? You will need to take certain steps, proven to work. The good news is that once you make a little progress, it only gets easier. Dr. Michelle P. Maidenberg writes, "Our brains form neural pathways that get stronger the more often we perform a task. When we perform a task enough times, we no longer must think about how it's done. It becomes an automatic habit."[11]

There are specific steps that must be utilized to create good habits in recovery or otherwise. Kristi DePaul, CEO of Founders, an agency focused on the future of work, has identified seven steps to creating a new habit.[12] As you scan this list, think about a new recovery habit you need to establish and how this applies to that habit.

- Set your intentions.
- Prepare for roadblocks.
- Start with nudges.
- Make a schedule.
- Set micro habits.
- Try temptation bundling.
- Show yourself compassion.

WARNING: LONG-TERM REWARDS DON'T WORK

Our focus throughout this book is on the positive steps we can take to secure long-term recovery. A huge part of that has to do with creating new habits. But to my surprise, one strategy that I would have liked to promote has been found to be less than ideal.

Initially, I expected that by focusing on the long-term rewards of successful recovery, we would be highly motivated to maintain that recovery. But this is not true. Stephanie Parker has studied the difference between long-term and short-term rewards in terms of their effectiveness for helping to develop new habits. Her conclusion: "Given dopamine's short timeline, strategies that rely on long-term rewards, like paying people weekly or monthly if they exercise more, don't build habits. They're not tapping into the brain's habit-learning mechanisms. So, you need a different strategy."[13]

I tell guys all the time, "Recovery is about giving up what you want now for what you want most." That sounds great. But that sentiment would matter a lot more if the temptation was to become a lifelong drinker or carry on a lengthy affair. But addiction doesn't work that way. We want the next drink, the next pill, or the next hit. It's all about the quick fix, the dopamine hit. So, a better strategy would be to focus on the *short-term* benefits of staying sober.

TEN HEALTHY RECOVERY HABITS

Now for the fun part. I have scoured dozens of studies in search of the very best habits we need to adopt to secure advanced recovery. While one size certainly does not fit everybody, I think you will go further in your recovery if you develop just a few of these habits. Some of them are already pretty much automatic for you. So, skip over those. Ask God to clarify a few of these that can benefit your unique journey into advanced recovery. Each of these will be some form of self-care, because you must love yourself before you can love anyone else. The following sentiment says it well: "Despite its importance, self-care is one of the most overlooked aspects of recovery."[14]

1. **Eat healthy.** If you want to feel good about yourself, visit just about any 12-Step group. About sixty percent of those in attendance also have another addiction. The one we talk about is alcohol. That is the mainstream addiction. With Alcoholics Anonymous having been around since 1939 and having AA groups all over the world, most people know an admitted alcoholic. But the other addiction we see a lot—that few people talk about—is food.

    I read somewhere that the average person weighs twenty-five pounds more than the average person weighed fifty years ago. Many Americans are clinically overweight. So, a great place to start is to do what most people only think about doing: Eat healthy. Food is fuel. If you are recovering from any addiction, you need healthy fuel to keep you strong. The simple formula for what you should eat is this—if it tastes good, don't eat it.

    The World Health Organization has a more detailed plan.[15] Specifically, they recommend:

47

- Include vegetables with every meal.
- Eat fresh fruits and raw vegetables as snacks.
- Steam or boil, rather than frying.
- Trim visible fat from all meats.
- Limit consumption of baked and fried foods, as well as pre-packaged snacks.

2. **Exercise regularly.** A few years ago, a doctor friend gave me some free, detailed medical advice that I try to put into practice every day, usually with pretty good success. Ready for this? Take notes. I'll go slowly.

Keep moving.

If you can't sprint, jog. If you can't jog, walk. Just keep moving. I'll never forget what my heart surgeon told me before my five-bypass open-heart surgery in November 2022. He said, "For five hours, your life will be in my hands. After that, it will be in your hands." I've long been a walker, but I took it up a notch after my surgery. I never miss my goal of 10,000 steps a day. I have averaged walking 5.5 miles per day since January 1, 2023. I won't set any records, but I keep moving.

An extensive study conducted in 2023 concluded that going beyond the minimum recommended weekly exercise pays huge dividends. While it is generally recommended that we get between two and a half to five hours of moderate exercise per week, doubling that number decreases cardiovascular mortality by 28–38 percent.[16] That represents five to ten hours a week, which breaks down to 45–90 minutes each day.

3. **Pursue activities that you enjoy.** Get. A. Hobby. Is that clear? For most people I know, this is a real problem. Part of the problem is that for many of us, our addiction was our hobby. It became our most reliable friend. We could count on it for a bit

of pleasure whenever we wanted it. Addiction never says no. So we put our time and resources into our habit. Once we get into recovery, we don't know what to do with our free time. It's been too long since we had a real hobby.

How much free time should you have? Between two and five hours per day. No, I'm not making that up. Dr. Max Alberhasky has done the research. He says that if you spend less than two hours a day in free time, you are working too hard. If you have more than five hours, you aren't busy enough, and your life may lack meaning.[17] There are a lot of ways to fill two to five hours. Think creatively—exercise, reading, woodwork, gardening, cooking, picking up a musical instrument, dancing (unless you are Baptist), wine-tasting (unless you are Baptist). Go to a museum, state park, beach, or lake. Get a dog. Take time off each day.

Get creative. Natalie Proulx, staff editor for The Learning Network, offers the following examples of creative things to do, simply to have fun, things we did as kids: study cloud formations, swing from a rope, or make a mud pie.[18] Create your own fun list. The biggest reason people get into trouble is that they didn't get into something else first. Don't let that be you.

4. **Get some sleep.** Eight hours a night is optimum; seven is minimum. Sleep gives your body a chance to recharge and recuperate from the stresses of life, especially those brought on by addiction. There are five basic triggers that make us vulnerable to our addictions. You can remember them with the acronym, BLAST:

   - Boredom
   - Loneliness
   - Anger
   - Stress
   - Tired

Don't forget that last one—tired. When you are tired, you are vulnerable. Your guard is down. You are not as alert. That is why you need sleep. But something matters more than the quantity of your sleep—the quality of your sleep.

Eric Suni and Abhinav Singh have done a lot of work related to sleep quality. They say that *how* you sleep matters more than *how much* you sleep.[19] The following are just a few of their suggestions on how to capture the best quality sleep possible: (a) create a bedtime routine, (b) choose a great mattress, (c) minimize bedtime distractions, (d) disconnect from electronic devices for the last hour before you go to bed, and (e) limit caffeine intake late in the day.

5. **Practice meditation.** Meditation is more than a mystical practice enjoyed by some people. It is a biblical command. The Old Testament tells us to meditate on God's Word day and night to find great success (Joshua 1:8). The Hebrew word used for "meditate" is the word used for the way a cow eats its food. With multiple stomachs, a cow eats the food, throws it up, eats it again, and repeats this a total of four times. To meditate is to chew on something over and over.

   Alice Walton, with Forbes Healthcare, says that mindful techniques such as meditation reduce stress, which helps to reduce relapse.[20] She cites several benefits of meditation, including a slowing of the brain's aging and reduced anxiety. In my experience, stress is the most common trigger of relapse. Anything that reduces stress—including meditation—is a huge friend to advanced recovery.

6. **Try journaling.** Okay, as a matter of full disclosure, I must admit that I don't journal. My explanation has always been, "Jesus didn't journal, and I want to be like Jesus!" But a lot of

guys I work with tell me that journaling is one of the best tools in their recovery kit. They journal every day. Research is on their side. Clearly, people who journal are able to grow in ways the rest of us may not.[21] The question, then, is not whether you should journal, but how.

By hand.

When you write by longhand, this forces you to think as you write. You are expressing emotion with the movement of your hand, as opposed to typing away on a keyboard. This will help you remember what you write, and it will enhance creative expression. If journaling is not your thing, perhaps you can try it for one week, just to see if it is a habit that you enjoy.

7. **Get organized.** Clutter can be a major source of stress in your life. Keep an organized environment at home and at work. Start by making your bed each morning. Create a daily schedule and stick to it. Work off to-do lists, as we discussed earlier. An organized person is a successful person. A habit of staying organized will serve you well in all facets of life. Here are just a few of the benefits of getting organized:[22]

    - Improves self-esteem
    - Increases a positive mood
    - Makes you more productive
    - Creates an overall sense of self-control
    - Instills confidence

If you aren't a particularly organized person, start small. Break your day into three-hour increments. Plan your two to five hours of freedom for the next day. Schedule your devotional times, recovery work, and family time. These things don't happen on their own. Make them happen.

8. **Practice gratefulness.** One of the reasons that we get depressed and anxious is that we fail to recognize the things in our lives that are healthy, warm, and safe. Keeping an attitude of gratitude is healthy for your mind. It can help you focus on the positive things in life, instead of feeling discontent and inadequate. "Gratitude acts as an integral part of overall happiness, enables you to see failures as opportunities, and helps you to face challenges with a positive mindset."[23]

   The Bible says to be thankful in all circumstances. Not *for* all circumstances, but *in* them. It is by maintaining a positive attitude that our focus remains on God, our purpose, and our future. When we lose gratitude, we go negative. And this is never good for advanced recovery. I'm sure that my experience has been yours, as well. The most positive, happy people I know are the ones who maintain thankful hearts.

9. **Give back.** One of the best ways to give your life purpose is to give back to others. This is the 12th Step. You can do this in many ways. Volunteer for a charity group or community organization. Better yet, sponsor someone in recovery. Recovery is the only thing you get more of by giving it to someone else. I've seen this happen dozens, if not hundreds of times. A guy in one of my groups sponsors someone else, and he gets more out of it than the person he sponsors.

   In 2015, I asked "Kevin" to be my sponsor. He agreed, but with an odd explanation. "I'm doing it for me," he said. He explained that every time he sponsors someone, it makes his own recovery better. I have seen that play out in my life, as well. When I lead 130 guys in my ten weekly recovery groups, when I take a man through my 90-day recovery program, and when Beth and I lead couples' groups, I always get the blessing. How does this work?

When you help someone else, you are essentially saying "thank you" to the people who helped you. As you help more people, you can make a difference in their lives, which will bring you a sense of happiness that is greater than any high.[24]

10. **Do daily devotions.** Jon Bloom, co-founder of Desiring God, writes on the benefits of daily devotions: "It's okay if there was no special spark in your Bible reading today. In fact, ordinary devotions are a good thing."[25] I love that. We don't need to feel a "high" or hear an audible voice to encounter God. By simply staying connected to the Source, we will experience growth in our spirits and find a peace that cannot be known any other way.

I am often asked to share my own routines. I hesitate, because our devotional lives are very private. What works for me may not work for someone else. But I will share my daily routine, as of this writing. Adapt this to what works best for you.

- Read a daily devotion.
- Read one page of recovery material.
- Pray the 3rd Step prayer.
- Pray the 7th Step prayer.
- Pray the Serenity prayer.
- Pray the ACTS prayer (acclamation, confession, thanksgiving, supplication).
- Read one chapter of Scripture.

Now, come up with your own plan. There is no more valuable set of habits than spiritual habits. The way you connect with God every day will set the foundation for the rest of your recovery work. There is nothing better that you can do today that tomorrow will thank you for.

DISCUSSION QUESTIONS

1. What is the worst habit you need to break?

2. What is the best habit you have established?

3. Why is it so hard to break bad habits?

4. If you could establish one new habit, what would it be?

5. How would you rate your daily physical routines?

6. How would you rate your daily spiritual routines?

7. What habits serve you best in recovery?

8. What recovery routine do you need to work on the most?

Chapter 4

COMPARISON TRAP

I t happens in 12-Step groups every day. At least I know it happens in my group. We are required to check in with our sobriety dates as we introduce ourselves early in each meeting. And while checking in with sobriety dates is not a bad thing, it does lead to an unintended consequence: *The comparison trap.*

We have all fallen into it. Some live there, incapable of digging themselves out. Hey, I get it. I remember sitting in on a group in Baltimore one time, while traveling. When I entered this room full of strangers, I felt good about my sobriety. When I left, I didn't feel so good. What happened to rock my sobriety? Several of the attendees had longer sobriety than me. I won't lie. It feels good to have the longest sobriety in the group. But that day, I was in the middle of the pack.

Of course, I was using the wrong scoreboard. Recovery should be measured according to *depth* more than *length*. But we can't measure depth. Hence, the comparison trap, all based on length.

The comparison trap is nothing new. In the Bible, Cain compared himself with his brother Abel. (Brothers have been comparing themselves to each other ever since.) Jonah didn't like God treating the Ninevites as if they had repented, even though they had repented. Jesus's disciples lived in the comparison trap. "I wanna sit next to you in the Kingdom!" "No! Pick me!" On and on it went.

Paul warned, *"We do not dare to classify or compare ourselves with some who commend themselves. When they measure themselves by themselves and compare themselves with themselves, they are not wise"* (2 Corinthians 10:12). The word translated "wise" is the Greek word *sophos*, which means "specially enlightened, sharp, or bright." In other words, "Comparing yourselves to others is not the sharpest or brightest thing to do."

Theodore Roosevelt's observation comes to mind: "Comparison is the thief of joy." I like what Oscar Wilde said. "Be yourself; everyone else is already taken." Still, we consistently fall into the comparison trap. Many of us *dive* into the comparison trap. One study found that ten percent of our waking thoughts involve comparisons to someone else.[1] So let's talk about it—the comparison trap. We will unpack the two kinds of comparisons, the effects of social media, fifteen ways out of the comparison trap, and more.

SOCIAL COMPARISON THEORY

Before we jump into the dangers (and benefits) of comparing ourselves with others, it might be helpful to look back to the genesis of the comparison trap, on a psychological level. In 1954, psychologist Leon Festinger initiated the discussion with the hypothesis that we make comparisons as a way of evaluating ourselves. His hypothesis became known as the social comparison theory.[2] The idea is that individuals determine their own social and personal worth based on how they think they stack up against others. At its root, the impulse is connected to the instant judgments we make of other people—a key element of the brain's social-cognition network that can be traced to the need to protect oneself and assess threats.

This plays out every day. Here are just a few examples:

- The gym. When you go to the gym, you are gratified to see someone of the same sex and of a similar age, who appears to be in worse shape than you.

- At church. You see a friend from a distance, wearing a new outfit. You draw close, taking careful note of whether their attire makes them look better or worse. Of course, "worse" is always preferable.
- The mall. There are attractive people everywhere. You are pleased when you see people of your gender who you deem less attractive than yourself.
- The beach. No further comment is necessary.

What do each of these examples have in common? They are all based on physical appearance. That's because we are a visual species. I suspect that kangaroos, squirrels, and chipmunks are less judgmental about one another's appearance and hygiene. We make comparisons the moment we meet someone. That is how we determine our own worth. It is mostly unhealthy, but almost impossible to avoid.

THREE QUICK QUESTIONS

Before we get into the two types of comparison traps, let's keep it simple. It might be good to respond to three questions that are common among those mired in comparisons. The answers to these questions will help frame further discussion.

- With whom do we compare ourselves?

  Our comparison targets tend to be those with whom we most closely identify and those in our personal orbit. We don't usually fixate on Elon Musk. Nor do we compare ourselves to the homeless guy we pass on the sidewalk. We compare ourselves to family members, friends, colleagues, and neighbors.

  When I see an NFL lineman, I never say to myself, "Man, I wish I had biceps like that!" Watching football games on television doesn't make me feel worse about myself. I never think, "If I wasn't such a loser, I'd be playing quarterback for the Dallas Cowboys!" On the other hand, the guy sitting next to me while

I watch the quarterback for the Dallas Cowboys on TV—he's a problem. For me, the same was true as a pastor. I didn't compare myself to Joel Osteen or Billy Graham. The pastor of some start-up church in East Texas wasn't on my radar, either. I tended to compare myself with other pastors of my denomination, whose churches had much in common with mine.

- Does it change with age?

Yes, it does. As we age, we tend to compare ourselves to others in our own age group. I'm no longer jealous of the thirty-year-old man who is in fantastic shape. Now I'm jealous of the sixty-year-old man who gets out of bed in the morning with minimum pain. Another thing changes with age. As we get older, we compare ourselves less to other people and more to ourselves. We ask questions like, "Am I further along than I was five years ago?" "Am I in better shape than I used to be?" "What do I need to do to be the person I want to be in ten years?" The comparison trap becomes the self-comparison trap.

- Why do we do it?

We are striving to become what professor Jeff Bilbro calls "the indispensable self."[3] We think about the other person who is in perfect shape, has the ideal job, or lives in an incredible house, and we say, "I can be that person," my indispensable self. When we give up on ourselves completely, we compare ourselves with others less. This is just one way we crawl out of the comparison trap.

TWO PROBLEMS WITH COMPARISON

Most of us intuitively know that comparing ourselves to others is generally a bad idea. No one had to tell us that. When we compare ourselves to others, we will always draw one of two conclusions. Either of them is dangerous.

Sometimes, we conclude that we are better than the other person. We have more money, are better looking, have a better job, a better spouse, or a better house, etc. This kind of comparison leads to pride. We become the man in the Bible of whom Jesus spoke. Remember the man who thanked God that he wasn't like others—that he was not a sinner? That didn't go well. It was his downfall. When we see ourselves as superior to someone else, we get a bloated opinion of ourselves, which leads to a lack of motivation to improve ourselves, since we feel like we have already arrived.

On the other hand, we might feel inferior to the person with whom we compare ourselves. They seem to have it all together. By comparison, we have failed to reach our goals, and our future looks bleak. This leads to low self-esteem and a loss of contentment. The end game is that we not only lose faith in ourselves, but in our God.[4]

Psychologists divide social comparisons into two categories—downward and upward. Downward comparison involves comparing yourself to someone you perceive as worse off than yourself, and upward comparison involves comparing yourself to someone you perceive as better off. The comparisons may be based on appearance, health, intelligence, ability, social status, wealth, or dozens of other things.

UPWARD COMPARISONS

Upward social comparison refers to how individuals evaluate themselves against those they perceive as superior in a particular area. Upward comparisons have traditionally been viewed as resulting in negative self-evaluations and lowered self-esteem. Now, it is thought to be more complicated than that.

Upward comparison can be a double-edged sword. On one hand, it can provide inspiration and hope, motivate us to improve our own situation, and provide useful information about how to overcome an obstacle. It can also give us a self-esteem boost such as when we bask in the reflected glory of a successful close friend or family member. On the other hand, upward comparison can fuel envy, low self-esteem, and shame. Like downward comparison, it can lead us to overlook the complexity of others' lives, such as the potential suffering beneath the surface of friends' idealized images on social media. And it can generate unrealistic standards of beauty or success that are unlikely to be sustainable or healthy sources of motivation.

Psychologist Juliana Breines summarizes the positive side of upward comparisons:

> Upward comparison may be less likely to elicit destructive emotions when we remember that even the most successful people struggle in some ways and are just as human and fallible as we are—and that, for all our foibles and shortcomings, we are just as capable of greatness.[5]

While any comparisons are generally seen as a negative force working against advanced recovery, psychologists have identified both positive and negative consequences from upward comparisons, as well as downward comparisons.

Positives of Upward Comparisons

Let's start with the potential upside to comparing yourself to someone you perceive as better than you on some level. If managed well, such comparisons can elicit a desirable outcome. Here are some potential benefits of such comparisons:

- They help you see where you want to go and who you aspire to be.
- They help you set new goals for your future.
- They can raise your competitive spirit in a healthy way.
- They can help you feel more motivated to achieve future success.

Negatives of Upward Comparisons

Comparing yourself to those ahead of you invites pain and anxiety. These predictable effects are the reason any upward comparison is generally discouraged. While such comparisons might have positive outcomes, negative consequences are almost certain.

- They initiate feelings of failure.
- They may lower your self-esteem.
- They create unrealistic standards that are exhausting to meet.
- They lead to delusional thoughts of becoming someone we can never be.

DOWNWARD COMPARISONS

Downward comparison is understood as the processes by which individuals evaluate themselves against those whom they perceive to be inferior in a particular area. This generally leads to a sense of superiority. Often, downward comparison is intentional, with the goal of self-protection. It makes us feel safer when we see ourselves as superior. Research suggests that we are more likely to make downward comparisons when our self-esteem is threatened. Sadly, they often depend on the failures of others.

As with upward comparisons, downward comparisons should be seen as largely problematic. We have already stated several reasons why we should avoid the comparison trap altogether. But some positive and negative outcomes are unique to downward comparisons:

Positives of Downward Comparisons

- They may leave you feeling better about your own situation.
- They can increase your sense of gratitude and hope.
- They may improve your self-confidence.

Negatives of Downward Comparisons

- You can lose your motivation to improve. ("What I have is fine.")
- You may become dishonest about your own level of suffering. ("It could be worse.")
- You may avoid getting the help you need. ("I'm already good enough.")

15 WAYS TO AVOID THE COMPARISON TRAP

Whether comparisons are upward or downward, we can agree that all comparisons are generally a bad idea. Psychologist Jim Taylor offers fifteen steps we might take to stay out of the comparison trap.[6] If you are to preserve your advanced recovery, these might help. Otherwise, you may catch yourself measuring your sobriety by someone else's standard. Here you go:

1. Accept that social comparison is a normal part of being human (but that doesn't mean you should keep doing it). As you know, recovery is about progress, not perfection. The same is true with comparisons. They're going to happen.

2. Learn to recognize the signs. Know yourself. If you need help, ask someone you trust. Look for the signs that you are not just admiring or criticizing someone else; you are comparing yourself to them.

3. Ask why you are comparing. Dig deep for this one. What is it that you feel you lack? Why are you comparing yourself to *this* person at *this* time?

4. Understand how comparisons make you feel. Remember, comparisons can lead to pride or low self-esteem. Remind yourself of those feelings when you are tempted to jump back into the quicksand.

5. Acknowledge that continuing to compare will only hurt you. The comparison place is a tough place to visit, but a horrible place to live. You know it's no good, so get out.

6. Ask yourself whether you have high or low self-esteem, so you can better understand how social comparison affects you.

7. Realize that you tend to compare your lesser qualities with others' best qualities, which puts you in a no-win situation. Remind yourself that what you are comparing yourself to is another person's highlight reel.

8. Put your comparisons into their proper context. Remind yourself that you are not who you appear to be in your worst moments, and the other person is not who they appear to be in their best moments.

9. Recognize that you only see the outside of a person and have little knowledge of who they are inside. And it is who they are inside that really matters.

10. Accept your humanity. God made you, imperfections included. You are special, not despite your shortcomings, but because of them.

11. Focus on your strengths. One of the tragedies of living in the comparison trap is that it takes us out of our strengths. You will never be successful because you improved your weaknesses, but because you magnified your strengths.

12. Focus on your goals and how to achieve them. Your goals are nobody else's. God has created you unlike any other person—ever. Use your unique wiring to determine your personal destiny.

13. Limit your use of social media. Remember, when you see someone else's profile on social media, what you are really seeing is the person they want you to see—not who they really are.

14. If you do compare, use comparison as motivation. Say things like, "If they can lose ten pounds, so can I." "If they can stay sober for one year, so can I." "If they can sponsor three people, so can I."

15. Shift your focus onto who you want to be and what you want to accomplish. Only you control where you look, how you think, and what you value.

A WORD ABOUT SOCIAL MEDIA

One of the things we do to achieve advanced recovery is the Three Circles exercise, which was developed by AA decades ago and continues to be used by most 12-Step recovery groups. Still, there are some groups, and even some therapists, who are not familiar with the Three Circles. I will give a brief overview here. Pay special attention to the middle circle.

Draw three circles on a sheet of paper. Start with a large circle. Then draw a smaller circle inside that circle. Finally, draw a still smaller circle in the middle circle.

Outer Circle

In the outer circle, write a few words listing activities that keep you in a good place. Here are a few examples:

- Daily devotions
- Church
- Date night
- Recovery groups
- Work with sponsor
- Physical exercise
- Meditation
- Scripture memory
- Healthy diet
- Hobby
- Step work

Middle Circle

In the middle circle, write the things that put your recovery at risk. None of these things represent a slip or relapse. They simply push you to the edge, against the guardrail. This is the circle we will look at more when we discuss social media. Here are some common middle circle activities.

- Unmonitored devices
- Bars
- Beaches
- Time alone
- Certain parts of town
- Toxic relationships
- R-rated movies

- Cash
- Traveling alone
- Missed recovery meetings

Inner Circle

In the inner circle, write the things that, for your addiction, break sobriety. Depending on your addiction, these activities may include:

- Taking a drink
- Popping the pill
- Masturbation
- Placing a bet
- Viewing pornography
- Eating certain foods
- Visiting certain places

What does any of this have to do with the comparison trap? Or social media? Let's go back to the middle circle. That is where social media belongs. Social media is a turbo-charged, precision instrument for social comparison unlike anything in human history. People share only their peak experiences and flattering news. They post their personal highlight reels. Nothing drives you into the comparison trap more quickly. Research confirms a direct link between excessive social media use and making unhealthy comparisons to others.[7]

I'm not suggesting that you should get off social media completely. What I do suggest is doing one of two things. If social media puts you in an unhealthy, unhappy place, get off for thirty days. If you feel like social media is safe for you, still limit your use to thirty minutes per day.

QUESTIONS TO ASK YOURSELF

Eric Owens has given us some questions to ask ourselves to process our feelings about ourselves and where we think we stand in comparison to where we think we should be.[8] Ask yourself these three questions.

1. Is the person you are now better than the person you were before?
2. If not, think about what improvements you'd like to make. Do you want to be more diligent in your work? Do you want to be in better shape?
3. What are you really good at?

This exercise will help you to process your feelings and set a standard for where you want to be. Make it all about yourself, not anyone else. The point is to compare yourself to where you have been and want to be, not to the accomplishments of anyone else.

A WORD FROM JACK WELCH

I'm always interested in what Jack Welch has to say about just about anything. The former CEO of General Electric is one of the most respected leadership experts in the world. He weighs in on the subject of comparison with some interesting insight, knowing that we all compare ourselves to others on some level. But the way we do it matters.

Welch suggests that if you are going to compare yourself to someone, don't stop there. Compare to ten other people. He says, "You become somebody else. You want to make yourself an amalgamation of the best ideas you can put together with your personality and your style."[9] In other words, draw from the positive traits of several people in developing your personal goals for growth and change.

HOW TO ESCAPE IF YOU'RE ALREADY HERE

In this chapter, you learned fifteen ways to stay out of the comparison trap. But what if it's too late? What if you have already fallen into the quicksand? How do you get out? Let's consider five ways to get out.

1. Seek connection, not comparison. When you're tempted to compare yourself to another person, focus instead on what you have in common with that person.

2. Look up, just a little. If you are going to compare yourself to others, always practice upward comparisons, and only compare to people who are one or two steps ahead of you, not 100 steps. For example, if you need to lose weight, make an example out of someone who has lost ten pounds, not the person on the TV ad who lost 150 pounds. Pick examples you can relate to.

3. Count your blessings. If you focus on the good things in your own life, you will be less likely to obsess over the things you lack.

4. Compare yourself to . . . yourself. Look for internal evaluation. Compare yourself to where you used to be and where you want to be.

5. Pursue upward joy. Only compare yourself to others if you are committed to using this as a catalyst for self-improvement.

GRATITUDE

My final word about comparison is *gratitude*. Gratitude is not a byproduct of happiness; happiness is a byproduct of gratitude. The reason we tend to fall into the comparison trap is that we are not fulfilled in our current state. But the problem isn't that we don't have enough. The problem is that we aren't thankful enough.

Therapist Hanna Rose writes, "There is nothing outside of you that can fill the internal void inside of you."[10] Comparison is rarely a good idea. When you compare yourself to others, you are essentially telling God he made a mistake. You feel that you come up short and are therefore dissatisfied. The answer is gratitude. The more you come to appreciate what you do have, the less you will obsess over what you don't have.

DISCUSSION QUESTIONS

1. Do you tend to make upward comparisons or downward comparisons?

2. Do you tend to notice what others do well or what they do poorly?

3. What can you learn from the person you most aspire to be like?

4. Are your comparisons mostly financial, physical, or recovery related?

5. How would you compare the "now you" to the "former you" from one year ago?

6. How do your comparisons motivate you in a positive way?

7. What are three things you are thankful for?

8. What do you do better than most people?

Chapter 5

SOBER ISN'T ENOUGH

Sober is a great start, but if that's all you've got, I give you an "incomplete" on your report card. One of the things you have learned on your journey to advanced recovery is that sobriety is critical early on, but it's not enough. You can't be still in recovery; you are always moving forward, or you are moving backward. If you are stuck in sobriety, you are moving backward.

With typical brilliance, Dr. Brene Brown writes, "Abstinence-based recovery is like living with a caged, raging tiger in your living room. If you open the door, you know it will kill you."[1] I like the term, *abstinence-based recovery*. We all want abstinence, and we all want recovery. But we don't want recovery that is simply based on abstinence. Just not doing something bad does not make us good.

Writing for *Psychology Today*, clinician Sarah Allen Benton adds, "An addict who is in true recovery is in remission from his addiction. His addiction is not cured, but he is able to be free of the cravings and mental obsession."[2] Again, sobriety brings a man or woman closer to the ultimate goal. But the addict is not yet "cured." Our task in this chapter is to break down the differences between sobriety and recovery, and to understand the need to stay as desperate for recovery today as we were when we first became sober.

Moving from short-term sobriety to long-term recovery requires a transition—in our thinking, recovery work, and entire approach to healthy living. Recovery expert Jonathan Strum, with the Recovery Village, writes, "Transitioning from sobriety to recovery takes both commitment and action. While most people can quit addiction for a short period, long-term sobriety is usually accomplished by traveling the road of recovery."[3]

Let's dig deeper. We will identify the marks of early sobriety, list the positive aspects of sobriety, and discuss the differences between sobriety and recovery. Finally, we will break down the challenges to advanced recovery and outline the steps to get there.

THE MARKS OF EARLY SOBRIETY

I don't miss the days of my early sobriety. It took me about a year to figure things out, even a little bit. I attended weekly meetings—usually two or three per week—for a year before I collected my first chip. I celebrated as if my team had just won the Super Bowl. (As a fan of the Houston Texans, I don't see that happening in my lifetime.)

I was in good company. Even my first sponsor struggled with chronic relapse. He said he was sober, but his definition of sobriety allowed for two instances of acting out each week. My response? I got a new sponsor. Then another. And another. "Please, someone help me figure this thing out!" I cried.

No one responded.

The days of early sobriety are not easy. For most of us, several signs emerged. While we all have different stories, there are some consistencies to our journeys. Common to early sobriety are the following.[4]

- Bottled up emotions
- Isolating

- Missing meetings
- Not sharing at meetings
- Poor self-care

Research indicates that several challenges are common to early recovery, much more than in later recovery. There are two categories of addiction—substance and behavioral. Though they may vary, depending on the category and precise nature of your addiction, these four challenges generally occur in the first year of recovery work:

- Strong emotions. In early sobriety, mood swings are common. "Emotions can be overwhelming during early recovery. Individuals may experience anxiety, depression, irritability, and mood swings as they learn to navigate life without their drug."[5] Of course, this will vary from person to person and from addiction to addiction. But strong emotions are to be expected for the first few months of recovery.
- Difficulty sleeping. Periods of anxiety and the fear of the consequences of our addiction can make sleep nearly impossible at times. The Insight Program has found that "most people who sober up have some sort of difficulty with sleeping, eating, or concentrating."[6] It makes sense. The regular tasks of daily life become far more challenging when we are in the midst of any kind of major change, especially one so profound as addiction recovery.
- Cravings. In the first months of sobriety, cravings persist. I wish it wasn't true, but you know it is. You have secured good sobriety yourself, or you wouldn't be reading this. You remember what the early days were like. Cravings and triggers can be powerful and difficult to manage during early recovery. Even the sight, smell, or thought of our drug can trigger intense cravings that can be hard to resist.

- Withdrawals. We can feel the pain in our bodies, in early sobriety. This is especially true for those recovering from substance abuse. The good news is that these don't last. Randy Smith, content manager for Monument Recovery, writes, "In the first few days of sobriety, it's not uncommon to experience varying degrees of acute withdrawal symptoms. They are not permanent."[7] Expect withdrawal as a daily part of your story but know that it does get better.

TEN REASONS SOBER IS GOOD

Before we move onto the benefits of recovery versus sobriety, let's establish that sobriety is good. Without it, there can be no recovery. While you have probably moved beyond the need to discuss sobriety, per se, let this be a quick refresher course. Never take for granted the amazing blessings of simply being sober for today. Here are ten reasons sobriety is good.[8]

- Being healthy feels good.
- It creates positive self-esteem.
- You want to stop the pain.
- It's less expensive.
- It lets you be the parent you want to be.
- You can stop feeling embarrassed.
- You enjoy little things again.
- Relationships with family and friends.
- Freedom is at your doorstep.
- Positive impact on future generations.

WHY ISN'T SOBRIETY ENOUGH?

Now that you are sober, you can think clearly—clearly enough, we hope, to understand there is more to come. Sobriety is like dipping your toe into the water; in recovery, you dive all the way in. Now that you are sober, you are capable of seeing things more clearly. And this, in turn, gives you the capacity to move further, dig deeper, and climb higher.

I learned early in sobriety that my biggest sex organ is my brain. Whatever your drug of choice, it starts there—in the brain. Praise God for the neuroplasticity of the brain. When was the last time you thanked God for your neuroplasticity? This simply refers to the brain's ability to change itself. This happens as we get sober. We rewire our brains. But this is just the first step. This allows us to unclutter our minds in order that we might transition to this exciting phase we will enjoy for the rest of our lives: *Recovery*.

THE DIFFERENCE BETWEEN SOBRIETY AND RECOVERY

Now for the nuts and bolts. What exactly is the difference between being sober and being in recovery? I like the way Joseph Skrajewski said it: "Sobriety is not simply just abstinence. It's a way of living. It's a way of thinking. It's a lifestyle."[9] Therapist Angela Pugh offers the more traditional definition. "Sobriety is stopping the substance or behavior; recovery is the healing process that follows."[10]

The key word is *process*. You have been to meetings when people checked in, "I am sober for today." Or "I have been sober since August 12, 2022." Sobriety points to a time when we last acted out. That becomes our sobriety date. We *are* sober. It's clear-cut. We are either sober or we aren't. There is no middle ground. You don't sort of act out. You don't kind of take a drink. You did it or you didn't. When you "do it," you aren't sober. When you do abstain from the behavior—no matter how you abstain—you are technically sober.

But recovery is a process. Have you ever heard someone say, "I am recovered"? I'm not a fan of that language. That implies the journey is over. Case closed. No more issues. The problem with that is the temptations don't just go away. Recovery is about far more than not acting out. It is a process that knows no end.

When I was a kid, we would drive from Houston to the big city of Pittsburg, Kansas, every summer to visit my mom's mother, my aunt and uncle, and five cousins for a week or two. But mostly, we'd go to the big city pool. I remember someone saying it was the largest pool in Kansas. As an aside, when I went back, thirty years later, the pool had shrunk. The pool I remembered was at least five miles long and two miles deep. But now, it was much smaller, and the thirty-foot high dive was down to ten feet. It's funny how we remember things from our childhood.

I learned to swim great distances (for me) in that pool. I took swimming lessons there. All I remember about the lessons is that the instructor transitioned through three stages.

- She showed me how to swim.
- She helped me swim.
- She watched me swim.

Think of the transition from sobriety to recovery like a series of swimming lessons. In the early stages, a sponsor or trusted leader shows us how recovery works. Then they help us do it. Eventually, we learn to do recovery work on our own.

Sobriety draws a line in the sand and says "no more" to things from our past. But recovery creates new thoughts, new patterns, new habits. Recovery rejuvenates. It creates. For that reason, it's more powerful than sobriety. But it's also more difficult. In early sobriety, you still experience mood swings, anxiety, guilt, sadness, insomnia, changes in appetite, tiredness, and lack of concentration.[11]

DROP THE ROCK

For most people, maintaining sobriety alone isn't sustainable. It's a well-intentioned choice. And a good one. But it's always looking backward. For that reason, it's easy to get too attached to guilt and shame. Sobriety doesn't look forward. It focuses on what's behind you. Recovery allows you to build something better. It engages with the future and allows you to remake yourself. Recovery paves the way for you to be at peace with yourself. In recovery, you can dig into what's beneath your addiction.

You can heal. You can realize hope. That hope can carry into your relationships and mend them. Recovery helps you see your life through a critical lens. It lets you be honest about your past choices, mistakes, and traumas. Only through dealing with past hurts can you experience healing. Remember, sobriety is good. But it's just the beginning for you. You've done well so far. Keep up the good work.

One of the best books ever written on recovery is *Drop the Rock.* I have all my 12-Step sponsees buy a copy and read through it as part of their 6th Step and 7th Step work. The gist of the book is that a man was standing on the shore holding a large rock, when the boat began to pull away. The goal was for him to jump into the boat. Instead, he jumped into the water, while holding onto the rock. The people on the boat screamed to him, "Drop the rock! Drop the rock!"

They knew that the man with the rock had to make a decision. Either drop the rock, thus freeing himself so that he could swim to the safety of the boat. Or hold onto the rock and go down into the water. That is the same decision every addict makes—every day.

Each day, we pick up new rocks. These may be middle circle activities. Or toxic relationships. Or new habits. The good news is that we have a chance to swim to safety, but we must act quickly. It is when we drop the rock that we can swim to safety. And that is what recovery does—it drops the rock. Sobriety wants to have it both ways. When getting sober, we want to stay afloat, but we don't want to let go of our rock. It's what I say often: "90 percent in is 100 percent out." Only in recovery do we finally let go completely. And that is when the magic begins.

CHALLENGES TO LONG-TERM SOBRIETY

We have established that sober is not enough. But we don't want to take our sobriety for granted. We've all seen it happen far too often that someone we looked up to lose their sobriety. After five or ten years, they slid into relapse. That's why I never promise anyone—not even my wife—that I will never act out again. My promise is, "It won't be today."

That's because today is the only day I can control. Why would I make promises for what I will or will not do on a day that God has never promised to give me?

It is critical that we remain on guard. Today is the most important day of your sobriety. Just like a wise coach prepares their team for the next opponent, we need to be ready for the next threat to our sobriety. Here are just a few challenges to our long-term sobriety.

- **Unrealistic expectations**

  Not Richard. Anyone but Richard. I had watched him as he led meetings. I heard his story. I admired the way he sponsored others with humility and grace. Richard knew more about recovery than anyone I'd met. He was the consummate encourager, full of faith and wisdom. If there was anyone who had been vaccinated against addiction, it was Richard.

  Yes, Richard. In a regular meeting, Richard broke down as he checked in. The man who would never fall did just that. The unsinkable did the unthinkable. Richard admitted to a relapse and to lying to the group for several months. He fell hard. That really affected me because I had based much of my own recovery on Richard's recovery. I did what he did, read what he read, and prayed like he prayed. Now he had let me down.

  But my problem wasn't Richard. It was me. I never had any business putting the hero mantle on a mere mortal. Psychotherapist William Berry, with Florida International University, said it well:

  > Initially, newcomers see hope in what long-time members offer. Newcomers may see old-timers, who have been sober for a decade, in a glorified light; it is as if they are meeting a guru for the first time. This glorified image may soon fade when the glorified makes mistakes and displays natural human emotions."[12]

One of the greatest threats to our sobriety is an elevated view of someone else's.

- **Just showing up to meetings**

We've all been there, just going through the motions. We are still doing the work, but with our heads more than our hearts. We might even work the steps, but again, we aren't really all in. Some addicts have the sophomore jinx. Think of your first year in recovery as your freshman year. It's all new to you, and you take it all in. You love the groups, new friends, and working the steps. You almost enjoy recovery.

Then the sophomore year hits. It may not be a chronological year, but you feel it. The newness begins to fade, and you start to slip in your recovery work—just a little. You don't even notice it at first. Ben Brafman warns, "Don't just show up at a meeting and play on your cell phone or daydream. Talk, listen, and engage with those around you. Don't waste your time or anyone else's time by going through the motions."[13]

- **Trying to do it alone**

A lone sheep is a dead sheep. That is one of the most accurate things I've ever heard in the arena of recovery. But I've seen it hundreds of times. It's a process that has become far too familiar:

- Addict gets caught.
- Addict gets help.
- Addict gets better.
- Addict gets confident.
- Addict gets overconfident.
- Addict gets isolated.
- Addict gets in trouble.

Jonathan Strum of The Recovery Village writes, "The recovery process is one of ongoing healing and is rarely accomplished alone."[14] I teach the Man Code whenever I get the chance. It's a concept introduced to me by my good friend, Dennis Swanberg. Jesus had certain numbers of people in his life; we need to follow his example.

- 1 = God
- 3 = inner circle (Peter, James, John)
- 12 = small group (Jesus's disciples)
- 120 = the church (Acts 1)
- 5,000 = the community (feeding of the five thousand)

That's enough to spark your interest for now, I will explain how you can use the Man Code in a later chapter.

You can maintain short-term sobriety on your own. But by the time you hit your sophomore year, you learn that you need others. When the newness of recovery wears off, you need a sponsor, sponsees, and a circle of friends to hold you accountable. You need a group. If you want to go fast, travel alone. If you want to travel far, travel with a group.

- **Old character defects**

Unfortunately, when we get sober, our character defects don't cower in a corner. In fact, it is my experience that most 12-Step members never finish the all-important 4th Step, which is the time we deal with our character defects. It's no wonder some of their defects return; many of them never left in the first place. Just because we aren't acting out doesn't mean our flaws mysteriously disappeared.

There's an old saying in 12-Step groups that "Sober is not well." The Sexaholics Anonymous website says it like this: "When I stop the acting out, old defects come raging to the fore again, and need to be addressed."[15] Who among us hasn't seen this play out in their own life?

The key is not to act as if we have no character defects, but to find ways to address them. Enter one therapist. Perhaps an intensive. Or a treatment center. Character flaws left unaddressed will always come back to haunt us. And that is a major threat to long-term sobriety.

CHIME

Sober isn't enough. But it's a good start, in fact, a necessary start. But now we need to build the bridge from sobriety to recovery. How do we do that? Dr. John F. Kelly offers this advice: "There can be many different pathways to remission. But the mechanisms by which people change are the same." Then he offers an easy-to-remember formula he calls CHIME.[16] Using this acronym, Kelly gives us five mechanisms for creating change:

- Connect with others: To move into the arena of advanced recovery, we need connections with people who are already there.
- Hope: A positive attitude is paramount to our success. Without hope, we're toast. A belief that we can overcome, and that setbacks do not define us, will carry us a long way.
- Identity: I encourage addicts to not use the term *addict* to identify themselves. It's not that they aren't addicts, but I don't think we should lead with that term. Instead, identify as a child of God and an overcomer.
- Meaning: To move forward, we need purpose. I suggest you write out your purpose and revisit it from time to time. This will keep you moving forward.
- Empowerment: Greater is he who is in you. When the Holy Spirit came, you received all the power you will ever need. Live *from* recovery, not *for* recovery.

HOW TO BUILD LONG-TERM SOBRIETY

Let's get really practical now. Sober is not enough; we all want more, and long-term recovery is our goal. But how do we get there? There are hundreds of volumes written in response to this one question. I have read many of those books. I've done the work, completed degrees, and poured over mountains of research. Plus, I have witnessed what works up close in the lives of 130 men with whom I am privileged to work every week, plus hundreds more who came before them. I will limit my answer to six simple steps.

1. Build a support system. Warren Phillips, with Lantana Recovery Center, writes, "Having a support system is crucial for individuals in addiction recovery. A strong support system can provide encouragement, accountability, and motivation to help individuals achieve and maintain sobriety."[17] It is never too early to start assembling your support system. In fact, you have one the moment you enter recovery. Who should be in your inner circle of support? I suggest the following people:
   - Recovery group
   - Therapist
   - Accountability partner
   - Spiritual leader
   - Sponsor

2. Pick up the phone. I heard a firefighter explain the best way to deal with housefires. "Call us *before* the fire," he said. He explained that calling the fire department before the fire begins would allow them to get there in time to limit the damage. Of course, he was being sarcastic. But his approach works well for recovery.

   Call someone *before* you do something stupid! Far too often, we call our sponsor or friend *after* the relapse. While it is better to call someone after a relapse than to not call anyone at all, it would be a thousand times better to call them as a deterrent to acting out in the first place. There is no better use of your phone. Why? "Friends in recovery can help you avoid high risk situations, relapses, and provide you with alternatives as you discover your new, sober life."[18]

3. Practice self-care. Tell a recovering addict to do something fun, something just for themselves, and they will look at you like you just landed from the planet Neptune. After all, it was self-indulgence that got them into trouble in the first place. True, but I'm not talking about self-indulgence. I'm talking about self-care. What does that look like? Dr. Maria Baretta has written a helpful article appropriately titled "Self-Care 101." She writes, "Self-care means identifying what you enjoy doing and what's fun for you and make a serious effort to integrate it into your day."[19]

   What, exactly, does self-care look like? Start with a healthy diet, a good amount of sleep, and spiritual disciplines each day. Spend time with people you enjoy. Go to church each week. And get a hobby. Find something you really enjoy and do it. Your options are unlimited. This matters because you can't be good for anyone else until you are in a good place yourself.

4. Learn to manage your triggers. Notice that I didn't say, "Learn to eliminate your triggers." You can't cut out the part of your brain that stores memories. You can't avoid every temptation. God wouldn't want that. Tests make us stronger. Every time you are triggered, but prevail, your recovery goes a little further. So, triggers aren't a bad thing.

   Trigger response begins by knowing yourself. Psychologist Stephanie Wright offers this counsel: "It can be helpful to pay attention to your mind and body and how it responds to the environment around you."[20] Your body will tell you when trouble is coming. Listen to your instincts. Trust your intuition. Pay attention to your senses. And be prepared to respond when the triggers hit.

5. Create routine. Routine is your friend. I don't know of anything I've ever done that helps my recovery more than routine—daily prayers, Scripture readings, recovery work, exercise. Even walking my dog twice a day helps. It's all part of building a life of stability. With routine comes balance. Without routine, you will find yourself reacting to life, rather than setting your own agenda.

   The leaders at Herren Wellness write, "Routines and patterns enhance your recovery, as it helps you prioritize recovery, shore up healthier habits, and reduce unpredictability."[21] Routines don't happen on their own. I suggest taking serious time out of your schedule to plan your week. And plan each day. Remember to build in two to five hours that are not accounted for, other than self-care. Include physical exercise, spiritual disciplines, and intentional recovery work.

6. Attend meetings. Since you have achieved long-term sobriety, I shouldn't have to tell you about the importance of going to recovery meetings. There is a lot of truth to the adage, "What it took to get you sober, you must do to stay sober." Initially, you may have attended ninety meetings in ninety days. For the first five years of my sobriety, I attended at least two meetings every week. Now, I have scaled it back to one. But I almost never miss that one.

   The Cabin Recovery offers several reasons to attend 12-Step meetings or some other kind of recovery group each week. These include: (a) support, (b) learning from others, (c) a nonjudgmental environment, and (d) a reminder of the consequences of relapse.[22] You can add a zillion other things to that list. If long-term recovery is your destination, meetings are the vehicle to get you there.

DISCUSSION QUESTIONS

1. Define sobriety.

2. Define recovery.

3. How long do you think it takes to get sober?

4. What are the benefits of long-term sobriety?

5. How well do you do with self-care? How can you improve in this area?

6. What are three things you enjoy most about going to recovery meetings?

7. Do you have a routine that works for you? What are the key components?

8. Do you have a relapse plan, in the event of a major setback?

Chapter 6

YOUR SPIRITUAL CONNECTION

"Without God, I can't; without me, God won't." That is something you hear in a lot of 12-Step meetings. In fact, seven of the 12 Steps refer to God in some way, usually with the phrase "higher power." Attendees are free to define their higher power according to their own perspective. Of course, as Christ-followers, we identify our higher power as Jesus Christ. But even those who don't know Jesus know themselves. They have learned that they cannot stay sober on their own. It is a partnership. You can't make it with God, but he won't force sobriety on any of us against our will.

Research confirms the connection between spirituality and long-term sobriety. People with high levels of strong religious faith report higher levels of life satisfaction, greater happiness, and fewer negative psychosocial consequences of traumatic life events.[1] In other words, people with a strong spiritual connection are able to navigate the choppy waters of life's turmoil better than those who have no faith.

A strong spiritual connection is critical to maintaining sobriety, but it is also an important force in responding to the trauma that often opens the door to addiction in the first place.

> A true awakening to spirituality comes from accepting that you do not have the answers to anything in recovery. Spirituality is not meant to frighten or scare people away. It is a tool that makes people stronger, more focused, and ever more engaged in their recovery. They needed to fall apart so they could come together again as a new person.[2]

Let's dig deeper. We will look further into the research of spirituality as a component of long-term recovery, then take a dive into the AA program. The biblical model of John 5 will be considered, along with the benefits of spirituality to recovery. We will also unpack a specific plan to develop our spiritual connection.

EVIDENCE THAT SPIRITUALITY HELPS RECOVERY

Let's dive further into the evidence, starting with a study published in the journal, *Substance Use and Misuse*, in 2013. Among its findings was this noteworthy observation: "Changes in the practice of prayer and meditation accounted for increased abstinence and reduced addiction intensity."[3] Notice the specificity of the study. The practices of (a) prayer and (b) meditation were uniquely aligned with both (a) abstinence and (b) intensity. This offers unquestionable support to the notion that spiritual connection has broad and deep ramifications.

Additional research considers "spiritual enlightenment" as a "crucial" component of the recovery process. Recovery expert Carly Benson, drawing from her own long-term recovery and academic studies, writes:

> To be truly successful in breaking the chains of addiction, we all need a spiritual path in recovery and a community of support to go along with it. The reason for this is that

the addict in us wants to remain alone in the dark, but a spiritual path and community shine the light for us. Once a light illuminates, the darkness cannot survive. Understanding the role spirituality plays in a solid recovery path is the cornerstone for treatment.[4]

While research clearly confirms the link between spirituality and successful recovery, it is hard to quantify specific spiritual practices, in terms of their direct benefits to recovery. The fact that seventy-three percent of addiction treatment programs in the United States include a spirituality-based element confirms that this link has become widely accepted among recovery practitioners.[5] As further support for this theory, "84 percent of scientific studies show that faith is a positive factor in addiction prevention or recovery."[6]

ALCOHOLICS ANONYMOUS

Of course, Alcoholics Anonymous has been the gold standard for 12-Step work since their inception in Akron, Ohio, in 1939. While there are hundreds of other 12-Step fellowships, most have followed the template created by AA. Many other groups read from the AA "Big Book," the *Twelve Steps and Twelve Traditions*, and use AA chips in their meetings, to recognize monthly or annual anniversaries of sobriety. So, any discussion of spirituality's connection to advanced recovery must include at least a cursory consideration of AA.

The AA People

Though not a drinker (let alone an alcoholic), I have attended several AA meetings. It doesn't take long before you see the emphasis on spirituality among recovering alcoholics, when you step into their meetings. But don't take my word for it. Dr. Stephanie Carroll of the California School of Professional Psychology surveyed 100 AA members and found that meditation, prayer, and other spiritual disciplines were significantly correlated with length of recovery.[7]

It is commonly understood that most addicts are dually addicted. For many, their second addiction is to alcohol. So, despite my expertise in the area of sexual addiction, I have been around a lot of alcoholics. My experience confirms Dr. Carroll's conclusions. I can count on one hand the number of alcoholics who do not claim a spiritual connection as part of their recovery program.

The AA "Big Book"

Look no further than the AA "Big Book." It contains 134 references to God. The founders, Bill W. and Dr. Bob, did not apologize for their faith. Rooted in the Oxford movement, Alcoholics Anonymous was a spiritual program from the very beginning. The stories in the first edition of the "blue book" concluded, "Essential to their recovery was a discovery of some personal power greater than themselves. This discovery of the reality of some kind of 'Higher Power,' some kind of beyond was, for most, the key to their newfound sobriety."[8]

Don't let anyone tell you that Alcoholics Anonymous is not a spiritual program. From its members to its written template, the spiritual component of recovery is indisputable.

HAVING A SPIRITUAL CONNECTION BENEFITS RECOVERY

You don't have to convince the faith community of the benefits of a spiritual connection to successful recovery from addiction. For us, it is foundational. The AA "big book" references God 134 times, and the 12 Steps mention "higher power" seven times; this clearly confirms what we already knew: One's spiritual connection benefits their sobriety.

But the faith community isn't alone in coming to this conclusion. In 2000, the American Psychological Association (APA) welcomed a report at its annual conference, which confirms this thesis. The study involved 236 recovering addicts and found that a strong faith component resulted in increased coping, greater resilience to stress, an optimistic life orientation, greater perceived social support, and lower levels of anxiety.[9]

Megan Hall, who works with Recovery Village, gets very specific. From her extensive work with recovering addicts, she has identified five powerful direct outcomes from a strong spiritual connection, coupled with sound psychotherapy.[10]

1. Healing: The addict finds sobriety, but also a deeper healing to his most deeply wounded parts.
2. Strength: Faith teaches the addict that he already has what he needs to stay sober—a strength to resist temptation and overcome his triggers.
3. Gratitude: This powerful tool teaches the addict to focus less on what he has lost, and more on what he has left.
4. Purpose: We all should live what Rick Warren calls "the purpose-driven life." Nothing gives us a stronger sense of purpose than a spiritual connection.
5. Connection: When we connect with God, we become ready to connect with each other. This connection is invaluable to our recovery.

There are two other factors worthy of consideration: isolation and pro-social behaviors. As for isolation, remember that addiction is an intimacy disorder. Emotional withdrawal pulls us away from our God and into our addiction. The answer is a spiritual connection. Psychologist Adi Jaffe writes, "Spirituality embodies values like trust, faith, respect, self-expression, and self-acceptance. These are exactly the things that are needed for people struggling with isolation."[11] Isolation is never your friend; connection is.

Finally, a pronounced benefit of a spiritual connection is the re-formed behavior that it helps to produce. Intuitively, the recovering addict, in tune with God, begins to give back. They feel compelled to help others. Researchers have found that a spiritual connection, especially when achieved with the context of a gathering with others, generates pro-social values, which counteract triggers to addiction.[12] We see a cycle: (a) spiritual connection, (b) community, (c) helping others, (d) reduced triggers.

89

THE BIBLICAL MODEL – JOHN 5

The Bible is full of recovery passages. Our ministry gives away copies of the Life Recovery Bible, which is the best resource of its kind that I know, as it walks readers through dozens of biblical passages, which are viewed through the lens of recovery. My favorite passage, as it speaks to recovery, is John 5. There, we read the account of miraculous healing. Jesus changed a man's life when he restored him from thirty-eight years of absolute agony that resulted from paralysis. In this passage, we discover four principles to restoration, each rooted in a spiritual connection.

1. **Desperation.**

   Until we are desperate for God, we don't find God. The same is true with recovery. I often say, "If you are 90 percent in, you are 100 percent out." Another way to say it is that if you want it, you'll get it. You are as sober as you really want to be. Let's dive into this passage:

   > Sometime later, Jesus went up to Jerusalem for one of the Jewish festivals. Now there is in Jerusalem near the Sheep Gate a pool, which in Aramaic is called Bethesda and which is surrounded by five covered colonnades. Here a great number of disabled people used to lie—the blind, the lame, the paralyzed. One who was there had been an invalid for thirty-eight years. When Jesus saw him lying there and learned that he had been in this condition for a long time, he asked him, "Do you want to get well?"
   > —John 5:1–6

   Did you catch that question: "Do you want to get well?" Of course, the man wanted to be well. Why else would he be there? But English fails to capture the full thrust of the question in its original language. Jesus was asking, "Do you *really* want to get well?" And notice, Jesus didn't ask if the man wanted to *be* well, but *get* well. Was he committed to the process, whatever it entailed? We all want to be over our addiction, but actually getting over it is something entirely different.

2. **Surrender.**

> *"Sir," the invalid replied, "I have no one to help me into the pool when the water is stirred. While I am trying to get in, someone else goes down ahead of me." Then Jesus said to him, "Get up! Pick up your mat and walk."*
>
> —John 5:7–8

Learn this: When we do the improbable, God does the impossible. It is in surrender that we become victorious. This is a purely spiritual step. When we take the Third Step, we decide to turn our lives and wills over to the care of God as we understand God. With Steps Six and Seven, we do just that.

Jesus commanded the man to prove his level of desperation and obedience. "*Pick up your mat and walk,*" he told him. Still paralyzed, the man would pick up his mat, but he could not yet walk. It would have made more sense if Jesus had said, "Once you are able to walk, pick up your mat." But again, we must do the improbable (pick up the mat) before God does the impossible (walk). It is in surrender that we are healed.

3. **Disclosure**

> *At once the man was cured; he picked up his mat and walked. The day on which this took place was a Sabbath, and so the Jewish leaders said to the man who had been healed, "It is the Sabbath; the law forbids you to carry your mat." But he replied, "The man who made me well said to me, 'Pick up your mat and walk.'"*
>
> —John 5:9–11

Here's the point. Jesus did not heal him in a vacuum. He could have easily dropped by the paralytic's home earlier in the day, while the man was still at home. Jesus could have stepped into his home and healed him away from the crowd, in a quiet and personal moment. But no, the Master waited.

Perhaps he is waiting in your life. You want to be healed now, but God is waiting. You want to be free now, but the wait continues. Sometimes, God waits. But he didn't wait forever. Once the man was in full view of others, he was healed. And that is how God heals us from addiction. The secrecy must go. We must be known, not by everyone, but by someone.

4.   **Community**

> Later, Jesus found him at the temple and said to him, "See, you are well again. Stop sinning or something worse may happen to you."
>
> —John 5:14

Remember, the opposite of addiction is connection. No one told this man to go to church. But that's what he did. Something in him said, "You need to be with others." You will not find—and keep—sobriety on your own. What is significant is not that this man went to church after he was healed, but that the Holy Spirit inspired the writer of the Gospel to let us in on that. God was saying, "Not only do you need community, I will remind you of that over and over again."

COPING WITH DIFFICULT SITUATIONS

A spiritual connection is integral in getting us out of our addiction. But it is also a valuable component in keeping us out of our addiction. No one chooses addiction. Addiction is the predictable outcome of a series of choices or events. For most of us, there is a string of abuse and trauma in our past. Even now, while walking in freedom, we remain a target of abuse and trauma. And that is where spirituality steps in.

Multiple studies verify that spiritual beliefs typically play a positive role in helping us adjust to difficult circumstances.[13] I have certainly found this to be true in my life. Like many of you, I have endured a series of setbacks and traumas in my life, some of which admittedly were self-inflicted. But looking back, I see the hand of God at work through it all. Here are just a few of the setbacks and challenges I have faced (and I'm sure I'm not done yet!):

- Dad suffered a severe heart attack when I was four months old; he never fully recovered.
- My legs did not develop properly as a child, so I wore painful steel leg braces as a preschooler. I was way behind other children my age in my physical activity.
- I was legally blind by age eight, requiring incredibly thick eyeglasses, which only partially corrected the problem. I had two eye surgeries by age nineteen.
- I was abused physically by a friend of the family, repeatedly.
- I was sexually abused at the age of ten.
- I stuttered badly until age fifteen.
- My Dad died with I was a teenager.
- I had to work my way through college with no financial support from home.
- I have been dismissed from two full-time jobs.
- I have had a major heart attack and a five-bypass open-heart surgery.
- I am a long-suffering fan of the Houston Oilers, and now the Houston Texans.

I'm sure you could make your own list. We all have endured unwanted and undeserved pain. But we are not abandoned in the midst of our suffering. God shows up in these times. How does this work, exactly? A large body of research has investigated the role of spirituality in dealing with stressful situations. In that context, religious and spiritual beliefs and practices appear to function as protective factors or buffers that mediate or moderate the relationship between life stressors and quality of life.[14] Whatever God allows, he redeems. God uses our most stressful situations. In all these things, he is there.

GENERAL QUALITY OF LIFE

I often tell sex addicts, "Porn isn't a bad problem; it's a bad solution." The reason we get into trouble is that we don't get into anything else first. Addiction is a reactionary disease. We turn to unhealthy and destructive behaviors because of some unmet need in our lives. We all want the same thing. We want to be happy, even if just for the moment.

An extensive study was conducted on the quality of life on two broad groups: those who self-identified as spiritual and those who did not. The research found that the non-spiritual people reported lower levels of quality of life and general satisfaction than did the spiritual group.[15] This only confirms what the faith community has always known. A spiritual connection enhances our chances for lasting recovery, but also a preferable quality of life, in general.

A SPECIFIC PLAN

It's one thing to want a spiritual connection. But it's another thing to pursue it. We all hope to have a walk with God, but hope is not a plan. Spirituality is not some vague concept beyond our grasp. We are as spiritual as our agenda. Things we do have a real impact on our spiritual lives. Specific disciplines are a part of our walk with our Creator. Spiritual practices have been proven to be tools that rid people of addictive behaviors.[16]

Dr. Joseph Nowinski gets specific. He cites a study, which concludes that "activities such as meditation, prayer, and reading recovery material were significantly correlated with length of recovery."[17] It is important to move from the philosophical to the practical. The difference between a spiritual connection and no connection is not will but work. Like anything else, we must plan our work, and then work our plan.

Let me lay out ten steps you might take to develop and maintain a strong spiritual connection.

- Put your connection with God ahead of recovery.
- Read Scripture for application, not information.
- Create a daily plan.
- Pray. Start with five minutes a day.
- Go to church every week.
- Repent often.
- Go on a spiritual retreat.
- Find ways to use your spiritual gifts.
- Exercise daily.
- Turn off your devices at night.

LONG-TERM RECOVERY

We have established that there is a spiritual connection to recovery. Better yet, there is an undeniable relationship between a spiritual connection and *long-term* recovery. A growing body of empirical research supports the notion that spiritual practices enhance the likelihood of maintaining long-term recovery.[18] While research doesn't delve into the specifics of how spirituality impacts long-term recovery, per se, we can draw a few obvious conclusions.

Spiritual disciplines are just that—disciplines. No one maintains lasting sobriety apart from working several consistent disciplines, such as attending meetings, daily prayer, devotions, check-ins, physical exercise, self-care, and much more. A strong spiritual walk cannot be maintained apart from these disciplines. So, it only makes sense that by developing discipline in one area, a person becomes more disciplined in other areas.

A closer walk with God naturally feeds the desire to stay sober. We do recovery work for an audience of One. Our motive is purer and our commitment is surer. The only motivation that will last is the one that comes from within. Billy Graham used to say, "There is in the heart of every man a God-shaped emptiness that only God can fill." As we seek the Lord with diligence and consistency, recovery results.

Another benefit of a strong spiritual life is that it connects us to those around us. The second greatest command—love one another—kicks in. We don't think less of ourselves; we just think of ourselves less. And as our focus shifts to those around us, we find our selfish nature fading into the background. A spiritual connection motivates us to be others-centered, and that benefits everyone.

MORE THAN A SPIRITUAL PROBLEM

We have established that successful recovery must have a spiritual foundation. Even the secularists and academics have asserted this. I can't imagine trying to secure advanced recovery apart from the guidance and power of God. I'm not sure it's even possible. But let's not drive off into the ditch on the other side of the road.

On one side of the road is the ditch that rejects all spirituality. But the other extreme is the thesis that recovery is only a spiritual issue. We've all heard the messages: "Repent!" "Just turn this over to God!" "Pray harder!" "Read your Bible more!" All these practices have their place, to be sure. But to view recovery as just a spiritual issue is shallow and counterproductive. Yes, recovery has a spiritual component. But it is much more than that.

Dr. Lance Dodes, former professor of psychiatry at Harvard Medical School, goes too far in his conclusion, but makes a good point:

> Addiction is not a spiritual problem. Saying that it is has caused a great deal of pain to many. Addiction is hard enough for people, without having to think they have shallow or tormented souls. Addiction is not a failure of religious devotion. It is a psychological symptom.[19]

Let that sink in, ye who struggle with shame! Again, I reject the notion that "addiction is not a spiritual problem." The way I would say it is, "Addiction is not *primarily* a spiritual problem." Dodes has done a service to all addicts with his work. You need to pray on your way out of addiction, but you will not pray your way out of addiction. To hold the shame of your past, and compound it with self-condemnation, will only drive you further into your addiction. You will find yourself self-medicating to cope with the shame from past self-medicating. Recovery is multi-faceted. It is complex. Is it a spiritual problem? Yes, but it is so much more than that.

CONCLUSION

If you ignore the spiritual aspects of recovery, you will do so at your own risk. From the highly respected *Journal of Substance Abuse Treatment,* we read these words: "Higher levels of religious faith result in more positive life orientation, more optimistic outlooks, higher resilience to stress, lower levels of anxiety, and better coping skills."[20] I suggest you run your recovery on multiple tracks—12-Step meetings, therapy, self-care, recovery readings, and more. But don't forget your spiritual connection. A systematic plan for consistently engaging spiritual disciplines will be a huge component, even foundational, to your chances for advanced recovery.

DISCUSSION QUESTIONS

1. Describe your relationship with God.

2. How does your spiritual walk impact your recovery?

3. Can you stay sober without God?

4. What is the one thing you need to change most about your spiritual walk?

5. Do you serve in a local church?

6. Do you have a daily time in prayer and Bible reading?

7. What keeps you from going deeper in your faith?

8. Do you meditate on God's Word?

9. Do you journal?

Chapter 7

GIVING BACK

My recovery was nearly derailed before it got started. New to recovery, I had begun attending a Friday afternoon meeting in Houston, which would become my "home group." Walking into my first meeting was more traumatic than my first colonoscopy. It might have actually been worse; for my colonoscopy I was given anesthesia. Admitting my addiction in a public setting was indescribably unsettling.

That is why I have always been sensitive to others who are new to recovery. It didn't take me very long to start helping others in their recovery, though I wasn't even aware I was doing that. So, here's what happened that knocked me on my emotional backside. In my third or fourth meeting, I sat with a newcomer. After the meeting, I went over the details of how our group operated, to the best of my early understanding. I gave him literature and my cell number. For that, he was grateful.

And then a more "seasoned" member attacked me. He berated me for "having the audacity" to tell another guy how to get sober. Of course, all I had done was to befriend a new attendee of our group. I was giving back. I'll never know why the man who scolded me was unhinged, but this reminds me, more than a decade later, that nothing matters more than giving back.

St. Francis of Assisi said, "It is in the giving that we receive." While Francis was not a sex addict, he seems to have understood recovery. Nothing speaks to this more clearly than the 12 Steps. The final Step is the one that never ends: "Having had a spiritual awakening as the result of these steps, we tried to carry this message to other addicts, and to practice these principles in all our affairs."[1]

The following testimony serves as a great example of the power of giving back.

A Personal Story
by Renee W.

While deep in my alcohol addiction, I was about as self-absorbed as I could be. All my thoughts and behaviors revolved around the center of my universe—me.

It wasn't until months of recovery that I began to realize just how much I thought of myself. I do not mean I thought a lot of myself, because my self-esteem was zero, but I thought about myself a lot.

I had a chance to care for others and how they felt. I found myself actually listening when other people spoke, like actually absorbing what they said, instead of rehearsing what I wanted to say next. This was all new to me because when I was in my addiction, I could not get outside of my own mind.

When I started to care for others, my recovery began to flourish. I wanted nothing more than to help people, especially those struggling with addiction. And through this process, my self-esteem and self-image improved.

I want others to know that there is another way to live, and it's a life full of peace and freedom. Helping others to help yourself sounds like basic Psychology 101, but it's not just a phrase to use. It actually works, and it's backed up by research.[2]

BENEFITS OF GIVING BACK

Helen Keller said, "The unselfish effort to bring cheer to others will be the beginning of a happier life for ourselves." The benefits to one's recovery, from helping others, are innumerable. Professor Marianna Pogosyan writes, "Research has found many examples of how doing good, in ways big or small, not only feels good, but also does us good."[3] Let's consider ten specific benefits to one's recovery that are derived from helping others.

1. **Mental Health**

   Advanced recovery is impossible if we are not in a good place mentally. Helping others is a proven way to maintain our mental well-being. A helpful article titled "The Benefits of Addicts Helping Addicts" notes the following:

   > Connecting with others is good for your mental health. Staying connected and engaged with people can be extremely good for your mental health. It can, at times, be even more beneficial if you are connecting with other people that share stories and struggles that are similar to yours. Many people who have become victims of drug and alcohol addiction also suffer from depression or other mental health disorders. Though a good treatment program should work toward addressing these concerns, it is always good to have a support system in place should you begin to struggle with them again.[4]

Millions seek therapy every day with stronger mental health as their goal. No one is a bigger fan of therapy than I am. I have several therapists among my closest friends and colleagues. I have three therapists on speed dial, ready to reach out to them when I need them myself. But mental health is not derived simply from *getting help* from others; it is dependent on *giving help* to others.

2. **Personal Sobriety**

While sobriety is not *the* goal, it is *a* goal. As we frequently hear in recovery meetings, "Sober is not well." I agree. But sober is a great start to "well." You can be sober without being well, but you can't be well until you are sober. And that is where giving back plays a role in your advanced recovery. The fact that giving back helps to secure your own recovery is well documented and beyond dispute.

Dr. Maria Pagano, an addiction researcher at Case Western University, has focused her life's research on the addict's social connections. During a ten-year study, Pagano and her colleagues followed 226 recovering alcoholics from nine outpatient treatment programs. They specifically measured the impact of AA attendance and service-related activities. Not surprisingly, Pagano and her research team found that those who attended more AA meetings and helped others in recovery through service work stayed sober longer than those who did not. The participants also reported a long-term increased consideration for others.[5]

Dr. Pagano's extensive research confirms our thesis. The service-related activities of 226 recovering addicts were integral to their lasting sobriety. The same is true for each of us. In "The Benefits of Addicts Helping Addicts," we read,

Giving back may help prevent relapse. Anyone in recovery faces a risk of relapsing. This risk is especially high in the transitional time when a person leaves rehab and enters back into their normal life. Leaving the comfort, structure, and support of rehab can be extremely intimidating, and some people find themselves relapsing because of this challenge.[6]

3. **General Happiness**

We all want to be happy. That's not news. Recovery speaks to this directly. Having attended hundreds of meetings for my own recovery, and as one who leads more than 450 recovery meetings each year, I have come to two irrefutable conclusions:

- The saddest people I know are addicts.
- The happiest people I know are addicts.

Let me explain. There are few things that are as painful as observing the depressed spirit of a man or woman who is an addict, not in recovery. I've been there. It's awful. An addict who is not working on their recovery is hurting, sad, and often hopeless. But the opposite is equally true. A person who has stepped from their addiction into successful recovery has so much to celebrate—freedom, connection, and hope, for example. Researchers confirm that giving to others makes us feel better, with a neural link between generosity and happiness.[7] Psychologists confirm the direct link of giving back to the reduction of depression.[8] While personal happiness should not be the primary motivator for giving back, it is a wonderful benefit.

4. **Reduction in Isolation**

Studies conclude that acts of kindness toward others reduce isolation and increase a sense of connection for those offering the acts of kindness. Writing for the Mental Health Foundation, Mark Rowland says, "Helping others helps to create, maintain, and strengthen our social connections."[9] Rowland cites such activities as volunteering at a food bank as an example of a way we can reduce isolation.

This matters, because isolation is at the root of addiction. I have written a lot about what I call the addiction pyramid. At the top of the pyramid are the acting out activities. The next layer of the pyramid consists of the five most common triggers for those behaviors—boredom, loneliness, anger, stress, and tiredness. The third layer is made up of those things that feed these triggers. And the bottom layer, beneath the surface, is a combination of trauma, abuse, and isolation. There's that word again—isolation. If we don't deal with our isolation, it will rise up and feed our addictive tendencies. But if we mitigate our isolation, we will be in a much better place to enjoy lasting sobriety.

5. **Curbing Boredom**

Helping others is an effective tool to combat one of our five primary triggers—boredom. The top reason we get into trouble is that we don't get into anything else first. Boredom is not your friend. But the mistake many of us make is to divert boredom by indulging in pleasure of some kind. This can lead to additional addictive behaviors. Of course, self-care often includes hobbies and other activities that make us happy. But one of the best forms of self-care is others-care.

Research revealed the following ways to combat boredom:

> After rehab, it is important to keep a somewhat busy schedule. Those who sit idle without having something to occupy their minds may have a hard time keeping their thoughts away from their addiction. Boredom may

also lead a person to experience a sense of loneliness or isolation that may push them toward a relapse, as they seek to displace these negative feelings.[10]

One of the most effective ways to overcome boredom is to develop a plan of helping others to find recovery. This plan should include calls, sponsorship, and going to meetings. Be creative. Use your spiritual gifts and passions to help others in their fight for sobriety.

6. **Physical Health**

Mark Rowland has identified one of the least noticed benefits of helping others—one's physical well-being. In his article, "What Are the Health Benefits of Kindness?" Rowland writes:

> Studies have found that acts of kindness are linked to increased feelings of well-being. This, in turn, improves our own self-esteem. It helps to keep things in perspective. The benefits of helping others can last long after the act itself, for those who offer kindness, not just those who receive the kindness.[11]

Many people don't realize the impact a different perspective can have on their own outlook on life. Giving back increases our feelings of happiness, optimism, and satisfaction, which in turn lead to better physical health. Serving others enhances our own sense of self-worth, and this is paramount to our personal health.

7. **Stress Reduction**

A recent study from Columbia University has found that when we help others navigate their stressful situations, we enhance our own emotion regulation skills, and thus, benefit our own emotional well-being. Over a three-week period, participants were provided with an anonymous online environment in which they could share their personal stories of stressful life events. They could also provide emotional support to other participants by replying to their entries with short, empathetic messages. Participants helped each other by identifying potential distortions in thinking, suggesting strategies, or providing words of acceptance. Responses were rated by their degree of helpfulness, and participants were given the opportunity to express their gratitude for the acceptance or reappraisal messages they received from others. The results showed that helping others to regulate their emotions predicted better emotional and cognitive outcomes for those participants who were *giving* the help. Moreover, because heightened levels of self-focused attention are common in depression, the more people helped others, the more their helping behavior predicted a reduction in their own depression.[12]

Further research supports this thesis. Dr. Emily Ansell of the Yale University School of Medicine authored a series of experiments on seventy-seven adults, ages eighteen to forty-four. Over two weeks, participants tracked their various daily activities, as well as their stress levels throughout each day. The conclusion of the study, in Ansell's words:

> Our research shows that when we help others, we can also help ourselves. Stressful days usually lead us to have a worse mood and poorer mental health, but our findings suggest that if we do small things for others, such as holding a door open for someone, we don't feel as poorly on stressful days.[13]

Ansell's research found that stress reduction was most notable during holidays and other times when we are susceptible to pressure.

8. **Positive Reinforcement**

When we get outside ourselves to help others with their recovery, it advances the stability of our own recovery work. This provides positive reinforcement to our own work. Remember what it was like when you first entered recovery. Whether your journey began with rehab, 12-Step meetings, group therapy, or individual therapy, you will remember that your early steps were marked by insecurity and fear. The early steps you needed to take to get solid footing in your sobriety were not easy. And you didn't do it alone.

Just as you needed others, someone else needs you. As you give back to someone new to recovery you will help yourself. The principles you share with them will strengthen your own work. I'll never forget what my sponsor said when I asked him to be my sponsor. "I'll do it, Mark, but I'm doing it for me." He meant that by helping me, he would be reinforcing his own recovery. In helping others, you will find purpose, satisfaction, meaning, and a greater sense of responsibility.[14] Remembering your own journey and using it to help those who need it now will help you on a successful path.

9. **Reminder of the Past**

Supporting another addict in their recovery provides a reminder of your past. This can be a good thing. Many people in recovery may find themselves facing days when they struggle to remember why their life spent under substance abuse or addiction was all that bad. As the days of addiction and the damage caused by it begin to fade within your memory, support systems are more important than ever. Reaching out to a group of people who can remind you of both where you came from and how much progress you have made, can help you to stay on a clean and successful path.

I've heard addicts describe their life before recovery as if they missed it. They had more to say about their addiction than their sobriety. That is human nature. We are all a little like the people of Israel of the Old Testament. They wanted nothing more than to get out of the oppression that was Egypt—until Moses led them out of Egypt. Before long, they whined and complained. They missed "the good old days" of bondage, having long forgotten what the past was really like.

Every time I take on a new sponsee or welcome a new person to one of my Freedom Groups, I am reminded of how low addiction once took me. I don't want to ever go back to that place again. Being with those new to recovery serves as a great reminder of my past, which motivates me to live out a better version of myself.

10. **Someone to Listen**

On September 22, 1994, *Friends* made its television debut. Over the next ten seasons, millions of Americans followed the antics of six young adults, over the course of 236 episodes. The title of the show was brilliant. Everyone needs a friend. But many of us struggle in this area. A recent study into the social dynamics of 2,000 Americans found that the average person hasn't made a new friend in the last five years. We have the most friends at age twenty-three, and then it goes down from there. Sadly, eighty-two percent say lasting friendships are hard to find, and forty-five percent say they need new friends, but don't know how to find them.[15]

New friends may come in handy. Like a lot of people in recovery, you may find yourself with fewer friends after you achieve sobriety. That's because a lot of your friends may have the same bad habits and damaging behaviors that you did. They may continue down the path of substance abuse and addiction, even if you choose to stay clean. Keeping them in your life can be too difficult and can even become dangerous as it threatens your sobriety by exposing you to peer pressure and a variety of triggers.

Having someone to talk who listens and understands what you are going through can be very important. While you may have friends and family offering you their support, they may not understand your situation and struggles the way that a person going through it will. The full benefit of helping others is realized when working with a fellow addict.[16]

SPECIFIC WAYS TO HELP OTHERS

Let's get specific. Let's pretend you know someone who needs recovery (since most people do). Let's assume this person is a friend of yours. Or someone in your home group. Or a coworker. Or a family member. It matters not. We know two things to be true: (a) you know someone who needs your help, and (b) you are fully equipped to help them—right now! Here are ten ways to give back, to help someone else (and in the process, help yourself).

1. **Say you want to help.**

    Don't wait for your friend to come to you, begging for help. Recovery coach Dr. David Susman offers this advice:

    > Sometimes a person in recovery will ask you directly for help. If so, that's great. But often they may be afraid or embarrassed to ask for assistance. If that's the case, go ahead and make the first move. Make a clear statement that you want to help. Keep it simple and just say, "I want to tell you I'm here to help in any way I can." [17]

2. **Be available.**

Your friend doesn't need your ability as much as they need your availability. I find it interesting that of the hundreds of clients with whom I have worked, far more cite their sponsor as a source of help than their therapist. That is for two reasons. First, we spend more time with our sponsor than our therapist. Second, you can't pick up a phone and call your therapist in the middle of the night when you feel like taking a drink. Your sponsor has a key role in your recovery because they are available. Follow that lead in the life of the person you can help. I'm not saying you should take every call that comes at two o'clock in the morning, but you can take most calls at two o'clock in the afternoon.

3. **Learn more about recovery.**

As with most worthwhile efforts, you will be more effective if you are better informed. Seek out reputable mental health resources to learn more about the individual's issues and ways to promote his or her recovery. Pick up a book by Patrick Carnes or Milton Magness. Or even Mark Denison. (Half of my material came from Carnes or Magness anyway!) Listen to a podcast on recovery; there are zillions of them out there. God uses sharp tools. And in this day of technology, you don't need a degree to learn something. Get informed on all things recovery. What you learn today, you can use tomorrow.

4. **Be their ally for their devices.**

If your friend struggles with pornography, encourage them to get on Covenant Eyes. More than that, offer to receive the daily report that will confirm that they have not looked at inappropriate material on their devices. Covenant Eyes calls that support person an "ally." This is a very simple way you can give back. You don't have to sponsor someone to receive their report. I currently receive about 30 daily reports on individuals I don't sponsor. It's a great form of accountability and an easy way to give back.

5. **Give honest feedback.**

Dr. Susman suggests that we "ask for permission to offer honest feedback. Once this approval is given, don't be afraid to offer feedback regularly. Keep it positive by providing frequent encouragement and abundant praise for progress toward a specific goal." [18] Don't wait for your friend to mess up before you talk to them about their recovery. No one was ever shamed into a better place. We all need encouragement. I read somewhere that the average person needs fourteen words of encouragement each day. There will be times when you need to offer critical feedback to the person you are helping, but give them positive feedback, as well. The last thing they need is for someone to convince them that they aren't measuring up.

6. **Empower the other person.**

Remember that you can't do recovery for the other person. My word to sponsees is always the same: "I won't work your recovery harder than you do." You can offer encouragement and instruction. Then their recovery must become *their recovery*. Offer all you can, then let them go. Don't try to prop them up. For me, this is hard. Really hard. One of the hardest lessons I have learned is that Step 12 tells me to carry the message, not the addict. Jesus asked the paralytic if he really wanted to walk (John 5:6). He wasn't going to offer the man two good legs if the man wasn't willing to use them.

7. **Be a good resource.**

When you get into the business of helping another person in recovery, you will become their expert. Remember, an expert is anyone who knows more than you do. You've probably heard the old saying—a man with one eye is a hero in a room full of blind people. You know more than someone new to recovery. You have unique experience and knowledge that they don't yet have. What you have learned, give away. Point the other person to a group, book, podcast, or therapist. Never hesitate to give someone else the benefit of what you have learned.

8. **Focus on the person, not the disease.**

You can't "fix" anyone. Neither can I. But we can help. That is only possible when we make our focus the person, rather than their disease. Said another way, don't define anyone by their disease. A friend called me in the middle of the night a couple of years ago. When I answered, he proceeded to cuss me out, using all kinds of words that aren't in the Bible. It was odd, given that we hadn't talked in weeks. What he said made no sense. I just listened, and I took it. When he was through, we hung up. He called back the next day to apologize. He said that (a) he was drunk, and (b) he called the wrong "Mark." He asked if I could forgive him. I said, "Of course. I learned a long time ago to never judge someone based on their worst day." Focus on the person, not their behavior.

9. **Don't give up.**

Not everyone is as brilliant as you are. Most of us don't figure out recovery at first. I attended meetings for over a year before I picked up my 30-day chip. After eight months, I relapsed. As of this writing I have passed nine years of sobriety. I found lasting sobriety because I refused to give up. But more than that, I have a group around me who refused to give up on me, starting with my wife. Then my sponsor. And my home group. And my therapist. And a whole lot of friends who are in recovery. You are here today because someone refused to give up on you yesterday. Return the favor by treating someone else the same way.

10. **Get them additional help.**

You will never have all the answers. As a senior pastor, I cherished the words of Rick Warren: "You can't pastor everybody." Warren was saying that not everyone is a good match. Friend, while you will be able to offer great wisdom, you will never have all the answers. I learn stuff from recovery newcomers as well as from the latest book or program. Be willing to point someone to a new sponsor, a different group, or another resource. I often tell guys in my Freedom Groups, "Maybe you should try a different group." I direct them to other leaders who do what I do, all the time. Be willing to offer other resources to those in need. We are all in this thing together.

TAKE ACTION

Weak recovery is passive recovery. In passive recovery, you wait for something to happen. Once you stumble upon the right group, right sponsor, right therapist, right podcast, or right book, you'll be home free. Recovery will find you. That would be great if it was only true.

Strong recovery, on the other hand, is active recovery. And no recovery is complete without working the Twelfth Step. It is in giving that we receive. "The Benefits of Addicts Helping Addicts" stresses that we become stronger than the person we help:

The joy of living is the theme of AA's Twelfth Step, and action is its key word. Here we turn outward toward our addicts who are still in distress. Here we experience the kind of giving that asks no rewards. Here we begin to practice all Twelve Steps of the program in our daily lives so that we and those about us may find emotional sobriety. When the Twelfth Step is seen in its full implication, it is talking about the kind of love that has no price tag on it.[19]

TIMING IS EVERYTHING

It is never too soon to begin helping others with their recovery. The moment you receive is the time you can start blessing others. Start by thanking the person who blesses you in your own recovery. Serve as a greeter in your local 12-Step meeting. Offer to read at the meetings. Pray for your leaders. Don't wait another second to begin giving back. Anne Frank said it well: "How wonderful it is that nobody need wait a single moment before starting to improve the world."[20]

Addressing this subject, author Jill Suttie writes, "It is important to begin helping someone else within six to twelve months of your own recovery."[21] Does that mean you are ready to lead a 12-Step meeting or sponsor someone the moment you step into recovery? Of course not. But the best time to begin giving back in recovery was yesterday. The second-best day is today. Then, as you grow in your recovery, the way you can give back will grow, also.

DISCUSSION QUESTIONS

1. What person has made the greatest impact on your recovery?

2. Do you have a sponsor? If so, how have they helped you in your recovery?

3. List the names of three people you can help with their recovery.

4. Narrow that list to one person you can begin to help this week.

5. Write out five things you have to offer in helping someone else.

6. What are three lessons you want every addict to know?

7. How can you pray for the person you will reach out to help?

8. What are the pitfalls you will avoid in helping others?

Chapter 8

SUBSTITUTE ADDICTIONS

While an addict is to be commended for seeking and finding help, they must always be aware of a common pitfall to recovery—substitute addictions. It is common for a person to do great recovery work in one area, only to fall into another addiction. This is referred to as a substitute addiction or replacement addiction. Some therapists prefer to call this condition cross addictions.

Several studies have demonstrated that a vast array of substance and behavioral addictions may serve similar functions such as relaxation, overstimulation, or escape. These replacement addictions, like the one they seek to displace, tend to desensitize the reward system.[1] In the early phase of recovery, the dopamine-starved brain will find compensation in euphoria-generating activities that are driven by their new drug of choice.

HOW COMMON IS THE PROBLEM?

The short answer is that substitute or replacement addictions are quite common. Steve Sussman is a leading researcher in this field. Along with his colleagues, he conducted a study of college students and found that seventy-five percent of the participants have at least one addiction, with fifty-eight percent of that seventy-five percent having two to four addictions, and thirty-one percent having five or more. This means that forty-four percent of the college population has more than one addiction.[2] The two numbers that should stand out are these: (a) seventy-five percent of the population has at least one addiction, and (b) forty-four percent of the population has multiple addictions.

The timing of replacement addiction onset is interesting. While substitute addictions can emerge at any point in recovery, they are the most frequent during early periods of recovery from the initial addiction.[3] By no means does this suggest that the addict is ever so far removed from the possibility of a replacement addiction that he can consider himself no longer vulnerable. But a study of 13,000 addicts in recovery found that only 13.1 percent turned to substitute addictions once they had achieved three years of sobriety.[4]

Another phenomenon is that sexual addiction is among the most common replacement addictions. Data suggest that the rate of sexual addiction is significantly higher among those who suffer with substance use disorders.[5] In other words, an alcoholic, for example, is much more likely to become a sex addict than a non-alcoholic.

As troubling as the data is for dual addictions, there is a silver lining. Sussman and his colleagues have found that most addicts who engage in substitute addictions seek out activities that are generally far less harmful than the compulsive behaviors they seek to replace.[6] What makes this fascinating is that most addicts progress in their addictive behaviors within their primary addiction. So, it is somewhat encouraging to note that they often seek to replace these behaviors with those that are less destructive. They make a choice to adopt an entirely new addiction that is less damaging than it would be to progress within the old addiction into areas that become increasingly deviant and destructive.

SUBSTITUTE ADDICTIONS

Addictions fall into two general categories: substance and behavioral. With substitute addictions, it is not uncommon for addicts to move from one category to the other. That is why so many alcoholics become sex addicts. The number of addictions recognized by the American Psychological Association and other groups is north of 150. While there are a few addictions we all recognize, there are some you would never think of. Your compulsive behavior doesn't need to be recognized by the APA to be an addiction. I've known people whose addictions were collecting toy trains, license plates, Pokémon cards, autographs, beer cans, and antique medical supplies. I have a friend who is addicted to mountain climbing. I read about a guy whose addiction was collecting meteorites.

While the number of potential cross-addictions is limitless, there are a few that are most prominent. Following are the ten most common substance addictions among Americans, with the number of Americans who are addicted to each.[7]

- Alcohol (28.3 million)
- Nicotine (23.6 million)
- Marijuana (14.2 million)
- Benzodiazepines (5 million)
- Opioids (2.7 million)
- Inhalants (2.4 million)
- Cocaine (1.3 million)
- Heroine (902,000)
- Barbiturates (500,000)
- Stimulants (500,000)

While these are the most prevalent chemical addictions in the United States, they are not all common as substitute addictions. Millions of people are addicted to these substances, but in many cases, only as their primary addiction. On the other hand, there are eight addictions that show up on most lists as the behaviors/substances that addicts are the most likely to turn to as a substitute for their primary addictions. These replacement addictions can be caused by a variety of factors, including the need to relieve anxiety, pain, or stress.[8]

1. Work
2. Shopping
3. Sex and relationships
4. Gambling
5. Food
6. Internet
7. Nicotine
8. Benzodiazepine

Shehan Karunaratne, who works with Eudaimonia Recovery Homes, adds an interesting addiction to this list—exercise. She writes, "Regular exercise is a great thing, but when it turns into an obsessive behavior, it can become unhealthy and result in physical injury or negative social, psychological, or interpersonal problems."[9] I cite exercise because I have observed many of my clients (who struggle with unwanted sexual behaviors) obsessing over exercise. Interestingly, many of them never worked out until they began to work on their primary addictions.

Why are some addictions so common as substitutes? Recovery expert Brittany Oliver explains:

> Almost anything can become a cross-addiction, but some activities are more common than others. That is because some cross-addictions can cause the same chemical reaction in the brain that substances do. They are able to create a euphoric high, much like what was achieved with drugs or alcohol. While in recovery, finding a new addiction that can produce these same feelings can alleviate discomfort, but in the process creates new, impulsive habits that can be equally destructive.[10]

WHY WE DO IT

As we have seen, most people who have one addiction also have at least one more. Why is this? The short answer is that our primary addiction writes checks it cannot cash. It takes us further than we want to go, keeps us longer than we want to stay, and costs us more than we want to pay. But it never fulfills. That's why we say that one is too many, and a thousand is never enough. One drink is too many, and a thousand never satisfy. So, most of us eventually turn to other addictions in search of our "high."

Dr. Shahram Heshmat, professor at the University of Illinois, writes, "Many addicts often substitute one compulsive problem for another. They become compulsive workers or gamblers or use sex as they once used chemicals to combat the emptiness, boredom, anxiety, and depression that constantly threaten to overwhelm them."[11]

SIGNS OF ADDICTION REPLACEMENTS

The indicators of a dual addiction are similar to those of a primary addiction. Dr. Lance Dodes, former professor of psychiatry at Harvard Medical School, writes, "Every addictive act is preceded by a feeling of helplessness or powerlessness."[12] Whenever you feel helpless or powerless over an unwanted behavior, you have crossed over into addiction. Unfortunately, most addicts don't recognize the symptoms of a second addiction, even though they have lived with their primary addiction for years.

Individuals often replace their addictions with what appear to be harmless or healthy activities and behaviors. On the surface, everything may seem to be going well. However beneficial these new behaviors may seem; they can produce similar consequences that alcohol or drug addiction cause. These are some signs of addiction replacements:[13]

- Continuously thinking about the new behavior or activity
- Losing sleep due to the compulsive behavior
- Problems at work, school, or home
- Disregarding self-care or personal hygiene
- Relationship problems with friends or family members
- Feeling stressed or anxious if unable to participate in the new habit

When in doubt as to whether a behavior has become an addiction, it probably has. If you aren't sure, ask two or three people who are the closest to you. Listen to the Holy Spirit. Ask God for wisdom. You can't treat a disease until you know (and admit) that you have that disease. Do what you have to do to diagnose your situation.

CAN THERE BE A POSITIVE SUBSTITUTE ADDICTION?

What if the substitute addiction involves a positive activity such as exercise? Does it become a positive substitute addiction? Although less harmful, if performed compulsively, the new addictive habit will fuel up an addictive personality all the same. It will continue to diminish self-control and one's sensitivity for dopamine. As a result, the addicted person will become even more vulnerable to additional addictions and relapse.

Some researchers have identified several examples of activities that do not generally lead to addictive patterns of behavior, such as reading a novel, gardening, or playing a musical instrument. There may be qualities inherent in a behavior that tend to prevent it from becoming an object of addiction, at least for most people.

Three primary characteristics can define a behavior as not likely to become addictive:

- If a behavior is consistent in flow and lends to a slow pace, such as gardening
- If a behavior involves deliberate, step-by-step planning and processing of information
- If a behavior leads to long-term gains rather than short-term gains that, over time, lead to relative losses[14]

Not all habits can be categorized under the substitute addiction label, and some could actually help in the recovery process. For example, I encourage my clients to do a recovery day once a month. This is a day filled with fulfilling activities as well as direct recovery exercises. For many, this includes a round of golf, a favorite hobby, or a familiar restaurant or museum. These can be habitual activities, but that doesn't make them addictive activities.

Take a hard, but fair look at the things you do to stay out of your addiction. Your substitute activities can easily slip into dual addictions, but not always. There are several things I enjoy doing for fun—playing my latest saxophone, walking on the beach, listening to old-time radio shows, reading books, and chasing crazy weather. As I write this chapter, I am in Grand Marais, Minnesota, which is about ten feet south of the North Pole. It is January. The temperature tonight will be −6 degrees. Tomorrow, the chill factor will be −30. And I'll be walking to my favorite lunch spot in town. No need for the car when the weather is so inviting! Does that sound crazy to you? If you're normal (whatever that is), it probably does. But I love it! That doesn't mean I'm addicted to bone-chilling weather or the six inches of snow we had today. If I was addicted to winter weather, I wouldn't live in Florida.

What I'm saying is that when we move into advanced recovery, we need to be aware of potential replacement addictions. But not every activity or habit is an addiction. Don't let your guilt tell you that everything fun is bad. God created you to enjoy life more abundantly (John 10:10). Avoid the ditch on either side of the road—addiction on one side and boredom on the other.

FOUR GREAT TIPS

Our target audience is those who have one year or more of unbroken sobriety. If you are in your first three years of sobriety, you are the most vulnerable to substitute addictions. You may try to fill the void that was created by ending one behavior by indulging in another behavior that is equally threatening, without even noticing it. Before we get into the weeds about how to prevent dual addictions and how to rebound from them, let's touch on a few simple ideas that will position you for success.

Tip #1 – Create a support group.

I lead ten recovery groups each week. For each group, we exchange cell numbers and email addresses. This enables us to support each other between sessions. Of course, this is not a substitute for individual therapy. But support groups can allow you to meet and talk with others who share similar experiences. Sometimes, the magic of a support group is what happens after the meeting. It is two members getting together for lunch. It is the pre-meeting gathering or connection that happens when the meeting is over. Create a support system within your group. This will establish a healthy infrastructure that will empower you to avoid new addictions.

Tip #2 – Get a new hobby.

The leaders of one addiction center say it like this: "Instead of swapping out one addiction for another, explore new hobbies and activities that bring you fulfillment. Staying sober requires you to shed old habits and unhealthy relationships that put you at risk of relapse."[15] Explore hobbies or activities you have always had the desire to try. If you always wanted to learn to cook or to play a certain instrument, now is the perfect time to do it. Sobriety will require you to leave behind old ways and possibly people who influenced your addictive behaviors. Now is the time to branch out and try new activities and meet new people.

Tip #3 – Recognize the difference between a hobby and an addiction.

To maintain a healthy lifestyle, you must learn how to have a sense of balance in your life. Exercising, eating healthy, and getting good sleep are essential in life, but they can easily become unhealthy if you become obsessive. It can be difficult for you to see when an activity you enjoy has become an addiction. Ask trusted friends in your life to observe your behaviors, to give you another perspective as to whether you are falling into a new addiction.

Tip #4 – Identify healthy coping strategies.

A helpful plan might be to pursue cognitive-behavior therapy (CBT), which can teach you new skills to help you cope with the urge to use, also known as cravings.[16] Talk to your therapist about activities that can be an alternative to your chemical or behavioral addiction, such as self-care habits. When you feel a craving, do something that has proven successful in the past. Self-care is a critical component to recovery, and a healthy lifestyle will empower you to cope with your addictive temptations, rather than simply creating new avenues to act out.

HOW TO PREVENT CROSS-ADDICTIONS

The Old Testament records the story of King Hezekiah. We read part of that story in 2 Chronicles 32. The king's first task was to protect his people. In those days, that meant building a solid wall of defense around major cities. Hearing of a pending attack from an outside enemy, Hezekiah did three things. First, he inspected the wall. Second, he fortified the parts of that wall that had weakened over time. Third, he built a second wall of defense.

For Hezekiah, remaining strong was all about prevention. He couldn't wait until the enemy was close to start building a second wall of defense. In recovery, we take the steps to prevent the enemy from taking us down, before we even see him coming. That applies to substitute addictions. Wisdom tells us to do all we can to limit the potential of falling into a new addiction.

Brittany Oliver shares these insights:

> It is not uncommon for those in recovery to try and find
> something to fill the hole addiction leaves, but it can lead
> to financial stress, emotional problems, and other issues.
> Finding new interests and hobbies is an important part of
> the recovery process, but it is critical to make sure there is
> a healthy balance established as well. Once those interests
> become excessive and compulsive, it may be time to take a
> step back and assess why that is happening.[17]

To create balance and ensure your hobbies do not become addictions, it is important to make sure you do not allow them to dictate your time. Neglecting your other responsibilities and relationships in favor of your hobbies can create a problem. Rather than allowing your hobbies to run your life, creating a schedule and relying on friends or family for feedback can help you stay organized, maintain control, and feel good about what you do.

If you are unable to find that balance on your own, it may be worthwhile to reach out for professional help. Experiencing a need to fill a void following addiction recovery is normal, but it does not make it easy to cope with. Talking to a therapist can help you uncover underlying reasons you may be struggling to feel fulfilled and work with you to create a plan moving forward. Recovery does not happen overnight, and dealing with difficult feelings and situations takes time. Allow yourself the space to explore these topics and find healthy ways to cope. By doing so, you can minimize the risk of developing cross-addictions and find better balance in your everyday life.

While there are probably hundreds of specific strategies that may be helpful in preventing dual addictions, research has landed on four strategies that will help to keep us out of the ditch.[18]

If you find that you tend to replace your addiction with another activity or substance, there are a few tested ways you can curb that habit and modify your behaviors both now and in the future:

1. Address the underlying causes of your addiction. Although you should have already done this in your recovery, returning to address the root causes of your addiction again will be an ongoing process. Just as recovery is a lifelong journey, you will have to remain vigilant and fight to overcome your personal struggles every day.

2. Become aware of your unhealthy habits and develop strategies to counteract them. Your recovery coach or sponsor can help you develop self-awareness of harmful habits and develop coping strategies to maintain your sobriety.

3. Mentally practice by visualizing yourself making healthy decisions. Enrolling in a recovery program provides you with an excellent opportunity to practice making healthy decisions. You should seek out guided structure and accountability. Then practice making healthy choices by visualizing yourself doing just that.

4. Recognize the difference between a healthy activity or hobby and an addiction. The key to living a healthy life in recovery is maintaining balance. You may not always be able to see when a hobby or activity turns into an unhealthy addiction, but a sponsor or therapist can help you see the trends you might otherwise miss.

HOW TO BOUNCE BACK FROM SUBSTITUTE ADDICTIONS

As you progress in your long-term recovery, it would be naïve to assume there won't be challenges. You may be among the many addicts who have wrestled with multiple addictions. The question becomes how to recover, not only from your primary addiction, but from the additional layers of compulsive behaviors, which have taken over. In your effort to overcome a cross-addiction, never minimize the need for therapy. Because the secondary addiction has received little or no notice, you are probably behind, in terms of confronting its origins and grip on your life.

It is generally suggested that you work on this addiction with a therapist and in a state of abstinence.[19] Most often, an underlying issue attracts the addictive behavior so it can act as a coping mechanism. The issue can be, for example, an anxiety-generating situation, an unfinished grieving process, or it might be linked to a past traumatic event. Identifying and uncovering these issues and trying to heal them will contribute to the recovery process and help to prevent new addictions from developing.

If you have replaced one addiction with another, an addiction treatment program that uses evidence-based therapy may be an ideal way to curb addictive behaviors and uncover the root of these behaviors. Sometimes it is also necessary to use medication in conjunction with therapy.[20]

Some of the most effective, evidence-based methods to fight addictions are:

- Cognitive and Dialectical Behavioral Therapy (CBT and DBT): Through CBT, one learns to identify and correct problematic thinking and behaviors by helping to develop more accurate thoughts and effective coping strategies.
- Motivational Enhancement Therapy: This is particularly effective with alcohol and cannabis addictions in engaging people to enter treatment.
- Trauma-informed approaches: This technique addresses consequences of traumatic experiences, changes problematic thinking, and develops coping strategies. It helps to recognize one's need to be respected, informed, connected, and hopeful regarding his own recovery.

Of course, overcoming a substitute addiction can't all be about therapy. You need to adopt some practical steps that can be implemented daily. All the therapy in the world will only help if you are willing to do hard work yourself. Here are a few steps you can begin to take today:

1. Accentuate the positive. Finding positive, healthy, and beneficial activities to replace an abused substance or behavior is one major way to make transitioning into recovery a less daunting process. Focus less on what you have lost and more on what you have left. Muhammed Ali told everyone he was the greatest before he was. That's the kind of positive outlook that will carry you through the hardest day of recovery.

2. Eliminate the negative. Replacing the negative behaviors of addiction limits the chances that relapse will occur. The triggers will still be there, but having ways to cope with them that don't include negative behavior patterns results in continued progress in your recovery journey.

3. Latch onto the affirmative. Being accountable to people who will celebrate the little victories is also immensely helpful in recovery. Everyone has an emotional need for affirmation. Especially in early recovery, when the feelings are very raw, being recognized for a positive choice will light up the reward center of the brain like a pinball machine.[21] A support system of friends, family, counselors, and friends in recovery will go a long way.

4. Don't mess with Mr. In-Between. Being halfway in is a dangerous thing with addiction and recovery. When excuses are made for lapses in judgment, or when one addiction is traded for another, it's a slippery slope downhill. What else is down that hill? Relapse. Staying sober requires having every angle covered: an understanding of addictive behaviors, positive alternative behaviors, and people requiring accountability. As I tell people every day: "If you are 90 percent in, you are 100 percent out."

DISCUSSION QUESTIONS

1. What is your primary addiction?

2. What are your two or three primary hobbies?

3. Have any of these hobbies become an addiction?

4. Having read this lesson, do you think you may have a substitute addiction?

5. What is there in your life that could become an addiction?

6. Have you done anything to work on your substitute addiction?

7. What steps will you take to be free from any cross-addictions?

Chapter 9

THE SILENT ASSASSIN: PRIDE

I have seen it happen far too often. A man or woman gets into recovery. After months or years of stumbling, slipping, and relapsing, they figure it out. Finally, the addict puts together an extended string of sober days. They eventually collect their one-year chip. They're on their way.

And then a relapse occurs along the way. How does this happen? Remember, any relapse is the predictable outcome of a series of poor choices. But in this case, the addict was still going to meetings. They were sponsoring others. So, what went wrong?

The silent assassin: pride.

I have seen pride take so many addicts out after they had achieved significant periods of recovery. Pride is as deadly as it is silent. There's a reason it makes the list of the seven deadly sins. C. S. Lewis called pride, "the essential vice, the utmost evil."[1] From pride, so many other problems flow.

Pride comes from the French word *prud*, which is often translated "arrogant, haughty." It is in that arrogance that addicts fall. They want to move on, check the box, and declare themselves "recovered." Past tense. Done. Mission completed. Recovery expert Steven Melemis said it like this: "Clients often want to put their addiction behind them and forget that they ever had an addiction."[2]

HOW WE GOT HERE

We know that pride comes before fall (Proverbs 16:18). But what comes before pride? How is it possible that an alcoholic can drink for thirty years, be sober for three years, and think they are beyond the possibility of relapse? How is it that the gambling addict can ever think they are safe inside a casino again? Yet, that's where so many of us live every day. It's called overconfidence. Or pride. The silent assassin.

Shernide Delva explains:

> Overconfidence may be a trait acquired in recovery, or it can be a trait a person struggled with before sobriety. Most addicts battle overconfidence their entire lives. For example, those times when you acted out and thought no one would notice. Sadly, this behavior can persist after recovery, even after hitting rock bottom. Even those with no history of overconfidence can start to become overzealous in their recovery program. They start to believe that they are above the rest of their friends and family because of the work they have done in their recovery."[3]

I'm sure that if we tried hard enough, we could come up with a hundred reasons addicts become overconfident and prideful in their recovery. But from my research, I have narrowed that list to three.

1. Fear of the loss of control. Dr. Randi Gunther, clinical psychologist and counselor, writes:

> One reason people act egoistically [great word!] prideful is that they are fearful that any admission of their wrongdoings will result in automatically giving in to being controlled. They can only think hierarchically; one person, and only one person can be in charge of the rules of the relationship."[4]

Addicts want to be in control; we all do. To lay down one's pride is to admit, "I'm not in control." This is the essence of recovery— admitting we are not in control. But it never comes easily.

2. Overcompensating for low self-esteem. Prideful behavior is the natural response to internal feelings of low self-worth. People who feel this way act prideful, while battling immense insecurity internally. They cannot bear the thought of being seen as inadequate, timid, or dependent. As such, they present themselves as needing nothing, autonomous, and untouchable. Often, they are boastful, sometimes exaggerating their accomplishments to maintain their outward influence over others.

3. Attachment to dominance and power. There are those who do not consider anyone but themselves to be in charge of the relationship. They not only want control of the distribution of all resources, but they take pride in being the only one who can do that "right." They will take care of those whom they see as less-than, which can include their partners and any dependents, but they will not tolerate any form of feedback in response.

SIGNS OF OVERCONFIDENCE

I call pride the "silent assassin" because it never rises up and declares itself. The proud never lead with that. We only claim to be proud of others, never ourselves. So how do you recognize it in others? More importantly, how do you see it in yourself? So far, science has yet to produce a blood test for pride. Even if they did, the more overconfident among us would see no need to take such a test.

But to identify one's level of pride or overconfidence is a worthwhile endeavor. Such an attitude has brought down too many recovering addicts for us to just ignore its powerful existence. So, let's unpack some of the more obvious signs of overconfidence. Check yourself on each of these. If you answer yes to any of these questions, you probably have an issue with overconfidence and pride:

- Do I reject suggestions from others?
- Do I judge others by their actions, while judging myself by my intentions?
- Do I seek immediate results?
- Do I think I have all the answers?
- Do I put in less time in recovery work today than I did a year ago?
- Has it been more than three months since I read a recovery book?
- Do I see my situation as unique from anyone else's?
- Do I talk more than I listen?
- Do I feel I deserve preferential treatment?
- Do I describe myself as "healed" or "recovered"?

Shernide Delva says:

It is crucial to understand that addiction will not simply disappear. Regardless of how long you have been sober, addiction can always creep up again. Addiction is not a curable disease; it is a manageable disease that does not have room for overconfidence."[5]

I love that sentence: "Addiction is not a curable disease; it is a manageable disease." Not only do I agree with that, but I am also grateful for that. It is my addiction that keeps me in a state of surrender. I pity those who don't have the benefit of an addiction; they have to find the motivation for complete surrender somewhere else.

THE DANGER OF PRIDE

Nothing is a bigger threat to advanced recovery than pride. Psychologist John Amodeo says, "A more genuine and stable self-worth is based upon validating, affirming, and valuing ourselves as we are."[6] The last three words are key: "as we are." Not "as we want others to think we are." Pride projects an image rather than a true self. I often tell people that when we meet someone new, we aren't really meeting the person; we are meeting their agent. We are seeing the person they want us to think they are. And we do the same thing. We are too proud to let anyone see us as anything less than our Facebook images would suggest.

Andrew Murray says, "Humility is the first duty and highest virtue of every creature. Pride is the root of every sin."[7] I doubt any of us would want to make the case for pride. We agree, at least on an intellectual level, that pride is not a good thing. But in a practical way, why is pride a danger to our sobriety? There are several reasons:

- When the addict is consumed with pride, they will find it harder to acknowledge their mistakes. Pride blinds them to the risk they are putting their sobriety under when they miss meetings or lapse in other recovery work. With pride comes a diminished priority of recovery work, which puts that recovery in danger.
- Pride builds a wedge between the addict and their support group. By show of hands, how many of you are more attracted to people when they are arrogant, prideful, and have to always be right? (Not seeing any hands go up, I'll move on.) When that wedge exists, the addict loses the connection with others, their greatest ally.
- When we struggle with pride, we are far less likely to ask for help. This means we will not have the tools in place to stay sober. Pride says, "I know it all." When you think you know it all, you are unlikely to ask for someone else's help.

- Pride is detachment from reality. From the American Addiction Centers, we read, "If people have an unrealistic sense of pride, it is likely to mean that they have lost touch with reality. To get the most from sobriety, the individual needs to face life on life's terms."[8]
- To gain the additional knowledge necessary for continued growth, the addict may need to put aside some of their preconceived ideas and beliefs. If a person is excessively proud, they may struggle to do this.
- Pride is a spiritual problem. Most spiritual paths require that the individual let go of their pride. Those who have an excessively high opinion of themselves will struggle to make progress on a spiritual path.

DOES PRIDE HAVE AN UPSIDE?

This is a tricky question. While the Bible is generally critical of pride, and while pride can be one of the greatest obstacles to advanced recovery, pride can have an upside. When we see pride as confidence or belief in our ability to overcome, it becomes an ally, rather than an enemy.

Consider these questions:

- Is it wrong to be proud of collecting your next sobriety chip?
- Is it okay to be proud of the achievements of your sponsees?
- How important is it for someone else to be proud of you?
- What accomplishment in life are you most proud of?
- Can you be proud without being overconfident?
- How can pride be an asset to your recovery?

I hesitate to suggest the benefits of pride, lest you forget the immense danger that it can bring. Being prideful is a huge threat to long-term recovery; never doubt that. But let's consider some upsides to healthy pride in recovery:

1. Pride may be seen as a reward for a job well done. Getting sober and building a new life is an incredible accomplishment, and you have every right to feel good about this.

2. Pride in one's recovery can be an encouragement to continue the hard work that is necessary to maintain that recovery.

3. A sense of pride can motivate a person to take on challenges, which, once achieved, result in a healthy sense of accomplishment.

4. Group pride can be helpful. You might partner with an accountability person or recovery group, to set corporate recovery goals. Achieving these goals as a group is something to be proud of, and it serves as a good motivator.

5. Pride in someone else's sobriety is a win-win. The need for respect is innate for each of us. When we earn that respect from a mentor or sponsor, it motivates us to take our recovery to another level.

Now, having said that, we must understand that pride is generally a detriment to our recovery. Think of healthy pride as that which motivates us to move forward, whereas unhealthy, more common pride leads us to get stuck in the past, as though our accomplishments guarantee an unspotted future. One of my 100 recovery rules is this: your past victory is no guarantee of future success.

HOW PRIDE LEADS TO RELAPSE

Confidence is generally recognized as an excellent quality. We are told to believe in ourselves in every endeavor we pursue. Whether it is a sport or a school exam, having confidence is touted as the key to success. However, when it comes to addiction recovery, can too much confidence become harmful?

Shernide Delva cautions:

> The reality is too much confidence is not great in recovery. While it is great to have confidence in your program, it is important to stay humble. The emotions that arise from overconfidence can block underlying issues. Having an overconfident mindset can hinder your recovery process. It is important to make recovery a priority regardless of how much time you have.[9]

Here are some ways that pride encourages relapse.

1. Distorted self-image. A major part of recovery is staying humble. Overconfidence makes people believe they are not as "bad" as newcomers. They may start to feel they no longer need their program and start to wonder if they are even an addict at all. Overconfidence encourages the belief that it is not a huge deal to have a drink, use casually, or take in an occasional porn image.

2. Irrational thoughts. Overconfidence can lead an addict to believe they deserve certain rewards in conjunction with their success. They might feel as if they are worthy of a celebration. They may quickly convince themselves that one drink is not going to hurt because they are "in control" of their addiction. This is risky behavior and can lead the addict down a slippery slope.

3. Complacent behavior. This is when an addict starts to believe that their addiction is not nearly as bad as they once thought. They start believing that they can live normally due to the length of time they have been sober. They think they are cured, so they slowly stop going to meetings and stop thinking of themselves as an addict. This leads to a relapse or substitute addiction.

THE BENEFITS OF HUMILITY IN RECOVERY

St. Augustine said, "It was pride that changed angels into devils; it is humility that makes men as angels."[10] Humility plays a huge role in recovery, with direct and indirect effects. The indirect effects are that a person who walks in humility will become the man or woman best equipped to face the temptations and triggers that are an inevitable part of recovery. Dr. Dimitrios Tsatiris, professor of psychiatry at Northeast Ohio Medical University, writes, "Humility has a positive effect on self-awareness and it strengthens social bonds."[11]

As for direct benefits, we will unpack several of those here:

- People with humility have no fear of admitting that they do not know something. This makes it much easier for them to learn and develop.
- The individual who shows a bit of humility is far less likely to experience conflicts in their life. Excessively proud people always rub others the wrong way.
- Being humble means having a beginner's mind. This means that the individual does not allow their opinions and beliefs to get in the way of learning new things.
- If people are humble, they are more able to help others in need. Doing some type of service is a wonderful way to strengthen sobriety.
- If people are humble, they will have fewer qualms about asking for help when they are struggling in recovery. This means that they will be less likely to relapse.
- Those individuals who exemplify humility find it much easier to make new friends.
- Those who are following a spiritual path will find humility to be a wonderful asset.

HOW TO AVOID PRIDE IN RECOVERY

It is important to know how to rid ourselves of the burden of pride. But better yet, we can find coping strategies that will allow us to not become prideful in the first place. Pride is a destabilizing force that must be avoided at all costs.[12]

There are things that the individual can do to avoid the dangers of excessive pride, including:

- Developing a beginner's mindset means that the individual is always willing to learn new things.
- Developing humility is a great way to temper pride.

- Learning to think critically will encourage the individual to challenge their own ideas about themselves.
- The individual should avoid taking themselves too seriously.
- Spending time helping other people can be a great antidote to excessive pride, but only if the addict is humble about it.
- Mindful meditation can allow people to become more objective about their own thoughts and behaviors.
- Practicing spiritual disciplines will maintain the foundation on which successful recovery is built.

WORKING STEP 7

Step 7 – "We humbly asked God to remove our shortcomings."[13]

Step 7 is the shortest Step—just eight words. Eight very powerful words. Notice, the genius of Step 7 is that it doesn't require us to admit our *addiction*, but our *shortcomings*. If you only address your addiction, your shortcomings will remain. But if you address your shortcomings, you've got a shot at overcoming your addiction. And if you are like every other human being on the planet, pride is one of your shortcomings. If you can't see that for yourself, that only proves it's a *big* problem!

John Amondeo, author of *Dancing with Fire*, writes:

> Pride is driven by poor self-worth and shame. We feel so badly about ourselves that we compensate by feeling superior. We look for others' flaws as a way to conceal our own. We relish criticizing others as a defense against recognizing our own shortcomings.[14]

The answer is Step 7—the Step that attacks our pride head-on. Whether you attend 12-Step groups for your substance abuse or some kind of behavioral addiction, the theme of Step 7 is central to all recovery. Within the larger recovery community, a common theme is that by the time a person reaches Step 7, considerable progress has been made in terms of developing the type of lifestyle that supports continued abstinence, but that lifestyle cannot be maintained without completing this step.[15]

Let's break this step down.

"We humbly"

Again, our pride is the issue. Even before we address the shortcoming of pride, we must address the attitude of pride. We start with humility. It is the only way to pray, the only way to approach the God of the universe. Yes, we are to come before his throne with confidence, but that confidence is no replacement for humility.

"Asked God"

We don't demand. We ask. Again, this is a picture of humility. Of course, God wants to cleanse us of our sins—including pride. But we leave the outcome in his capable hands. We ask him. And only him. No one else can do what he can do. Only God can remove our shortcomings.

"To remove"

We don't sugarcoat our issues. We don't dance around the subject. Nothing short of removal will do. To ask God to forgive us would be commendable. But that is not enough. You wouldn't slap someone, and then ask them to forgive you for slapping them while you continued to slap them. The behavior must stop—completely. Our shortcomings must be removed—completely.

"Our shortcomings"

We all have shortcomings. There is nothing to apologize about for that. It's what you do with your shortcomings that matters. Step 7 says to give them to God. Ask him to remove them all. Of course, how he does that is his business. Some of your shortcomings will go away immediately. Others will require work, time, and patience. Addiction usually falls into this category. As does pride.

Patrick Carnes writes that successful recovery requires the addict to adopt this mantra: "I exercise humility and embrace my mistakes and needs." That is the essence of Step 7. And that is how we overcome pride.[16]

HOW TO LET GO OF PRIDE

As we have established, pride can be highly debilitating. While the right kind of pride, practiced in the right kind of way, can be helpful, Henry Ford had it right. He observed, "A man given to pride is usually proud of the wrong thing."[17] Given that history has only produced one man who never fell to pride, and you aren't him, you are among the 100 percent who need to learn how to let go of pride from time to time.

Dr. Randi Gunther, clinical psychologist, has contributed to this cause. He identifies eight steps to a healthy response to our pride.[18]

1. Be willing to recognize what has contributed to your pride and share those experiences with your partner. Being vulnerable that way can encourage your partner to want to help you change.
2. Open your mind and heart to the joys of authentic transparency that allow you to give up the burden of controlling and owning others.
3. Recognize that humility is a beautiful state, and once achieved, can be amazingly liberating.
4. Commit to taking down the barrier between what is thought and felt inside and what is expressed to your partner.
5. Trust that your partner will feel compassion and support for who you are trying to become.
6. Recognize what the price of humility may entail and make certain you are ready and willing to pay it.
7. Recognize the positive impact of letting go of your unhealthy pride will have on the people you love.
8. Have the courage to stay the course even though discouraging obstacles may arise.

Too many men and women struggle with pride as they move deeper into their recovery. A lack of humility is at the root of most relapse among those with long-term sobriety. Nothing is as heartbreaking as receiving yet another call from a friend who has five or ten years of sobriety, only to tell me of their recent fall. It doesn't have to happen. True humility is no guarantee that you will never fall, but a lack of humility virtually guarantees that you will.

DISCUSSION QUESTIONS

1. Is pride always a bad thing? If not, when is pride a good thing?

2. What can you justifiably be proud of?

3. On a scale of 1–10, how much do you struggle with pride?

4. How does pride affect your recovery?

5. Do you think you could ever suffer a relapse?

6. What areas of your recovery still need the most work?

7. Would others say you are more humble or more prideful?

8. Will you take a moment to humbly ask God to remove all your shortcomings right now?

Chapter 10

ADVANCED SCOREBOARD

I love baseball. I always have. It goes back to April 15, 1968. As an eight-year-old boy, I attended my first Major League game with my Cub Scout group. The Houston Astros beat the New York Mets in the famous Astrodome, in the longest game in history at that point—24 innings.

I was hooked.

One of the things I've always loved about baseball is that it is a game of statistics and analytics. You can spend the entire game just taking in the numbers on the scoreboard:

- Score
- Hits
- RBI
- Home runs
- Batting average
- Errors
- ERA
- SB

- Passed balls
- AB
- Walks
- Strikeouts
- OBP
- SLG
- Speed of pitch
- Attendance

As you consider all those statistics, which is the only one that matters? Of course, that would be the score. Can you imagine a team claiming to have won the game because they had a good attendance number that day? Well, that is exactly how churches measure success every Sunday. What matters isn't what the players are accomplishing on the field, but how many people showed up to watch that day.

Ouch!

Now, let's apply this to advanced recovery. Could it be that we need a new scoreboard? Now is as good a time as any to say that I'm not a big fan of the check-in method of most 12-Step groups. "My name is Mark, and I'm a _____-aholic. My sobriety date is January 29, 2015." It's not that my length of sobriety doesn't matter. It does matter—a lot. But it's not the *only* thing that matters. Have you ever sat in a meeting, when someone checked in by saying something like, "My name is Rob, and I've been sober for 2,163 days"? While I celebrate the length of recovery, I often wonder, "How much could Rob have accomplished if he could reclaim the four hours it took him to do that math?"

Again, length of sobriety matters. But I want to make the case that a good scoreboard has far more on it than that. There are several other factors to be considered when measuring the success of one's recovery.

12-STEP GROUP

Let's start with an easy one. Do you go to a group each week? One of my 100 recovery rules is, "If you aren't in a group each week, that might explain the mess you're in." Another rule: "The best group is the one you actually attend."

I have known a lot of guys who have quit meetings. They say something like, "The meetings are repetitious. We do the same thing every week. We can't even engage in cross talk. Blah, blah, blah."

I agree with all of that. If I were king for a day, I'd change many things about the typical 12-Step meeting. But here's the thing. Not every meal consists of my favorite items. I'd love it if ice cream was an appetizer at every restaurant. Get rid of all foods that are green. Quit calling chicken a "meat." (I'm from Texas, where "beef" and "meat" are synonymous.) But I still eat vegetables. And I eat three times a day. That includes boring meals. I've been making the same meatloaf recipe for forty years. I've been making my mom's biscuits and gravy recipe every Christmas morning for forty years. I do it because, for me, it works.

Let's return to the guy who quit meetings because he doesn't think he needs them anymore. Fast forward. That story rarely ends well. The person who quits meetings usually quits recovery soon after. According to the American Society of Addiction Medicine, "12-Step recovery programs offer a proven approach that addresses a person's psychology, spirituality, and personal values. These programs encourage connectedness to others, a willingness to engage with others, and the courage to humbly ask for help."[1]

I obviously believe in 12-Step meetings; otherwise, I wouldn't go to so many of them. But I'll let the gurus of 12-Step meetings make their own case. Alcoholics Anonymous has been doing this for eighty-five years, as of this writing—since 1939. These are five benefits of attending meetings, according to AA:[2]

1. You learn new strategies for overcoming addiction. AA meetings are the ultimate setting in which to learn new tricks and tips for overcoming alcohol addiction. At nearly every 12-Step meeting, you'll have the opportunity to listen to other addicts describe and share their personal experiences with addiction.

2. You connect with like-minded people. Nearly everyone you meet at 12-Step meetings understands what you're going through as a recovering addict. This bond allows you to get through difficult roadblocks on the path to recovery, especially on days when you're feeling lost, hopeless, and alone.

3. There is an absence of judgment. Judging others is not a part of the 12-Step philosophy; therefore, you can attend meetings with peace of mind, knowing that you won't be judged for your actions, past or present. When you attend 12-Step meetings, the general focus will be on honesty, sincerity, and a willingness to help other addicts overcome their addictions.

4. You get help where you need it. The early stages of recovery are often perilous and extremely difficult. You might feel a strong urge to act out, and face problems with breaking old habits. Joining a group gives you access to help whenever you need it.

5. Meetings are free. 12-Step groups take an offering, but you don't have to give. The only requirement for membership is a desire to stop acting out in your area of addiction.

Now, I ask any therapists who are reading this to turn away for one paragraph. Here it is. A Stanford professor and her collaborators conducted extensive research, which concluded that the fellowship of a 12-Step group helps more people achieve sobriety than therapy does.[3] Don't misunderstand. I'm a huge believer in therapy. It's not an either/or proposition. Do you need 12-Step groups, or do you need therapy? The answer is yes.

LENGTH OF SOBRIETY

I've already said that the length of sobriety isn't the only thing. But it is a *big* thing. We can fall into either of two ditches. On one extreme, we have the guy (or gal) who can't say it enough: "My name is Jim, and I've been sober for three years, seven months, and fifteen days. I work at a manufacturing center, and I've been sober for three years, seven months, and fifteen days. I have a wife and two kids, and I've been sober for three years, seven months, and fifteen days."

I know the sobriety dates for several guys because I hear them every week. That's great! But if the only way you measure your recovery is by a sobriety date, your recovery is suspect.

Then we have the ditch on the other side of the road. "My name is Alicia, and I have embraced recovery for two years now." What does that mean— "embraced sobriety"? A man in my 12-Step group recently picked up a chip, marking the anniversary of when he first "embraced sobriety" (his exact words). If I had been the guy with the chips at that meeting, I wouldn't have given him one. I would have said, "Give me a specific date, man! I need to hear a date!"

Length of sobriety is probably the clearest way to measure your recovery. Again, it's not the only way, and I'm not even sure it's the best way. But it is the clearest way. Lyle Fried, CEO and President of The Shores Treatment & Recovery of Florida, says, "Sustainable recovery requires improvements in the recovering individual's relationships, living situation, finances, employment, and overall well-being." Then Fried goes on to lay the foundation of "tallying the number of days sober."[4]

There are specific benefits to counting sobriety days and celebrating milestones. One of the most obvious benefits is that it builds confidence and positivity for the addict, when he can identify tangible evidence for his recovery. Addiction expert April Smith writes:

> The reasons for counting vary, but the most obvious is that not wanting to lose "time" can provide a reason to stay away from that first drink or other drug that could lead us to more. Seeing those days of sobriety rack up on the Sobriety Calculators that are now on many people's phones can be gratifying, and keep people motivated to do what it takes to achieve their goals.[5]

The public nature of celebrating sobriety dates should not be dismissed. When a recovering addict collects another chip, this motivates the rest of the group. Many tell themselves, "If he can do it, I suppose I can do it, too." A recovery center in California makes the rowdy celebration of sobriety dates a centerpiece to their recovery process.[6] April Smith says it like this:

Reporting sobriety time in meetings can be a happy occasion. The congratulations one receives on every day, every month, and every year may be the only positive reinforcement that some people get when their lives have been so destroyed by the wreckage of addiction and the stigma around it, that they feel proud of their time achieved.[7]

Achieving measurable goals brings an enormous sense of accomplishment and hope to most men and women in recovery. With the focus of this project being on advanced recovery and with my criteria of advanced recovery including at least one year of unbroken sobriety, I was interested in learning how having one year of sobriety affects recovery. While there is little evidence for such a narrow example of sobriety, the *Journal of Substance Abuse Treatment* sheds a little light on this. Egan Hagen and his colleagues have done extensive research, which showed that one year of sobriety improves overall satisfaction with life.[8] Hagen concluded that by measuring his first year of sobriety, the addict enjoys an improved lifestyle, is better able to make sound decisions, and becomes relatively free from psychological distress.

Again, the length of sobriety isn't the *only* thing. But it's a really *big* thing.

EMPLOYMENT AND FINANCIAL STABILITY

Typically, women draw their self-esteem from their relationships, while men draw their self-esteem from their work. Usually, when women meet each other, their first questions are about family and children. Men lead with, "What do you do?" Women are human beings; men are human doings, but that's how we are generally wired. And I'm not likely to rewire the entire male persuasion with one chapter. As we say in recovery, let's face life on life's terms.

Employment and financial stability are key factors in advanced recovery. We keep score. The questions are endless:

1. What do you do for a living?
2. How long have you worked there?
3. How much money do you make?
4. How big is your house?
5. What car do you drive?
6. How do you invest your money?
7. How did your retirement portfolio do last year?

Of course, most of us are slick enough to not ask those questions. But the information is easy enough to find. How many of us have googled someone to find their address, simply so we can look up the value of their home? Have I ever done that?

Guilty as charged.

Let's quit apologizing for this. The fact is, when our jobs or finances struggle, we struggle. Financial issues are one of the major causes for stress, and stress is never your friend. So, getting your financial house in order matters for your recovery—a lot.

I've lived on both sides. I've been poor, and I've been middle class. I have come to this conclusion: poor is overrated. It is a good thing to feel comfortable and stable financially. I heard about a study that found that Americans are happier if they make more money—up to a point. Once their income hits $70,000 per year, anything above that does not make them any happier. In other words, financial independence is helpful. Being debt-free and living within our means is good for our recovery. But as far as recovery goes, having a boat, exotic car, and second home do not result in happiness—or recovery. Lyle Fried says, "After leaving treatment, individuals in recovery should take steps to secure employment and improve their financial situation."[9] Note that he didn't say to get rich, just to become secure.

As far as the scoreboard goes, I'm not going to give you a specific goal for financial security and employment. Set your own goals. Make them S.M.A.R.T. (specific, measurable, attainable, realistic, timely). Psychotherapist Sherry Gaba says that the challenge of financial responsibility is one of the greatest obstacles addicts face on the road to recovery.[10] Take that challenge seriously.

Let me offer seven reasons that your work and finances are important to your recovery.

1. They build routine and structure.
2. They establish accountability.
3. They create achievable goals.
4. They stabilize and build success.
5. They grow self-reliance.
6. They gain trust and purpose.
7. They teach responsibility.

It is hard to put employment and finances on the recovery scoreboard. How much money is enough? How do you measure a sense of enjoyment at work? I suggest that a feeling of security in these areas is something that you know when you see it. Regardless of how you measure it, you need it—reasonable success in your professional and financial life.

PHYSICAL CONDITIONING

One of the phenomena that I have observed while working with hundreds of recovering addicts is the correlation between physical exercise and successful recovery. Lyle Fried notes that "physical health is a key to maintaining recovery."[11] Of all the markers for successful recovery, this may be the one that most of us miss. In fact, many addicts go the opposite direction. Rather than caring for themselves physically, they eat too much and exercise too little.

How do we measure success in this area? One study concluded, "Recovery is indicated in part by improvement in overall physical health. This may be measured by physical examinations."[12] And a review published in the journal *PLOS ONE* looked at forty-three studies with more than 3,000 participants. In addition to a reduction or cessation in addiction activity, the studies found that improved markers of physical health decreased depressive symptoms. Further, regular exercise was associated with decreased addictive behaviors in about seventy-five percent of the studies.[13]

There is also an interesting connection between exercise and the pace of recovery. Writing for *Psychology Today*, Dr. Lantie Jorandby reports, "Recent research has found that regular vigorous exercise such as fast walking, swimming, running, or cycling can significantly shorten that brain-recovery timeframe."[14] A level of recovery that might otherwise take five years to attain may be accomplished in much less time, if we simply engage an effective program of physical fitness.

A more direct connection between exercise and recovery may be drawn. In the arena of drug abuse, research has shown that "exercise boosts the mood, protects against illness, and increases the rate of abstinence, while reducing cravings and lowering the likelihood of relapse."[15] This alone should be enough to convince any addict to get into the gym, take up cycling, or engage in some form of regular exercise.

Researcher and author Martin Preston addressed the subject of physical care in its connection to recovery extensively. He writes:

> Exercise produces protective effects during the different transitional phases that occur when someone is recovering from addiction. Experts believe this could be due to similarities in how exercise affects the brain. Physical activity increases euphoria and well-being in the same way as taking drugs or drinking alcohol because it works on our pleasure and reward system, releasing the same feel-good chemicals. Exercise can also help to reduce withdrawal symptoms, replace triggers, and boost self-esteem.[16]

Preston identifies the following benefits to physical conditioning:

1. Relieving stress and improving focus

    Stress is one of the leading causes of addiction. Any form of exercise increases endorphins, which helps you to feel good, inside and out. Physical activity gets your heart pumping, muscles moving, and energy soaring, thereby helping to reduce the negative effects stress puts on the body. Physical activity also provides an escape from focusing on harmful thoughts and physically removes you from environments that may trigger a relapse.

2. Improving the quality and quantity of sleep

    Addictions and sleep disorders go hand in hand. Many people turn to their addictions to help them sleep, but the high levels of dopamine released can interrupt the body's natural sleep-wake cycle, making it difficult to fall asleep and stay asleep. Unfortunately, during the withdrawal process, people also find their sleep quality is affected. Moderate to vigorous exercise increases the amount of deep sleep you get, allowing the mind and body the time it needs to heal and recover. People who engage in as little as thirty minutes of exercise can see a benefit to sleep quality that same night.

3. Supporting mental health and emotional well-being

    When someone stops taking drugs or acting in their behavioral addiction, the body has to make a wide range of adjustments. It's no surprise that withdrawal from any addiction can bring about challenging mood swings, including feelings of anxiety and depression. Physical exercise provides a natural high that helps to replace the effects of substance abuse, lifting your mood, improving self-esteem, and making you feel more capable of dealing with recovery. A recent study found that running for fifteen minutes a day or walking for one hour reduces the risk of major depression.

4. Reducing the risk of chronic disease

    Long-term addiction takes its toll on the human body. Substance abuse slowly destroys vital cells and systems, leaving lifelong effects. This includes weakening the immune system and leaving it open to illness and disease. Strong evidence suggests physical activity reduces the risk of many conditions. Moderate to vigorous exercise was found to lower the risk of breast, bladder, lung, and colon cancer; exercise may also reduce the risk of existing conditions getting worse over time and improve overall quality of life and physical function.

5. Preventing cravings and relapse

    Adjunctive treatments such as mindfulness, wellness, and exercise have proven to be successful when used in combination with traditional psychotherapies, such as Cognitive Behavioral Therapy. Exercise training can help to reduce cravings and focus the mind to prevent a return to destructive addictive behaviors. In a trial involving young people at an addiction treatment clinic, those who enjoyed exercise were found to have improved self-esteem and perceived physical health, as well as greater confidence to resist drugs and alcohol.

FRIENDSHIPS WITH HEALTHY PEOPLE

I have found that three things are generally at the root of addiction: trauma, abuse, and isolation. Isolation is never your friend. You need people, and people need you. One of the common mistakes people make in recovery is to try to go it alone. One of my recovery rules is this: if you want to go fast, go alone; if you want to go far, go together. This isn't to say that the number of friends you can count provides a direct correlation to the success of your recovery. It is the quality of those connections that matters more than the quantity. Specifically, you need to build friendships with positive people; it is important to cut off toxic relationships.[17]

For some wise counsel about friendships, we can go all the way back to about 350 BC. There was a fellow you may have heard of who was pretty smart. His name was Aristotle. The ancient Greek philosopher had a lot to say on this subject. He called friendship the most important relationship one person can have with another. The right friends, he argued, can make us become better people because they can help us to improve our moral character by giving us more opportunities to practice virtue. And the opposite is also true. The wrong friends can bring us down.[18]

Of course, our human connections alone can't carry us to sobriety. The best outcome for advanced recovery is an integration of relationship recovery with addiction recovery.[19] Recovery is too complex to be reduced to a silver bullet. It is all about integration. The scoreboard includes a multitude of numbers. The various factors that feed long-term sobriety are nearly limitless.

Physician Kristen Fuller lays out six benefits of healthy relationships:[20]

- Friends are there to lift you up in joy and comfort you in sorrow.
- Friends help you develop social skills.
- True friends will give you a reality check.
- Friendships at a young age can help you develop healthy romantic relationships.
- Couple friendships can help your own relationship.
- Friends can improve your health and longevity.

FAMILY RELATIONSHIPS

The first step in recovery is admitting you have a problem. This is a common expression. But it applies to more than the addicted person. If you are a family member, this phrase should have meaning for you as well. It is normal to try to avoid conflict and stressful situations. Admitting there is something wrong in the family and that you can't fix it is hard to do. Perhaps you don't want to confront an addicted family member because you are worried about making matters worse.

Sometimes it is easier to reassure yourself that their problem isn't that bad or tell yourself that at least they are safe at home. Too often, family members freeze up and do nothing. The result can be the addict's downward spiral into depths they have never known before. Johann Hari, author of *Chasing the Scream*, says it like this:

> Communicating effectively with the recovering addict, creating a safe environment for all family members, including the recovering loved one, and gradually rebalancing the frayed family dynamic while providing ongoing support and encouragement to the one in recovery comprise a core element in his or her recovery—as well as contribute to an overall meaningful and purposeful life for all concerned.[21]

There are several benefits that strong family connections bring to the person in recovery. For starters, the family can offer emotional support. They also provide accountability, helping to put healthy boundaries in place. And wise families educate themselves, in order to give guidance and wisdom to the addicted family member. Finally, the close-knit family can provide an ounce of prevention. By establishing a stable environment, the odds shift toward the addict's favor.

Let's get specific. The Ashley Recovery Center has identified five strategies the family can embrace in their effort to protect and encourage the person who is battling for her sobriety:[22]

1. Offer encouragement and emotional support. Your loved one needs to know that you are in their corner, that they have your love and support. Make sure you communicate these words of encouragement often as they go through their recovery journey.

2. Provide space for open communication. Your loved one will need a safe, accepting place to communicate the emotions, struggles, or fears they experience during early recovery. When inevitable setbacks occur, they will benefit from your input and counsel.

3. Offer logistical support in early recovery. Many times, the loved one in recovery has to pick up the pieces of their lives and start over. They may need a ride to work, meetings, or legal appointments or someone to pick up or drop off their kids at school. The family can pitch in and help with these logistical needs.

4. Set healthy boundaries. Establishing realistic boundaries helps both the family members and the loved one in recovery. When all parties understand the need for boundaries and clearly articulate them to each other, including any consequences if boundaries are breached, it becomes a safeguard against family dysfunction.

5. Include them in family events. Strive to rebuild cohesion in the family by including your loved one at your family gatherings. You can also show them your support by excluding any substances from family events or gatherings.

SPIRITUAL DOMAIN

The role of spirituality in recovery must not be overlooked. Those of us who have a faith bias will always celebrate any recovery story that proclaims the power of the gospel. We love the story of a man or woman whose faith in Christ has set them free. At the very least, we see an integration of faith and recovery. I like to remind skeptics that seven of the twelve Steps refer to a "Higher Power." We cannot divorce the spiritual connection from advanced recovery.

Even the APA, which certainly takes no position on religion, has documented the value of spirituality for recovery. They have posted an insightful article titled, "Religious Faith and Spirituality," which makes the following case:[23]

- Among people recovering from addiction, a new study finds that higher levels of religious faith and spirituality were associated with several positive mental health outcomes, including more optimism about life and higher resilience to stress, which may help contribute to the recovery process.
- The study involved 236 people who were recovering from alcoholism and/or drug addiction. This study represents the largest self-report study ever undertaken examining the relation between religious faith, spirituality, and mental health outcomes among people recovering from substance abuse. The findings show that higher religious faith and spirituality are associated with increased coping, greater resilience to stress, an optimistic life orientation, greater perceived social support, and lower levels of anxiety.
- Other studies have found similar outcomes, with those enjoying long-term sobriety more likely to self-identify as "spiritual" than "religious." The APA study went even further. It found denominational effects. Protestant groups appear to maintain a closer relationship between faith and psychological health than Catholic groups in terms of anxiety management, but Catholic groups tend to be more stress resilient. Too few Jewish and Muslim participants were available for comparison.[24]

While Christianity is certainly not the only religion that advocates the values of recovery, it offers a wonderful lens through which to view recovery as a long-term, attractive, and sustainable lifestyle. And there is evidence to support implementing faith and spirituality into recovery treatment programs. Scientists have found that spirituality combats addiction in the following ways:[25]

- Bolsters accountability and resilience in many areas of life
- Increases situations that require collaboration
- Decreases substance abuse and use in teenagers and young adults
- Decreases instances of addiction, dependence, and substance abuse in both men and women

Unfortunately, some strains of Christianity still stigmatize addiction, making it hard for some Christians to feel comfortable seeking treatment. This is why many who attend recovery meetings will refer to these as "more of a church than church." Slowly, progress in the organized Church seems to be evolving. But what seems undeniable is that spirituality is a key component to advanced recovery, whether it takes place within the context of organized religion or not.

SUMMARY SCOREBOARD

We have only scratched the surface in identifying the factors that should be included on the recovery scoreboard. If we have accomplished nothing else, we want you to understand that while celebrating sobriety anniversaries is important, the scoreboard is bigger than that.[26]

We have identified just a few lines that belong on the advanced recovery scoreboard: engagement in groups, length of sobriety, employment/financial security, physical fitness, friendships, family relationships, and a spiritual connection. Research confirms that recovery is difficult to measure and has different meanings for different people.[27] But it is crucial to create some sort of scoreboard, so we can measure the progress of our recovery.

DISCUSSION QUESTIONS

1. Give yourself a grade in terms of your commitment to a recovery group.

2. How long have you been sober?

3. How secure are you with your employment and finances?

4. Give yourself a grade for how well you are doing with fitness and your diet.

5. Do you have a close circle of friends who know your story?

6. Are you doing your part to engage your family in the recovery process?

7. How is your spiritual connection?

8. Is there anything else that belongs on your recovery scoreboard?

Chapter 11

THE MAN CODE

This is where advanced recovery gets fun. Consider this amazing experiment conducted by Canadian psychologist Bruce Alexander, several years ago. Rats were placed in empty cages, alone, with two water bottles to choose from—one with pure water and the other with heroin-infused water. Those experiments showed that as time passed, these rats would uniformly get hooked on and eventually overdose from heroin. So, the researchers unsurprisingly concluded that the potential of extreme pleasure, in and of itself, is addictive. Closed case, right? No! Alexander was bothered by the fact that the cages in which the rats were isolated were small, with no potential for stimulation beyond the heroin. Alexander thought, of course they all get high. What else were they supposed to do? In response to this perceived shortcoming, Alexander created what we now call "the rat park," a cage approximately 200 times larger than the typical isolation cage, with hamster wheels and multi-colored balls to play with, plenty of tasty food, and spaces for mating and raising litters. He put in not one, but twenty rats (of both genders). He added both water options. The rats ignored the heroin. They were more interested in community activities such as playing, fighting, eating, and mating. With the social stimulation available, addiction disappeared. Even rats previously hooked on heroin left it alone.[1]

What is true about rats applies to humans as well. Dr. Glenn Altschuler is a professor at Cornell University. From his research, he has identified what he calls "the surprising benefits of social connections." Altschuler concludes that "social isolation is a major factor in physical as well as mental health."[2] This confirms what we in the recovery community have known all along.

Recovery is all about connection. The opposite of addiction is connection. We can't say enough about connection.

> Connection.
> Connection.
> Connection.

I tried, but I still can't say it enough—*connection!* Convincing you of the need for connection isn't hard. What is more difficult is not *whether* we connect, but *how* we connect. To that end, I want to introduce you to something my good friend came up with several years ago. Dr. Dennis Swanberg calls it "The Man Code." You can read about it in his book by that title.[3] "The Swan" unlocks the code to relational success, all around five numbers, which we see demonstrated in the life of Jesus—1, 3, 12, 120, and 5,000. Let's dive into The Man Code. It will take us further into advanced recovery than any of us have been before.

THE ONE

Blaise Pascal (1623–1662) is credited with saying, "All of humanity's problems stem from man's inability to sit quietly in a room alone."[4]

Jesus had a habit of turning down ministry opportunities to be alone with the Father. He passed by countless open doors—chances to heal the blind, preach to the lost, and feed the hungry—to focus on the One who mattered most. What did Jesus do after "his fame spread everywhere" (Mark 1:28) and "the whole city was gathered together at the door" (Mark 1:33)? He slipped away by himself.

Very early in the morning, while it was still dark, Jesus got up, left the house and went off to a solitary place, where he prayed.
—Mark 1:35

After he had dismissed them, he went up on a mountainside by himself to pray. Later that night, he was there alone.
—Matthew 14:23

One of the best things you can do is to learn from others. Pastor Bobby Jamieson writes, "Find the godliest men you can, get as close to them as you can, and learn as much from them as you can."[5] Start with Jesus. Follow his example.

Let's consider three aspects to our connection with the One. First, what is the purpose for such a connection? I suggest that the highest calling of every believer is to practice the presence of God. This can be done anywhere and at any time. It's simply calling to mind that God dwells within us through his Spirit and his Son. Being aware of God in our daily lives takes being intentional. Welcome Jesus into whatever you are doing. You might want to set a timer at various intervals to remind yourself to call to mind the presence of Jesus.

Charlie Riggs, who worked for the Navigators and then the Billy Graham Evangelistic Association, defined the purpose of daily connection with God:

The goal of the quiet time is to get acquainted with our heavenly Father—to enjoy his presence, peace, joy, wisdom, strength, forgiveness, guidance, and much more. In a lifetime, we cannot know all there is to know about God, but we can enjoy his presence every waking moment of the rest of our lives.[6]

Second, we see the practical communication of God to us. Prioritizing our One means listening to his voice every day. We need to learn the Word, love the Word, and live the Word. It all starts with setting aside time each day to read it. While there are a zillion plans for reading Scripture, I want to suggest a few guiding principles that have served me well since 1975 at Dairy Queen.

It was at a local DQ that my first mentor, Jimmy, presented me with my first study Bible, a Thompson Study Bible. King James Version. I still have it today. But unfortunately, while I had the best Study Bible available at that time, I had no plan. I wish I had known then what I am sharing with you here. These are six simple guidelines for reading God's Word.

- Choose a translation that you can understand.
- Don't start with Genesis; start with the Gospel of John.
- Pick a book of the Bible and work your way through it.
- Read a little each day.
- Pray before you begin.
- Write out your thoughts as you read a passage.

I like the SOAP method. Read a *Scripture*. Write down a few *observations*. Then write a couple of points of *application*. Finally, *pray* over what you have written.

Third, you need to pray. Nothing will bring your connection with the One closer than prayer. Again, let's turn to the example of Jesus. Several aspects of Jesus's prayer life stand out. He prayed for others (Matthew 19:13). Jesus not only prayed for others, but he also prayed with others (Luke 9:28). He also prayed alone (Luke 5:16). Our Lord prayed in nature (Psalm 19:1). And Jesus prayed regularly (Luke 5:16).

Perhaps you've heard of Ignatius, founder of the Jesuit order of priests. He practiced a five-step process called the *examen*. This was a step-by-step prayer practice, which he taught to the Church. The purpose of this daily regimen is to free us from the effects of unconfessed sin. It was intended to make us more sensitive to God's voice and less likely to live as slaves to our sinful desires. The formula is simple, but profound.[7]

- Give thanks.
- Ask.
- Review.
- Repent.
- Renew.

THE THREE

The next number in the Man Code is three. Jesus focused on three men in ways that were unlike any other relationships he had in his life. These men went with Jesus where others did not go, they saw what others did not see, and they experienced what others did not experience. They became known as his "inner circle." The three men in this group were Peter, James, and John. It was these three who walked with Jesus to the Mount of Transfiguration (Matthew 17:1). These were the only ones taken in to witness the raising of Jairus's daughter from the dead (Mark 5:21–24). And only Peter, James, and John were invited to the Garden of Gethsemane for prayer (Matthew 26:36-46).

The three represent accountability and transparency. These are the people in your life (same sex as you) who know you better than others. You let them in. There are no secrets. Why three? You don't have time for more than three, if you do it right.

The value of the three is hard to overstate. The American Society of Training and Development (ASTD) found that people are "65 percent more likely to meet a goal after committing to another person." The number jumps to ninety-five percent with an accountability partner.[8] We are more productive in life, work, and recovery, when we have about three others to hold us accountable and to encourage us. When others walk out of the room due to your bad behavior, these three walk in. They are there for life.

With the three, there is a level of accountability that cannot be found elsewhere. And studies indicate that personal accountability improves performance and eliminates the time and effort you spend on distracting activities and other unproductive behavior.[9] For Jesus, the three was a strategy. Leadership expert and author Michael Hyatt asserts that the special attention Jesus gave to Peter, James, and John was part of his leadership strategy. By building these three men up, Jesus knew he could expand the kingdom's work.[10]

Paul would become the greatest leader and influencer of first-century Christianity. Clearly, Paul bought into the notion of the three. And for Paul, each of these men filled a unique role. First, he had Peter in his life. Peter had gone before Paul and helped to disciple him. Then he had Barnabas, who walked alongside Paul in his life and ministry. And then there was Timothy, whom Paul mentored. Like Paul, you need someone who is ahead of you, someone who is beside you, and someone who is behind you.

You need a Peter. You need a Barnabas. You need a Timothy.

Let's assume you've found your inner circle. You have your three. What's next? How do you foster these relationships of accountability? Author and researcher Peter Bregman has identified five ways to foster accountability within the context of such a group.[11]

1. Clear expectations. The first step is to be crystal clear about what you expect. This means being clear about the outcome you're looking for, how you'll measure success, and how people should go about achieving the objective.
2. Clear capability. What skills does the person need to meet the expectations? What resources will they need? If the person does not have what's necessary, can they acquire what's missing? If so, what's the plan?
3. Clear measurement. Nothing frustrates leaders more than being surprised by failure. Sometimes, this surprise is because the person who should be delivering is afraid to ask for help.

Sometimes, it comes from premature optimism on both sides. Either way, it is completely avoidable.

4. Clear feedback. Honest, open, ongoing feedback is critical. People should know where they stand. If you have clear expectations, capability, and measurement, the feedback can be fact-based and easy to deliver.

5. Clear consequences. If you've been clear in all the above ways, you can be reasonably sure that you did what's necessary to support their performance. At this point, you have three choices: repeat, reward, or release.

THE TWELVE

Jesus focused on the twelve. *"One of those days Jesus went out to a mountainside to pray, and spent the night praying to God. When morning came, he called his disciples to him and chose twelve of them, whom he also designated apostles"* (Luke 6:12–13).

As important as small groups are, the church drifted away from them for centuries. Historians trace the genesis of the current small group movement to the seventeenth century.

One warm Sunday morning in 1669, a thirty-four-year-old minister named Philipp Jakob Spener mounted the pulpit in the principal church in the city of Frankfurt and looked out over a congregation that seemed to have the form but not the power of godliness. Young as he was, he was the senior Lutheran pastor in this important city of 15,000 people, and he supervised several congregations and at least eleven other ministers.

As he stood in the pulpit that morning, though, he longed for a deeper spiritual renewal of the people gathered there. They seemed sermon-proof.

But instead of using the old ways, this young minister reached out on this Sunday morning with a daring proposal. In his student days, he had been part of a small group that met for Bible study and hymn-singing, and he knew about various house groups common in other places. How about if here in Frankfurt, then, after Sunday service, a group of friends might meet for conversation? But instead of playing cards, they might read devotional books together or discuss the sermon.

By the following year, these weekly private meetings were established and began to attract women and men from all classes of society in growing numbers. It was the beginning of the small group ministry within the church.[12]

Dr. Bruce Hindmarsh, professor of spiritual theology at Regent College, traces the origins of the evangelical small group. In addition to the work of Philipp Jakob Spener, an Anglican named Anthony Horneck started groups that would spread among Moravians and Methodists, eventually feeding the First Great Awakening.[13]

You would need a small group whether you were an addict or not. But being in recovery exacerbates that need. The benefits of a small group for recovery are limitless. Addictions.com identifies fourteen such benefits, especially noting that small groups help prevent relapse, create sober relationships, and prove corporate strength.[14] Again, this only scratches the surface.

Saddleback Church is well-known for the effectiveness of their small groups. Pastor Rick Warren has identified five things these groups do well.[15] Each of these is a mark of a strong recovery group as well.

1. Small groups study God's Word together: *"They devoted themselves to the apostles' teaching"* (Acts 2:42).
2. Small groups practice how to love: *"They devoted themselves to the apostles' teaching and to fellowship . . . All the believers were together and had everything in common"* (Acts 2:42, 44).
3. Small groups eat together: *"They devoted themselves . . . They broke bread in their homes and ate together with glad and sincere hearts"* (Acts 2:42, 46).
4. Small groups pray for one another: *"They devoted themselves to . . . prayer"* (Acts 2:42).
5. Small groups help one another: *"All the believers were together and had everything in common"* (Acts 2:44).

THE ONE HUNDRED TWENTY

Let's review. You need the One—your spiritual connection. You need the three—your inner circle. You need the twelve—a small recovery group. And you need the church, the 120. When the number of disciples had swelled to 120, the Church was launched. *"In those days Peter stood up among the believers (a group numbering about a hundred and twenty)"* (Acts 1:15).

The Church is often referred to as "the bride of Christ" in Scripture. Think about that. Imagine that you invited me to your home for dinner, and I said, "I'll come on one condition—that your wife isn't there. I love you, but I don't want to be around your wife."

Of course that would never happen. I can't accept you without also accepting your bride. Yet, many believers do just that. They are fond of the Groom (Jesus Christ); they just aren't too fond of his Bride. Sorry, but that's not how it works. To embrace the Groom is to embrace the Bride. You need the 120.

Dr. Kelly Green, holistic restorative coach, says it like this: "Relationships impact quality of life and present opportunities to practice skills essential for addiction recovery."[16] Green is saying two things here. First, the relationships, such as we find in church, improve our quality of life. The fellowship of believers is fun! It's a great place to hang out, laugh, grow, and worship. Jesus died for the Church because he knew how impactful she would be. Second, these relationships encourage recovery. The skills we learn in church, such as Bible study, prayer, and connection drive our recovery.

There is another aspect to church you probably never thought of—the health benefits. Did you know that being committed to the 120 makes you healthier? Psychiatrist Dr. Harold Koenig, Director of Duke's Center for Spirituality, has found that "religious people have more resilience, more reserve as they face the stressors of life."[17] You will recall our acronym which represents the five basic triggers for acting out. The acronym BLAST stands for boredom, loneliness, anger, stress, and tired. None of these is more prominent among addicts than stress. This makes Dr. Koenig's study more encouraging. Those of us with a strong faith component, which includes a commitment to a local church, are better positioned to face the stressors that threaten sobriety.

Kevin Makins, founding pastor of Eucharist Church in Hamilton, Ontario, concurs. Through extensive research and reflection on his ministry, Makins has listed what he calls, "11 incredible benefits of going to church."[18] Two of these benefits apply directly to recovery: stress reduction and access to personal resources.

Remember, the opposite of addiction is connection. Therefore, the opposite of recovery must be isolation. Rick Warren writes, "Here's the truth: Christians need each other to grow. Many people think spiritual growth is a private matter, but God calls believers to live out their faith in community. You can't develop a deep faith in isolation."[19] The way I like to say it is, "God has called you into a personal relationship with his Son, but he hasn't called you into a private relationship with his Son."

THE FIVE THOUSAND

The Man Code is nearly complete. Sadly, for too many of us, we stop here, at the 120. But there is more. So much more.

Jesus focuses so much of his attention on the next numbers. The 5,000. The number pops up twice in the New Testament. First, we read about the feeding of the 5,000. *"The number of those who ate was about five thousand men, besides women and children"* (Matthew 14:21). This is the only miracle found in all four Gospels, aside from the resurrection of Christ.

We also read about the 5,000 in the Book of Acts. Counting the number of converts, the Bible says, *"The number of men who believed grew to about five thousand"* (Acts 4:4). It didn't take long after the issuing of the Great Commission before Jesus's followers got after it.

The 5,000 represent outreach. As important as it is to secure our One, three, twelve, and 120, nothing sustains us quite like giving back. It's called the Great Commission, not the "Good Suggestion." Bill Bright wrote, "One Christian with a personal strategy, focusing all his efforts, can magnify and multiply his fruitfulness beyond measure."[20]

There are several ways to fulfill the Great Commission:

1. Pray for the nations. Prayer is one of the most powerful tools we have as believers. Praying for the nations expands your heart toward least-reached people and keeps you active in the Great Commission. Commit to pray for one country each week this year.

2. Volunteer at a local missions agency. One tangible way to engage in God's mission is to serve those in your community. Ask your church about opportunities or outreach needs like clothing drives, lawn care, and befriending newly resettled people in your area.

3. Invest in a missions project. Mission projects abound all over the world. There are hundreds of organizations with whom you can partner and serve. You can go on a medical mission trip, do construction projects for foreign countries, feed the hungry, or share the gospel in another part of the world.

DISCUSSION QUESTIONS

1. Do you have a personal relationship with God in Jesus Christ?

2. What can you do to make your connection with your "One" stronger?

3. Do you have a group of three who know you intimately?

4. Are you accountable to your three?

5. Are you in a church small group? If not, why not?

6. Are you committed to a recovery group?

7. Are you active in a local church?

8. Are you serving in a local church?

9. What are you doing for your community, the five thousand?

Chapter 12

FIVE DEADLY SIGNS

One of my recovery rules: No matter how far you go down the road of recovery, the ditch is still just as close on either side of the road. For many of us, that is offensive. We want to call ourselves "recovered." Past tense. Done. Over it. Steven Melemis captures this sentiment well. He says that people with long-term sobriety "feel that they should be beyond the basics. They think it is almost embarrassing to talk about the basics of recovery. They are embarrassed to mention that they still have occasional cravings."[1]

I see this a lot with men and women who give disclosures to their spouse. They want this to be the end of the process. We always tell them that a disclosure is the starting line, not the finish line. Recovery has no finish line. There are no graduation ceremonies, no certificates, no ribbons. The prize doesn't go to the man who finished well, but to the one who simply keeps running. *The race is the prize.* We must never forget that.

Here's another recovery rule. Your relapse was the predictable result of a series of bad choices. Relapse is never an event; it's a process. There are signs of the relapse well before the fall takes place. As my wife tells spouses, "Trust his behaviors, not his words." It is those behaviors, stretched over time, that give a clear picture of what is coming. Your current strategy is perfectly suited for the results you are getting. So, if you see slippage, change course.

Specifically, there are five warning signs we all need to remember. I call them "five deadly signs." If you see one or more in the life of a loved one—or yourself—respond appropriately and immediately.

SIGN #1 – MISSED MEETINGS

The first sign of trouble is missed meetings. I don't know of a more obvious warning sign than this. When someone begins to miss recovery meetings, they are in trouble. One of two things is generally happening. As a result of missed meetings, they lose their sobriety, or because they have lost their sobriety, they begin to miss meetings.

Jay Westbrook, award-winning clinician and scholar at Harvard Medical School, writes, "Meetings provide the chance not only to get to know others, but to truly be known by others, and both are equally important to sobriety and a sense of being connected."[2] Westbrook identifies five reasons to keep going to meetings:

- You would never want a newcomer to show up to an empty room.
- Addiction is a disease of loneliness; meetings overcome that.
- For many, our Higher Power is best experienced in community.
- Meetings provide the opportunity for connection.
- Meetings are instrumental in helping to keep us sober and prevent relapse.

Tim Stoddart emphasizes the need for making meetings a lifelong endeavor: "Recovery is a lifelong process. Meetings keep us connected in our recovery."[3] If there were other ways to get sober, I'm pretty sure I would have found them. I tried to get sober for thirty years without ever attending a meeting. Once I committed to meetings, sobriety was not far behind. Milton Magness said it so well: "Is there another way of doing recovery instead of a twelve-step program and attending meetings? Yes, but there is nothing as effective for sex addiction as twelve-step based recovery."[4]

I have observed that, on average, when a person misses three consecutive meetings, they don't come back. And as I follow up on these people, almost always, they have returned to their addiction. Sometimes, I'm not sure why meetings matter; I just know they do. Research indicates there are several benefits of going to meetings.

1. Meetings provide a sober community.

    One of the biggest advantages of 12-Step programs is their sense of community and support. A strong sober network is a good predictor of successful long-term recovery, yet many addicts spend thousands of dollars on rehab, then they struggle to find a good group when their rehab is complete. As a result, many return to the toxic relationships that preceded rehab.

    Dillon McClernon from Recovery Centers of America writes, "12-Step programs provide a safe space to connect with people who are also striving for sobriety. It provides an opportunity to form strong relationships with people who understand addiction."[5] Clearly, the need for a community of sober men and/or women on the road to recovery is reason enough to get into meetings.

2. Meetings provide structure and goals for sobriety.

    The 12 Steps provide a clear and structured path to recovery. You can use the Steps as a guide to help you identify your risk factors, thoughts, and behaviors that may lead you back to old behaviors. Groups provide personal structure and examples of how to stay sober. Brandon Duncan cites two ways in which the structure of recovery meetings benefits advanced recovery: (a) meetings help to mitigate stress and anxiety, and (b) they establish a structure which promotes long-term sobriety.[6]

3. Meetings offer support and accountability.

    The Steps emphasize the importance of involving a support system during recovery. You will be paired with a sponsor who can help guide you through the process and provide emotional support when needed. The program also encourages participants to attend weekly meetings where they can share their experiences in an environment of understanding and acceptance. As a result of these steps, accountability and self-discipline help reduce the risk of relapse, which is one of the main goals of these programs.

    Rhett Power writes, "Research found that individuals who participated in groups were more likely to adhere to their treatment regimens and make positive lifestyle changes, compared to those who did not have an accountability group."[7] Sean Galla, a seasoned worker with men's groups, adds, "Groups comprise like-minded people going through similar issues, and some have overcome the hurdles you are experiencing. Their advice helps you to achieve personal growth."[8]

    Of course, the ultimate support is from above. Dillon McClernon asserts, "People are encouraged to develop a connection with a higher power, which helps them cultivate hope and acceptance during their recovery journey."[9] There is a saying you hear in meetings all the time: "The measure we gave was the measure we got back." The support and accountability offered by meetings is unlike anything else, but only if you really want it.

4. Meetings empower people to take responsibility for their recovery.

    Meetings emphasize personal responsibility and ownership for one's addiction. This helps people realize that they are not powerless victims of uncontrollable disorders but active participants in their recovery process. The program encourages individuals to learn how to practice self-care and manage temptations that threaten their sobriety. The message of those who have achieved great sobriety includes a common theme: your past may explain your behaviors, but it doesn't excuse your behaviors. Until you take ownership for your disease, you won't take responsibility for your recovery.

From the Hanley Center we read:

> Going to a regular meeting is a good way to keep renewing your commitment to recovery. Just as people go to church every week to be reminded of their values and beliefs and see their fellow parishioners, going to meetings regularly reminds you of the many hard-earned lessons you have learned in recovery."[10]

That's a great line: "keep renewing your commitment to recovery." This is a journey that has no end.

5. Meetings are accessible.

Programs such as AA, NA, and SA are easy to find. Meetings are widely available and easy to access. There are meetings in most cities, as well as online communities, that allow people to connect with like-minded individuals from all over the world. This ease of access is convenient and eliminates excuses for not participating in meetings.

The AA General Service Office estimates that there are 64,000 groups with 1.4 million members in the United States and Canada, and a worldwide estimate of more than 114,000 groups and 2.1 million members.[11] And that is just for alcoholics. There are over 150 recognized addictions; nearly all of them have groups and meetings that offer help to those who suffer.

SIGN #2 - GRADUATION

The second sign of trouble is all about attitude. The addict says, "I've arrived. I don't need to do any more work." While most addicts will not say that with their words, many say it with their actions. Like the rest of us, they want to come to a point where no more work is needed. They want to be "cured." But unlike the rest of us, they think this is likely.

Of course, God can completely remove any compulsion or addiction. But it is rare. Addiction is like darts thrown at a dartboard. You can remove the darts, but not the damage. Scars are left behind. Recovery is about *becoming*, not *become*. We are all a work in progress. In theology, we call this "sanctification." Michael Formica is right when he says, "One of the greatest obstacles to recovery is overconfidence."[12]

The leaders at Granite Recovery Centers write:

> Overconfidence is one of the most dangerous obstacles to remaining sober. The reason this is true is that overconfidence causes you to feel as if you do not need to be as vigilant about your efforts to remain sober as you were at the beginning of your treatment. However, when you let your guard down, you can easily relapse into your addictive behaviors.[13]

This is profound. What it takes to get sober is usually necessary to stay sober. Shernide Delva identifies seven signs of overconfidence which affect sobriety. Delva writes, "Confidence is supposed to be an excellent quality. But when it comes to addiction recovery, too much confidence can actually become harmful."[14] These are the signs of overconfidence, which undermine successful recovery:

- Rejecting the suggestions of others
- Seeking immediate results
- Belief in having all the answers
- Always seeing your situation as unique

- Feeling that you deserve preferential treatment
- Feeling "healed"
- Always wanting to lead instead of listening

An addict goes through five stages, from a total lack of readiness for recovery work to the stage in which he or she maintains solid sobriety and commits to a lifetime of sustained success. If the addict stalls out in stages 1–4, they will eventually fall. A sense of "graduation" will keep them from moving into the final stage. Let's review these stages.

1. Precontemplation Stage

   People who are in the first stage of addiction recovery aren't yet ready for any addiction treatment program. This phase is characterized by defensiveness and endless justification of their behavior. There's a clear lack of insight into the negative impact of their behaviors and a strong focus on the positive effects they experience from using their drug of choice.

2. Contemplation Stage

   The next phase is characterized by contemplative readiness. This means the person is ready to bring about change in the future, but not immediately. Unlike the previous stage, they are aware of the pros of becoming free. However, they are also still acutely aware of the benefits they perceive from their addictive behaviors.

3. Preparation Stage

   When they come to the preparation stage, the individual is building a sense of urgency regarding their desire for sobriety. They have usually made steps toward taking action, such as intending to join a gym, see a counselor, or attempting to quit addiction on their own without attending real treatment.

4. Action Stage

During the action stage, the person has made significant changes in their life and is committed to change. This stage of change is characterized by prolonged periods of abstinence and the inclination to turn to professionals for help before or after relapse. It won't just be a case of halting the destructive behavior; change will be apparent in multiple aspects of their lifestyle.

5. Maintenance Stage

During the maintenance stage, the individual is working hard to prevent addiction recovery relapse. They are also keeping up the lifestyle changes they have made, like getting regular exercise, recreational activities, staying sober, paying attention to sleep hygiene, and attending support groups. They don't feel the urge to relapse as frequently as people in the action stage, so their confidence grows, and they truly believe in their ability to maintain sobriety long-term.

Clearly, this is the stage we should all strive to attain. The maintenance room is one we never leave. There is no "next step." Remember, your past success is no guarantee of future sobriety. I tell clients, "My sobriety today is not based on what I did ten years ago, but what I did last night." It is when the addict becomes overconfident and looks for an exit from recovery work that they are most vulnerable.

Even when someone has reached maintenance, it doesn't mean they are cured of addiction. Like diabetes or heart disease, addiction is a chronic condition that requires major lifestyle changes to keep under control. As such, it's crucial that people in addiction recovery make continuous active efforts to maintain sobriety. Complacency or a sense that the work is done once you reach maintenance is often a one-way ticket to relapse.

SIGN #3 - SECRETS AND LIES

You're only as healthy as your secrets. Addiction cripples, but secrets kill. Addiction thrives in secrecy.

I'm not sure how many ways I can say it. Secrets are bad, and truth is the antidote. But how common are secrets? More common than you might imagine. Researchers have identified thirty-six common secrets, and the average person keeps twelve of them at any given time.[15]

Ruben Castaneda has conducted interesting research on the power of secrets. Participants were tested on the effects of a total of 13,000 secrets they held cumulatively. It was found that when people mask who they are or what they've done, they have feelings of inauthenticity that are associated with a lower quality of relationships and lower satisfaction levels with personal connections.[16]

Dr. Josh Gressel adds, "A lie is like a parasite that lives off of real things, a kind of spiritual disease that creates distortion in the fabric of reality."[17] It is wise to view secrets as Dr. Gressel suggests— as a disease, whose effects are deadly. Like any other illness, to cover the secrets will only make them worse; they need to be brought to the light and treated seriously.

Secrets don't just *create* a problem; they *are* a problem. In his classic book, *Facing the Shadows*, Patrick Carnes writes, "Secrets themselves are a problem. First, you may carry the emotional stress of knowing you are being dishonest. Then you have the anxiety of trying to remember who you told what so that you do not trip yourself up."[18]

One of the problems with holding secrets is the stress and time involved just thinking about it. One study found that people with secrets found themselves thinking about the secret about three times more often than actively hiding it. Secrets decreased people's overall sense of well-being. However, the decrease in happiness was related to the number of times people thought about the secret, and not the number of times they actively had to hide it from someone else.[19] Thinking about secrets was also associated with poorer health.

Darlene Lancer, a licensed marriage and family therapist, has written on the ways that secrets and lies destroy relationships. She writes, "Most people who lie worry about the risks of being honest, but give little thought to the risks of *dishonesty*." She has identified eight ways in which lies and secrets cause harm.[20] Each of these, by themselves, should be all the deterrent necessary to keep us honest.

1. They block real intimacy with a partner. Intimacy is based on trust and authenticity—the ability to be vulnerable or "naked," not only physically, but also emotionally.
2. They lead to cover-up lies and omissions that can be hard to remember. Secrets mount up, and if the truth comes out, it may be more hurtful than the original secret. The longer the truth is hidden, the hurdle of revelation becomes greater, for it would bring into question every instance of cover-up and all the times the innocent partner relied upon and trusted the betrayer.
3. The secret holder feels guilty, or at least uncomfortable, during intimate moments with the deceived person. Closeness and certain topics tend to be avoided. Avoidance may not even be conscious and can include things like being preoccupied with work, friends, hobbies, or addictive behavior, and doing activities that leave little opportunity for private conversations. The deceiver might even provoke an argument or create distance.
4. Honesty is valued as a moral norm, although the context and specifics may differ among cultures. When we violate religious or cultural norms by hiding the truth, we experience anxiety generated by guilt. Despite our best efforts at hiding, our physiological reaction is the basis for electronic lie detectors.
5. This violation of our values not only leads to guilt; it also affects our self-concept. Over a long period, deception can eat away at our self-esteem. Ordinary guilt that could be reversed with honesty now becomes shame and undermines our fundamental sense of dignity and worthiness as a person.

6. Our ways of managing guilt and shame create more problems. We hide not only the secret but more of who we are. We might build resentments to justify our actions, withdraw, or become critical, irritable, or aggressive. We rationalize our lie or secret to avoid the inner conflict and the danger, which we imagine awaits us if we come clean. Some people become obsessed with their lie.

7. Lying leads to health problems. Not surprisingly, beyond mental distress, research reveals that repeated episodes of deception result in various struggles with health, similar to those brought on by other points of stress. These tend to grow worse with time, until the secrets are brought to the light.

8. The victim of deception is traumatized. The person who has been robbed of intimacy from the one holding secrets may begin to react to the avoidant behavior by feeling confused, anxious, angry, suspicious, abandoned, or needy. They may begin to doubt themselves, and their self-esteem may suffer. Often, victims of betrayal need counseling to recover from the loss of trust and to raise their self-esteem.

SIGN #4 - DEFENSIVENESS

This may be the surest sign of trouble. When you become defensive (those closest to you will notice), you are screaming, "I've had a relapse!" At least, that is the message that will be received. If you are married, remember the trauma you have brought on the person who loves you the most. There will be times, especially in the early stages of recovery, when your spouse will question you. "Where have you been? Who were you with? Why are you late?" You caused this situation, so own it. There is never a good time to be defensive.

The opposite of defensiveness is vulnerability. Vulnerability will be your greatest asset in rebuilding the relationships most damaged by your addiction or betrayal. Rachel Miller, a family therapist in Chicago, writes, "Vulnerability is your key to connection, change, and good communication."[21] Miller suggests several signs of defensiveness:

- Feeling attacked
- Shifting the focus from our own behaviors to the mistakes of others
- Insisting on talking about our intentions, rather than behaviors
- Condescending tone
- Making excuses
- Believing that others just need to understand you better
- Listening to respond rather than listening to understand

Psychologist Seth Meyers addresses the question, "Why are some people so defensive?" His answer: "Someone gets defensive as a means of avoiding accountability and getting the other person to back off."[22] Meyers says that defensiveness takes the following forms: attack, denial, fabrication, avoidance, and gaslighting.

Most of us have had an experience with a person who has the tendency to get defensive. At their root, all defensive behaviors have this in common: sending a message to the other person that what the person is saying is wrong or a problem. What's more, the message is that the person is "out of line" for addressing the other person or attempting to hold them accountable for something in the first place. The takeaway message is that such confrontation—as fair or appropriate as it may be—is unacceptable and will not be allowed.

Perhaps the most common way addicts manifest their defensive tendencies is by gaslighting. The term "gaslighting" comes from a 1938 play, *Gas Light*, and its film adaptation. Gaslighting can occur in personal or professional relationships, and victims are targeted at the core of their being: their sense of identity and self-worth. Manipulative people who engage in gaslighting do so to attain power over their victims, either because they simply derive warped enjoyment from the act or because they wish to emotionally, physically, or financially control their victim.

The writers at *Psychology Today* offer a more academic description of gaslighting. "Gaslighting is an insidious form of manipulation and psychological control. Victims of gaslighting are deliberately and systematically fed false information that leads them to question what they know to be true, often about themselves. They may end up doubting their memory, their perception, and even their sanity. Over time, a gaslighter's manipulations can grow more complex and potent, making it increasingly difficult for the victim to see the truth."[23]

SIGN #5 – CRITICAL ATTITUDE

Bruce Tulgan, founder of RainmakerThinking, writes, "If you want to do your best work, you must bring your best attitude."[24] Addicts all have an attitude. Let me say that again. We (me included) *all* have an attitude. We are either humble or critical. Sometimes, we can be both within minutes. But one of these two extremes will eventually manifest itself as our dominant attitude. And one thing is sure—a critical attitude is a glaring sign of trouble.

John Gottman has offered his now-famous *Four Horsemen of the Apocalypse*, which he uses to predict divorce with ninety percent accuracy. The first "horsemen" is criticism. (The others are contempt, defensiveness, and stonewalling.)[25] If you are married to an addict, you have come to recognize the signs of relapse. All four of these attitudes are usually prevalent. But none is so obvious as the first one—a critical attitude.

Through thirty-one years as a senior pastor, I observed a lot of people. I learned a few things about human nature. For example, when someone is critical, the issue is never the issue. The problem was never really the color of the carpet or that we stood too long in worship or that my sermon missed the mark somehow. The issue is never the issue.

I also learned that hurt people hurt people. We become critical out of pain. An injured person never responds the same as the person who has not been injured. So, when you are hurting, you will act differently. You can't be expected to say, "God bless you!" to the person who slams a hammer into your pinky.

I also learned that a lot of people—way too many—just have the spiritual gift of criticism. Of course, it's from the wrong spirit! We need encouragement, but some people didn't get that memo. They are just naturally critical—about everything. You know people like that; you avoid them. You are that person if you notice others are avoiding you!

There's something else I've noticed. I judge you by your actions, but I judge myself by my intentions. You said an unkind word to me; that's bad. But if I said an unkind word to you, I didn't mean it. Or you took it wrong. Or you're just too sensitive. I want you to be judged by your actions, but I want to be judged by my intentions.

Where does a critical attitude come from? Steven Berglas addresses this in detail:

> Harsh critics are often talented, intelligent, and productive people. Unfortunately, they have a flaw that compels them to disparage others—almost, at times, as though they are diagnosing an illness in need of eradication. It seems they're living according to the famous quip by Mark Twain: "Nothing so needs reforming as other people's habits." In the language of the self-help and recovery movements, these folks are often suffering from a disorder known as, "If you spot it, you got it." It works like this: you notice that colleague X has what is, in your mind, an affliction. You then take it upon yourself to castigate him for his affliction—irresponsive of whether or not it impairs his on-the-job performance or has a negative effect on group morale.[26]

Often, a spirit of criticism comes from a heart of jealousy. I know. I've been there. I can't tell you the number of times I found myself, as a pastor, criticizing another pastor. The funny thing is, the only churches anyone ever throws darts at are huge. No one criticizes the little church in East Texas that hasn't grown or reached anyone for Christ since the

Great Depression. We aim high. We criticize out of jealousy. In her helpful article, "Four Truths about People Who Are Overly Critical of Others," Lauren Edwards-Fowle touches on this. She says we criticize others to deflect our own issues. She calls this act of jealousy a "psychological defense mechanism."[27]

In your quest to maintain advanced recovery, keeping your attitude in check is a must. There are several ways to combat a critical spirit. John Piper offers seven steps a person can take to keep their attitude on a positive trajectory.[28]

- Recognize your own faults.
- Remember what you've been saved from.
- Give thanks.
- Grow in love.
- Ask yourself how criticism helps.
- Look at the larger world.
- In everything, give praise.

If you are married to an addict with a critical attitude, be warned. Their recovery may be in question. If you are the addict with a critical mindset, take a closer look at your program of recovery. There is probably something missing or something you need to shore up. Remember, relapse is the predictable outcome of a series of bad choices. A critical attitude is one of those bad choices to be avoided.

DISCUSSION QUESTIONS

1. Do you see any warning signs for your ongoing recovery?

2. How many recovery meetings do you attend each week?

3. How often do you miss meetings?

4. Do you feel like you can "graduate" from recovery?

5. Do you currently have any secrets you have not told anyone?

6. When was the last time you lied to your sponsor or recovery group?

7. Do you become defensive when someone questions your sobriety?

8. Do you find yourself being overly critical of other people?

CONCLUSION

You have made mistakes; we all have. But what matters most is what you do next. You can't go back and write a new beginning, but you do still get to write a new ending. You can stay sober for the next twenty-four hours. And if you can stay sober for the next twenty-four hours, you can do it for twenty-four days, months, and then years. Advanced recovery is the inevitable result of doing the next right thing.

It starts with your attitude. No one was ever shamed into stronger recovery. The words of Walt Whitman ring true: "I am larger, better than I thought. I did not know I held so much goodness."[1] Without a positive outlook, you will never finish strong. Whether you think you can make it or you think you can't, you are probably right.

To live in advanced recovery, it may be helpful to understand something known as the "arrival fallacy." This term originated with Dr. Tal Ben-Shahar, author and lecturer at Columbia University. The "arrival fallacy" is the false assumption that once you reach a goal, you will experience enduring happiness. The theory is that people start off unhappy with themselves, then reach for a goal that is designed to cure their sadness. When they find success doesn't fix their unhappiness, they are driven into despair.[2] In short, the fallacy is the idea that we can move so far into our recovery that we "arrive."

Let's consider some practical ways to keep the ball moving forward, ways to avoid the arrival fallacy.

First, focus on the process. Remember that in recovery, direction trumps destination. Do the right thing today, and tomorrow will take care of itself. Go to meetings, make calls, read literature. Robert

Schuller was right: "Spectacular achievement is always preceded by unspectacular preparation."[3] It's the little stuff you do today that will reap big benefits tomorrow.

Second, be present with those around you. Put the phone down. Make eye contact. Ask lots of questions. Make each conversation about the other person. Stay engaged. There is nothing that will help you more than helping others.

Third, keep a gratitude journal. While recognizing that you aren't all you are going to be, rejoice that you aren't who you used to be. Express thanksgiving to God and others—every day. Count your many blessings—every day. Focus on what you have left, rather than what you have lost—every day. Refuse to let the activities of tomorrow steal your joy today. Pray for a heart filled with gratitude.

There is more that I don't understand about addiction than what I do understand. But I do know this. And it is true for each of us:

> *"He who began a good work in you will carry it on to completion until the day of Christ Jesus."*
>
> —Philippians 1:6

PERSONAL STORIES

A nyone who has spent any time with the AA "Big Book" is familiar with the inspirational personal stories that fill 400 of the book's 550 pages. Similarly, I can think of no better way to encourage you on your path toward Advanced Recovery than to share the personal stories of fellow travelers. The stories that follow offer strength and hope to all of us; I go back through these stories often. For me, this has become the most powerful part of this *book*.

The thing is, people relate to other people. That's what makes my Freedom Groups work. As of this writing, I have over 150 guys from all over the world who join in groups that I lead. Are they there to hear a weekly lesson from my *Life Recovery Plan* workbook? *Maybe*. Are they there to hear from each other? *Definitely*. I suspect that most of the guys haven't looked at their workbooks all week. But they know the power is in connection.

What follows will really bless you. I asked thirty-four of my friends to be vulnerable enough to tell their stories. I have asked them to share their stories—life before recovery, how they found recovery, and how they stay sober today. Of course, I have masked their names and locations to protect their anonymity. The names and locations given are not their actual names and locations. Combined, these men have over 200 years of sobriety; that is an average of over five years per man.

You might consider reading one story each day for a month. They are short and very impactful stories. These recovering saints come from many states and countries. What they have in common is a commitment to sobriety and recovery—and a story that will encourage you.

Let's get started . . .

Cole N.
Nashville, Tennessee
Sober 17 Years

I celebrated seventeen years of sobriety this past Christmas Eve. That amount of abstinence from my acting out behaviors would not be possible for me on my own. I needed help from a powerful and loving God, experience, strength and hope from fellow recovering addicts, guidance from wise and skillful counselors, and the support and mentoring from a patient and encouraging sponsor.

My recovery looks a little different today than it did seventeen or even ten years ago. In the beginning, my strongest motivator was the fear of losing everything when the therapist told me that I needed to attend at least three 12-Step meetings a week. I did that, and the stories I heard of powerlessness and unmanageability sounded so much like my own failed attempts to stop my behavior that I assumed they were stories of healing. Victory and growth must also be true; I kept coming back as they recommended.

For me, the first months of recovery were about not going back, and replacing the addictive rituals and habits of mind with routines that align with my values. My sponsor met with me at a fast-food restaurant every Monday before my Monday night meeting. He listened to me share about my recovery and gave me practical assignments for my 12-Step work.

Having men that I can call when life is too much, when my wife is furious and threatening to walk away from the marriage, or when I feel like quitting, has been invaluable. During the strongest seasons of my recovery, I have taken daily inventory of my recovery and emotions, attended at least two 12-Step meetings a week, met with my sponsor or sponsee, and attended individual therapy sessions.

In the past three years of my recovery, the most important resources have been podcasts about betrayal trauma. They've been life-changing. For the first decade and a half of my recovery, I focused on understanding my addiction and its impact on my brain. These resources have expanded my capacity to empathize with my wife, and to understand the damage caused by my behavior, rather than resenting her for not forgiving me or trusting me sooner. I am learning to see just how necessary her pain and distrust are to her healing. I no longer want to rush her back to some previous place in our relationship, but I want to help her co-regulate and co-metabolize the trauma I inflicted on her and her nervous system as I abused her trust and left her without a firm emotional foundation to build upon. Today she is being treated for trauma and grief, and we have a deeper understanding of one another than we ever had before.

Fred O.
Green Bay, Wisconsin
Sober 11 Years

God has blessed me with advanced recovery by consistently working basic recovery, or the fundamentals. Recovery takes courage—to show up to the first meeting. Next, and the most important part of my recovery, is daily phone calls. This helps to bring the inside out, surrender lust in the moment, maintain boundaries, make friends and accept guidance. Advanced recovery takes humility. When I showed up, I knew nothing. I leaned on the old-timer veterans. I got a sponsor. I did what I was told. I had to, because my own way of thinking got me into the mess I was in.

Failure was a great mentor in my recovery. Don't let any failures go to waste. After each slip I experienced, I made calls, told my wife, wrote about it, and made adjustments so that to the best of my ability, a slip like that would not happen again. Amazingly, after a handful of failures, I was able to maintain sobriety, one day at a time, by God's grace for the past eleven years.

When I got my first sponsor, he asked me if I was willing to go to any lengths to stay sober. I replied, "Yes." By God's grace, willingness has been by my side through all the ups and downs. Being willing to do the next right thing is a must for early and advanced recovery.

When I found sobriety from lust, I realized how dishonest I was. I lied for any reason, but primarily for self-protection. I was great at lying. It took years to clean that up, but rigorous honesty is critical for advanced recovery.

Boundaries made a big impact in my recovery. First, with devices that lead to acting out. My phone caused me issues, so my sponsor suggested that at the end of the night, I walk it outside and leave it in the glove compartment in my car. I did that and it worked! I took Safari off my phone for four years, as well as dangerous apps that had a back door to the web. Next, boundaries were huge for my marriage. See, I had one foot in my marriage and one foot in with my parents and family of origin. I took steps to be all in with my wife even though that upset my parents and brothers.

One of the best ways I've been able to stay sober is by giving it away. It's what everyone else did for me. Sponsoring others is of great benefit to my own recovery. Coaching others has expanded my learning of recovery in general. As St. Francis of Assisi said, "It is in giving that we receive."

Finally, one of the biggest downfalls of men in recovery is empathy. I grew up so inwardly focused that it was hard to see my wife's pain. I had to learn how to become outwardly focused. I had to learn that it's not about me. It's about her. It's about living the relationship that God called us to.

Edwin W.
Owasso, Michigan
Sober 4 Years

I can now see all the things that led up to my addiction and the explosion of it all in 1992. I had been married for seven years but there had been multiple affairs and acting out that led to my divorce in 1994. My children were seven, five, and three years old. And I did all of that still telling myself that "I could do what I wanted" and not affect others. I literally had the ability to just block out of my mind those whom I devastated. It just kept going. I had multiple relationships with employees and friends. Again, not caring about the pain I may put into their lives as a consequence.

I met my current wife after I had been divorced and after multiple other relationships around 1999. There were several periods of total commitment, but I eventually began to fall back into my old patterns with other women. When my current wife caught me cheating after many years of dating, we broke up and had no contact for a year. After much discussion I convinced her and myself that I was done with that lifestyle. We got married in 2007, and I believed I could stop. But I was wrong.

It only took one year! In 2008, my wife discovered my other life. With intensive work with a counselor, I had to come to terms that I was indeed a sex addict. We found a CSAT therapist and did a full disclosure followed by a polygraph. At least as full as I was willing to give at the time.

Following this I had a period of four and a half years of sobriety. I had a sponsor, worked the steps, and passed many polygraphs. However, I refused to attend or participate in meetings; therefore, there was no recovery community. From here, there were major lapses. I became totally out of control again.

In 2019, I was discovered again, did another intensive with disclosure, but I again left out details and failed the polygraph. My wife was pushed to the edge and admitted that she was done. I could see it all falling apart, including myself. I finally decided to completely surrender in order just to save my own soul. Several months later I went to Arizona for a two-week intensive. I began work on my family of origin issues, to re-work the Steps, and form a community with others. I began with weekly Zoom meetings with There's Still Hope, a weekly 12-Step Zoom meeting, found a local CSAT therapist, started couples counseling, then added a weekly group therapy meeting on Tuesday nights. I am also currently sponsoring two people in working the Steps. It is a must that you have a CSAT therapist that will call you out to your face. My wife did much work on her own to heal herself, including intensive therapy and she also has a group of women for her support. Her having the same intensive therapy has helped us learn to recover together; however, we both had to heal ourselves first.

I currently have four and a half years of sobriety, knowing that the ditch is always right there. I must work each day to not go near the slippery slope; that slippery slope is what I just couldn't and didn't want to see, until I did.

In addition to the things I've listed above, I suggest the following strategies in order to stay sober. Find a sponsor and work the Steps. Do couples therapy. Grow relationships with others in recovery. Sponsor others and lead them through the Steps. Never ignore a call from a fellow addict. Have an accountability partner for at least the first two years of your recovery. Review Step 1 and your other work frequently.

Raymond L.
Casper, Wyoming
Sober 13 Years

As is the start to so many of our stories, I found my first porn laying around my apartment complex at the age of four. I still remember the image on that calendar I found. I soon discovered a steady supply of those same images by regularly diving in the apartment trash dumpster. This private world became my secret escape.

My name is Raymond, and I am a recovering sex addict.

I have come to realize that I am not an evil person, I am not a monster, God is not mad at me. I now realize I have a disease—the disease of addiction. I came about it honestly. I am a child of an unrecovered sex addict, the grandchild of an alcoholic who died from that disease. I was born in a chaotic family, which I have come to learn is the soup of addiction. For a time, my secret was my hiding place; it helped me deal with the life I was given. I learned to use it to medicate my feelings, my fears, my stresses. It was my one coping skill that I turned to often.

What started out as an addiction to porn and masturbation, ended up much more than that. I have come to realize that the disease of addiction is progressive. And my addiction did progress. It went from magazines to videos to massage parlors. I thought marriage and having a regular partner would fix me.

It didn't. I thought church and getting prayed for and repenting of my "sins" would fix me and make me stop. It didn't. I read self-help books, even books on stopping this addiction, and I tried to do it alone without ever telling anyone of my secret life. But nothing worked. My disease progressed to phone chat lines, and eventually meeting the people I was talking to on those lines.

My disease led to so much loss. I lost a marriage, relationship with a child, and embarrassment in my community. I hit what I thought was rock bottom many times, yet realized the bottoms could get lower. I went days with very little sleep, so obsessed with looking for my next image or encounter. What I was really doing was looking for a high. I now realize I was addicted to the chemicals in my brain. I wanted that "moonshot," that buzz, that ultimate escape that would fulfill me. So many times I told myself this is the last time. It never was. I stole, I lied, I deceived so many people with my behaviors.

I was very involved in church in my early teens and at some point, I ran into a Life Recovery Bible. I liked the simplicity of it, but more than that, I liked the footnotes that talked about recovery and the 12 Steps. I looked more forward to reading those footnotes than any other part of the Bible. Over time and through reading, I came to realize I needed help. So I found the courage to call a Christian counselor and spent a year sitting in his office for an hour a week, with him just listening, and hearing, "How does that make you feel?" It was cathartic to finally tell my story, but I didn't get better. I just lied better. The one thing I got out of it was that I realized I was an addict and later came to realize I was also an alcoholic. I made the decision to walk through my first door to a 12-Step meeting. I was petrified someone would recognize me. But what

I found was a bunch of real people who were broken, struggling, and on a journey to find answers to why they couldn't stop doing the things they no longer wanted to do.

I started going to AA meeting at six o'clock every morning. I did ninety meetings in ninety days and was able to get sober from alcohol and never relapsed to this day. My sex addiction was another story. In those early days of recovery, I was a chronic slipper.

What changed? Pain, loss and more pain. I got an incurable STD, and finally had to come clean to my then wife. I ended up losing that marriage for many reasons, one being that I couldn't stay sober.

I asked myself a really hard question. What would I do if I really wanted to get sober or had to get sober? I said to myself, I will find the person who has the most sobriety that I know of and ask them how they did it. Trembling, I found that person in a 12-Step room. In fact, I found two of them. One became my counselor, the other my sponsor. I finally began to work on a real program of recovery.

I started working the 12 Steps. I started doing what my counselor and sponsor suggested. I really wanted recovery. I was sick and tired of being sick and tired. I didn't want to pass on this STD to anyone else. I didn't want to hurt anyone else. I went to meetings often. I shared in meetings what I didn't want to share.

One of the biggest turning points for me came when I made a call to another addict when everything inside me wanted to act out. That person talked me through turning around, throwing away the phone number. It was the first time I realized I didn't have to act out. I now had help, and a choice.

I remember working my first 4th Step, when I finally told another person everything that I vowed I would take with me to the grave. I survived; I realized I am not the worst person in the world, I am not a demon, nor am I an angel, I am a human.

I was told that I get things backwards. I have come to realize that the worst thing that I thought was happening to me, was really my best thing. I was given a whole new way to look at life. One day, one hour, one minute at a time. I learned that no matter what I was going through, "This too shall pass." I learned that by helping others, I was helping myself and reinforcing my own recovery. I learned that recovery is a one day at a time thing. The shower I took yesterday was good for yesterday, but I need to take another one today if I want to be clean.

So too with Recovery. I need to pray every day. I need to read recovery literature every day. I need to stay in touch with others in recovery regularly. I learned the hard way that this addiction has a misery back guarantee, that if I go back, my disease will pick up where it left off. But I have also realized that I don't have to go back. Today I have a choice. Before recovery, I didn't. I was a slave to my addiction.

I was given some tools. One is Internet accountability. I choose to have the reports sent to my wife (I was given the gift of a second marriage), because I don't ever want to hurt her, and she has given me the gift of being willing to get those reports.

I don't think I would be sober had I not been given the gift of an STD, because I don't want to give that to anyone else. This is not everyone's path, but it has been mine. Isolation without accountability is the biggest danger to my sobriety today. There is no magic pill, no panacea, no "I'm cured."

What I get is a one day, one hour at a time reprieve from this disease by staying connected, realizing that sex is not a biological imperative. I won't die if I am abstinent or even celibate. It's scary as hell to ask for help, but it is the very act of facing that fear that has been my salvation.

Ben W.
Springfield, Missouri
Sober 20 Years

My story begins with me experiencing a chaotic and trauma-filled childhood which included physical, emotional, and sexual abuse. I went off to a Christian university and met my future wife. Soon after marriage

I started acting out by visiting pornographic stores to watch movies, then I would visit strip clubs. I would cruise, looking for prostitutes. This went on for many years with periods of three to six months refraining from those activities.

After the introduction of the Internet my sexual activity exploded. I visited chat rooms to meet women and have phone or video sex. I then would meet women in person for sex. I participated in sex clubs and eventually had a long-term affair with a woman. My acting out behavior had gotten out of control. My wife ended up divorcing me and for two years we had little contact. But God didn't give up on me and he chased me until I had a religious experience that changed my life. After my wife saw the dramatic change and that it lasted for over a year, she remarried me.

In looking at what practices have since kept me sober I believe the first one is committing to resolve trauma from my past. That entailed dealing with anger and resentment toward those who have offended me and forgiving them. Second is making a commitment to do whatever it takes to remain sober, and that starts with a commitment to God and to my wife. Having mentors in my life has been a huge contributing factor to me staying sober and making myself accountable to other men one-on-one and in groups.

As I think about those skills that I've learned over the years that are necessary for me to stay emotionally healthy, one is transparency to those that I'm accountable to and who are in my family. Those in my family and circle of friends have been given permission to challenge me at any time when they see behavior or attitudes that may contribute to a slip or relapse.

During the years I've resolved to deal with any guilt and shame that stem from my past acting out behavior. I seek to not allow any resentment or anger from my past or in my current life to build up to the point of acting out. Every night I ask my wife if I have acted in ways that disrespect, offend, or bother her in any way. And then we pray before we go to bed. Another thing that helps is developing intimacy skills that I did not develop in my childhood. Some authors see addiction as an intimacy disorder. Learning skills to have good emotional dysregulation—this is something I still struggle with at times in my life. Learning more effective communication skills is also important as I am open and honest with others and display an attitude of vulnerability instead of being so self-protective. Honesty is of vital importance.

Tim G.
Longview, Texas
Sober 5 Years

My story starts with an abusive, demanding dad, an emotionally ambivalent mother, and sexual abuse at a very critical age. I began finding validation via sexual contact with women that were not my wife. This form of validation started at age twenty-three and escalated until I was discovered at age seventy-two.

I am a very successful and prominent businessman and inventor. My sex addiction was a totally separate life from my marriage and my business life. I never let the three separate lives touch, that is until discovery. Discovery by my wife forced the once separate lives to collide and the outcome was the total collapse of myself. After weeks of depression and deliberation, I decided my best path forward was to accept that I was screwed up, and that I needed help to resolve the issues facing me.

Sobriety was job one; to accomplish that, several guardrails were put in place to penalize any attempt to act out. Covenant Eyes was installed on all my devices, a location tracker was installed on my phone, I started attending 12-Step meetings, and my wife joined me in any out-of-town trips. Also, an annual lie detector test was scheduled. Any places I picked up women were out of bounds, and I learned I must control my eyes.

This forced sobriety was working, but was not considered a long-term solution. Seeking a long-term solution to my compulsion to seek validation by means other than believing in my God-given power and his desire to have me be whole, I sought out a therapist appropriate to my needs. My wife found such a therapist, and I began weekly meetings with her.

I discovered very quickly that as I had hidden my acting out activities from the world, and I could also hide the me that I was ashamed of, from my therapist. After a few sessions of playing hide-and-seek with her, I decided this was not going to get me where I wanted to go. I confessed that I had been playing games and she replied, "Yes, I know. I'm hoping you'll start the real work soon."

From that point forward I was fearless and painfully honest about how I was feeling. After many very deeply hurtful sessions, discovering so many things I believed about myself and my family that were false, healing was taking place. As healing progressed, more advanced therapies were introduced, accelerating the healing process. All the following therapies are enhanced by my meditation, which I've been practicing for several years.

Next, I used neural feedback to further enhance my recovery. All these therapeutic treatments have opened my heart to the love of my spouse, friends, and most importantly to God's care and love. I had a very profound and spiritual experience with God that still feels as if it happened today. I pray that everyone can experience it.

Once I started feeling love, I found the need for validation from needy women diminished to a random thought rather than a compulsion. Now that recovery, rather than sobriety, is the focus of my attention I find that a routine of healthy recovery work is essential to continued progress. Included in my routine are morning prayer and meditation, evening review of the day, evening look into tomorrow's activities, weekly church, weekly recovery reading/podcasts/group meetings, at least one new recovery book monthly, an annual lie detector test, and meetings with my therapist as needed.

Bob W.
Tucson, Arizona
Sober 3 Years

I have been a sex addict for over forty years and did not recognize it until I received a shocking divorce summons from my wife after thirty-eight years of marriage. I was devastated and contemplated suicide, but I realized I could not do that to my two sons. I googled sex addiction and found Sexaholics Anonymous (SA). I started going to three meetings a week and realized that I was not alone. I also found a Certified Sex Addiction Counselor (CSAC) and met with him weekly. I also started working the 12-Step program and realized in Step One that I am powerless over lust and not in control and cannot recover on my own. I learned to surrender to God.

It was vital that I understood how I became a sex addict, and I gradually realized that my addiction was not just physical; it was also a spiritual and emotional defect. I was going through a difficult divorce, but I knew I had to work the program to begin my recovery. I struggled with sobriety during the first eleven months. I would have thirty to sixty days of sobriety and would lose it. I was still trying to control my addiction.

During my last acting out session, I was physically assaulted and had to testify as to what happened. I have been sober since, which is over two and a half years to date. I have attended over 500 recovery/SA meetings and over 150 therapy sessions to date and am the happiest that I have ever been.

These are the key things I have done to maintain my sobriety:

1. Going to three recovery meetings a week and regularly participating and volunteering to help run the meetings.
2. Working with a Certified Sex Addiction Counselor to understand the root cause of my addiction and help guide me to sustaining sobriety.
3. Working the 12-Step program rigorously and thoroughly, for me and no one else. The First Step was very important.

4. Working with a respected sponsor, one who has significant sobriety and who I like and trust to provide me with advice and counsel.

5. Connection with other recovering sex addicts. I regularly talk to at least six guys during the week, and sponsor two. It is vital to my recovery.

6. Do healthy activities. I bike and work out every day and have a great group of friends that I socialize with. I have replaced all the time I acted out with this.

7. Elimination of stress. I got rid of cable over three years ago and minimize discussions of politics and other controversial topics. I also stopped seeing a few toxic friends.

8. Avoid triggering places. I do not go to the beach and will strive to drive routes that avoid places I acted out.

I know I will never be fully recovered and, therefore, I need to continue to go to meetings and all the other things outlined above.

Tom T.
Birmingham, Alabama
Sober 2 Years

My name is "Tom." After two divorces in a three-year period, my drug of choice became chatrooms. Digital interaction issues were exacerbated with the advent of social media and later smartphones which put the world in the palm of my hand. Sadly, this was a struggle I brought into my marriage. After several painful discoveries, my wife and I separated, and I got into a Celebrate Recovery (CR) group. But at Step 5, I asked two guys to sponsor me, and both said no. My wife and I got back together, I left the program, and I closed all my social media accounts.

This guardrail worked well for about four years until it didn't work anymore. I found myself in the depression that COVID-19 brought many of us, and I succumbed to my old habits. I found a chat partner on a website and found myself the victim of a sextortion scandal that nearly cost me everything I had ever worked hard for.

This rock-bottom experience, though, is what led me to what has been lasting recovery. After that two-week bender, I said, "Never again," and was willing to do whatever it took to get lasting recovery. This began with therapy. I found a new CR group and this time I was able to get a sponsor. He wasn't even a sex addict, but he understood addiction, and he was my phone call when I got the itch to act out.

Then, my counselor got me in touch with Mark Denison at There's Still Hope and I began attending weekly meetings online. In the meetings, Mark led us through his 52-week *Life Recovery Plan* which has daily readings. I also got connected to a group chat of guys in the meetings. This became a place where I could check in prayer requests or talk about struggles and triggers, and could pray for my buddies who were going through difficult experiences. I'm still in this group and we have a lot of fun there, too, sharing jokes and laughing together.

It was in this season that the daily "quiet time"—I felt I had always struggled to do, because I didn't have time, or slept too late, or just got lazy about—became something I just learned to enjoy. This doesn't work for everyone, but one key for me was journaling. Since I can't write as fast as I think, simply writing about the stress in my life, my triggers, my joys, my fears, became a wonderful exercise in prayer and taking inventory of my life.

Then a Methodist friend turned me on to John Wesley's 22 daily questions for self-examination, and this became a part of my daily spiritual routine along with recovery reading (usually from the *Life Recovery Plan*), devotional reading, and prayer. I also meet with three other guys (they are not in recovery, but know I am) once a week when we talk about the struggles and successes of life and share our sins and secrets.

If I had to say there has been one key, it has been reminding myself every day that I am an addict and I'm still in recovery and I must do work daily.

Dave L.
Jacksonville, Florida
Sober 1 Year

My Discovery Day was easily the worst day of my life. Upon learning of my behavior, my wife left me within two hours, never to return. I had a choice to make. I could continue with my addiction (and my double life), or I could change who I had become. I had reached a point where the pain from my lost marriage exceeded the pleasure of my addiction. With the help of a good friend, I found a 12-Step meeting. I remember how I felt at that first meeting, but I quickly realized I was where I needed to be.

I started going to multiple meetings a week. I got a sponsor and began working the Steps. The program showed me what was the cause of my addiction and what I needed to do to break its power over me. At the same time, I began going to church, praying daily, and reading recovery material. I could feel the change inside of me and others saw it too. Going to the meetings encouraged me to be open and vulnerable with people in the room. I found strength and support there. I was embraced and not made to feel guilty or ashamed of my behavior. I developed real friendships, often meeting with other people for lunch or dinner and fellowship.

After completing the 12 Steps, I became a sponsor to others. And I gave of myself by doing volunteer community service work twice a week for homeless people in my area. I finally found self-confidence and value in myself. I realize that I will always be an addict, that I have to continue going to meetings and work the program. But now I am a new person, the man God always intended for me to be. I have the right people in my life, and my thoughts and actions are where they belong. My purpose is to do God's work.

Samuel R.
Barberton, Ohio
Sober 11 Years

My redemption story begins at the age of three. Like all redemption narratives, one must examine the fall of the individual so as to see the redemption at hand. I was sexually abused by a girl a little older than me for four years. She controlled everything. She was my best friend. She was my first "love," an unhealthy, abusive love.

At age four, I found my father's pornography collection, first magazines, then videos. I even learned how to operate an 8mm projector at the age of five to satisfy my lust. Around this time, I learned to masturbate. I cannot remember a time in my life that was not filled with sexual fantasies or actions.

I continued to watch pornography daily for almost thirty years. All through grade school, college, and in the workforce, I watched pornography, up to eight hours a day. It didn't end with pornography. I was physically unfaithful in every relationship, including my marriage. I even had a daughter out of wedlock, which my wife and I are raising as our own. Our intensive therapist told my wife and me that I was one of the worst sex addiction cases he had ever experienced.

I found recovery fifteen years ago with over a decade of sobriety thanks to working the steps. My life has dramatically improved, and the constant siren call of sex and pornography no longer come through as a megaphone, but as an occasional small whisper, and not the good kind.

There are a couple of pieces of advice that I can give to those new to recovery that have helped me along the way. The first one is to dive into your recovery community, and the second is to learn to laugh about your addiction. Although anonymity works well for those early in recovery and those still acting out (giving them a safe place to confess), community becomes a much bigger part of the recovery journey in the long term.

Many have stated that the opposite of addiction is not sobriety, but community. I wholeheartedly agree with this statement. My life revolves around recovery. I am not anonymous to the men in my group and openly enjoy our "food, fun, and fellowship" after recovery meetings. I also hang out with brothers in recovery outside of the meeting room. Even our families spend time together, and I openly introduce my family to the men in my recovery group when we see each other in public.

Laughing at oneself is not the easiest thing to do, especially if we are buried in the shame and guilt of our addiction. For too long we have been held hostage by our shame and guilt, unable to laugh at ourselves or our mistakes. In recovery, I learned that the enemy wanted to keep me in a state of shame and guilt, and the easiest way for me to escape that prison was to be able to laugh at the things I had done and help others laugh at our shared insanity. Laughing works. It releases Oxytocin, reducing our stress. It's okay to laugh with your brothers in recovery. Enjoy your recovery, learn to laugh at yourself and your mistakes. It will make your life and recovery a lot easier.

Mark B.
San Jose, California
Sober 21 Years

I will never forget my first sex addiction recovery meeting. At forty-six, my life was at a dead end. Hearing the 12 Steps for the first time was like a miracle. I could certainly identify with being powerless and my life being unmanageable. I did not reach this point until facing horrible consequences not just once, but over and over.

But I still wanted my fragile world of make-believe, always afraid that it might come crashing down. Protecting my acting out at all costs, powerlessness and unmanageability got worse.

I always felt I had the best excuse for doing what I did. Between age eleven and thirteen, I was sexually molested by a church youth leader and Boy Scout Master. My own dad never had time for me, so I delighted in this attention and closeness for over three years. He was my caring father figure. On the other side, my mother was a control freak.

Memories are full of childhood terror and powerlessness. I was abused, neglected, exposed to domestic violence and dysfunctional behavior. Sex addiction became my way to escape to a different and exciting life.

Developing two personalities, I was a popular high school teacher by day sex addict by night. I thought that I was so clever and smart. I loved the intrigue and the game. I was able to minimize the guilt. I tried to not allow myself to feel ashamed of my actions.

Before computers became popularized as a useful tool for acting out, I sought certain prostitute types in bars, hotel lobbies, parks, beaches, and even on the street. I loved to act out with more than one victim a day. During all the craziness, I was almost arrested three times.

I will never forget the detail of what happened in each of these dreadful events. I put my beloved marriage, career, and family in the balance. I could have easily lost all three.

These progressive scary circumstances eventually brought me to my knees before God in Steps 3–5, to confess my addiction and the depth of actions that got me there. My beginning of lengthy sobriety began with total honesty before God and my sponsor, stripping away fear, pride, grandiosity, and self-will.

I was sick and tired, and couldn't continue this life, knowing if nothing changed, nothing changes. God was ready to free me of this sad existence when I stopped and was willing to let go. This came after truly witnessing the horrible new progression to my acting out and doing things I said I would never do, going places I at first would never be seen in. Getting lost in dark/weird surroundings, waking up and not knowing the way or how to get home. God had shown me how the addiction was all-consuming.

Then came the rest of the Steps, 6–12, to deepen my resolve to change my life and maintain sobriety and recovery. Defects of character play such a part in reinforcing addictive acts. Family relationships contribute a strong role as well.

How do I stay sober long-term? Knowledge of past failures, one day at a time, accepting God's love and acceptance, and simply knowing that freedom from sex addiction is priceless. A must for each day of recovery are these maintenance steps:

1. Prayer and meditation to improve close contact with God every morning
2. Putting others first
3. Work with sponsees
4. Quietly witnessing to God's amazing love, mercy, and forgiveness.

I embrace five *s*'s:

1. Submit to God
2. Stay focused
3. Stick with the game plan
4. Support system
5. Strive for self-care

David W.
Worcester, Massachusetts
Sober 2 Years

Sadly, it took over forty years to come to this place of peace and joy in my life. I am forever grateful for the struggle I had to endure during my attempt to walk out of this horrible addiction. I have often told brothers in my group that discovery day was the best/worst day of my life. On September 19, 2021, my life was forever changed. My bride, with tears in her eyes, approached me with pictures and information she found on my phone.

The hiding was over, the lying was over, and the secrets were over. My sin was revealed. My attempt to fix myself before my bride found out had failed.

I can openly and freely say today that I live with no shame, no guilt, and my past does not define me. I have some regrets naturally, but the blessings I continue to receive are priceless. I learned that the godly sorrow I experienced would lead to true repentance. Without it, I would not be where I am today.

Immediately, the Holy Spirit began speaking to me about surrender. To begin walking the road of recovery, I realized the need to give up many things in my life. I recognized the need to surround myself with safe people in safe places, which would lead me into setting up healthy boundaries and a strong game plan.

This soon would be impactful for me and my wounded spouse walking this out by my side. Helpful to us along the journey was giving up social media, and mainstream television (except a ballgame).

Looking back, God's hand was in everything, and what unfolded was amazing and beautiful. Formerly, the only thing I had the ability to read was the sports page. Desperately and eagerly, I began to dive into one recovery book after another. In doing so, I acquired some newfound knowledge and information that would be valuable in my quest for purity.

Craig Groeschel's *Winning the War in Your Mind* taught me how to take back ownership of my brain. I learned the four key principles that helped me rewire my brain. I was encouraged to download Covenant Eyes on my phone. Then the purchasing of a brand-new phone, and changing my email helped me be removed from all the garbage coming through my previous phone.

I believe the connection of a recovery group is imperative in the life of an addict. James 5:16 states it clearly for us. I need to confess to my new brothers, they begin to pray, and God begins to heal the wretched sinner I was! In my daily devotion time, I began to ask God to partner with me in a brain covenant prayer each day. (If I forget, my new phone reminds me at 8:55 a.m. each day.)

The ability to take thoughts captive and release them to the foot of the cross is a refreshing new habit for me. I have to be ready for when, not if, the enemy attacks. I gracefully surrender my phone to my wife before entering a bathroom. I no longer carry over $50 in my wallet at any time.

I deposit into my bride's bank of trust a text message or phone call before I ever advance to another location during my workday. I believe the content coming through my radio at work has kept my mind and heart on a path of purity. I am grateful today for the ability to recognize my surroundings in this world, but not be conformed to it.

The road of the "long game" can be tough at times, but is extremely worth it. It is now time to carry out the 12th Step and help other brothers in need. My new identity is in Christ; I am a new creation. I am redeemed, restored and rewired. Thank you, Jesus!

Lord willing, I will get to share my story of his glory to many men before he calls me home.

George T.
Baltimore, Maryland
Sober 3 Years

I walked into the bedroom the morning of May 4th and I felt a shift in the atmosphere, as I was packing to go out of town with my youngest son. The look on my wife's face was that of devastation, as if someone had just violated her, and I could feel the intense trauma she was suffering. I thought, let me fix this. What happened? The violator was me.

Then it hit me like an unexpected avalanche; it really shouldn't have been so unexpected, but I thought I had done such a good job of lying to my spouse for years. This was discovery day. She found my history, my messages of a secret life I had hidden from her. I was always able to lie my way out every time she suspected my dirty little secret of hidden porn, masturbation, and massage parlors of happy endings. This was my escape, my numbing out, this was my coping with stress, for unhealed childhood abuse, from trauma I had endured, and I justified it believing it's my release.

That day I saw something different in my wife's eyes. She was done with me and with the marriage, and she told me to get help. I realized the biggest person I was lying to was myself. My life was crumbling fast and I didn't know how to stop it. I was an overcomer, high achiever in so many ways in my life, playing college football for the infamous Lou Holtz as my head coach, I achieved top in the nation powerlifting records, top in the nation in breaking sales records. Give me a goal and I will achieve it, set a record and watch me break it. I had such a drive of overachieving and getting the recognition always in my life. I had accumulated great wealth and possessions over the years, all the while keeping my dirty secret to myself, carrying deep guilt and shame over it.

I didn't know how to break free from it. I was the guy people looked to because no matter what was thrown at me, I would figure out a way to succeed. I never thought I needed a therapist, as I can muscle my way through anything. My wife told me there was about a two percent chance of us making it through this, she was finished, and I had put her through enough. I had worn all her brake pads off and her grace was lifted. I knew if I was going to get well, I had to do the work.

I called a man I had known who had a sex addiction recovery program. I couldn't believe this was what I was—a sex addict. How did I get here? I was raised in a Christian home, I loved God, I go to church, I serve, I love my wife and family. How did I allow this thief to come in and it's now controlling and robbing my life? This isn't what a sex addict looks like, or at least I thought I had an image of what that looked like. Now I just had to look in the mirror! I arranged for my wife and me to do an intensive therapy for the next week. I didn't know until hours before it started if she was even going to show up. The therapist was direct and hard on me, but it was exactly what I needed.

The first day was truth day, I had to lay it all out there and get honest about everything. I was a liar and a sex addict, and it was time to come clean with myself and her. Through the counseling process I discovered the deep root of where the brokenness came from, reality of the damage I had unknowingly caused and how to begin to heal. We got equipped to walk this journey out with tools to repair. My wife has given me the grace to walk through and repair the damage I did to her and our family. I discovered how many areas of my life were impacted by my unhealthy behaviors. It has now been almost three years of sobriety, and I owe my recovery to God truly being my foundation, my weekly sobriety meetings, my yearly lie detector tests, my openness and honesty, and the grace of my wife.

The temptations have mostly left, but I am extremely aware of boundaries I must keep in place for success. I also realize the patience and grace I have needed to give my wife while she recovers from the damage I caused. The meetings I attend are not only for myself, but they have shifted now to be that accountability and strength to others who are walking through this process.

I can now say because of my sobriety, my marriage is the best it has ever been, our sex life is thriving, our friendship is invaluable, and my finances are the most solid and stable they have ever been. I found through recovery I have become a better businessman, I have learned to be a better friend, and to show the grace to others who are struggling. I nearly lost everything that mattered to me that day because of my own behaviors, but it was the turnaround for me gaining everything to an incredible life. I am forever grateful for my recovery!

Jeff L.
Pueblo, Colorado
Sober 5 Years

My story began when I found pornography in my house at a very young age. My best estimate is that I was six or seven years old, and from that moment forward, I was hooked. It was something I immediately knew to keep secret. And I protected that secret by all means possible by lying and deceiving others. My path was set, and it only got worse from there. I started living a double life. On the outside I was a good student, athlete, and well-mannered kid. Inside,

I couldn't wait for the next opportunity to have an empty house or free time to seek out pornography for an escape. It continued to get worse as I got older. I'd snoop through the houses of families where I'd babysit, discover adult bookstores, and finally Internet pornography. None of my relationships could ever compete with my fantasy life. The woman I married had zero idea about my secrets. After catching me with pornography for at least the third time, she put a phone in my hand and said, "You need to get help."

Recovery has been a process of learning and changing. Learning about the reasons I seek out pornography and changing the way I live and react to those triggers. It's not easy. But it's changed my life and saved my marriage in the process. My recovery has not been without failures. The key for me is learning from each of my slips so I don't continue to make the same mistakes again. What did I do wrong? What do I need to do different? I'm also fully committed to a different way of life which includes 12-Step meetings, sharing my story and my feelings with others who have the same struggles that I have, and also sharing my feelings with my wife. No more secrets.

I can safely say the path I started on in my youth is not the path I am currently following.

Edwin D.
Kingman, Kansas
Sober 9 Years

At the genesis of my addiction were trauma and abuse. As for abuse, as a young boy, Dad's best friend watched me several times while my parents were out to dinner or a movie. He was physically abusive, throwing me up against the ceiling and making me jump off a refrigerator, while not catching me. At about the age of ten, I was sexually abused by a boy in our apartments, when I spent the night with him.

I suffered from several physical struggles, as well. Due to bone issues in my legs, I was forced to wear painful leg braces until the age of five or six, which severely slowed my athletic development, as I was unable to run. I was legally blind by age eight, so I wore embarrassing eyeglasses, which made me the brunt of jokes and bullying. And I had a severe stutter until age fifteen. Add to that a father who, while well-meaning, seldom offered hugs or words of encouragement. This left me an isolated, insecure boy.

As a teenager, I came to faith in Christ, but this did not deter my growing sexual desires. Married at age twenty-three, I was hopeful that this would take away my illicit desires. Of course, this didn't happen. I began seeking out sexual fulfillment by visiting women in sexually oriented businesses. This escalated to frequent visits to escorts and prostitutes, a practice I continued for thirty years. I was a senior pastor the whole time, so this double life tormented me daily.

At the age of fifty-three, I was discovered by my wife. I finally got into recovery, finding sobriety through a 12-Step fellowship. I gave my wife a full clinical disclosure, accompanied by a polygraph. I took three more polygraphs over the next few years, passing all of them.

As of this writing, I have been sober for more than nine years—zero porn, masturbation, or sexual contact with anyone other than my wife. Several things have helped to keep me sober. Every morning, I pray the Serenity Prayer, the Third Step Prayer, and the Seventh Step Prayer. I read recovery material every day. I attend two recovery groups every week, I have a sponsor, and I sponsor about fifteen guys from my groups and through other contacts. I have a Recovery Day every month or two. I practice the 20-minute miracle and the three-second rule daily. Other tools which I find effective include phone calls, thought replacement, and remembering the end game.

I remind myself daily that my sobriety tomorrow will not be determined by what I did over the last nine years, but what I do today. I can't gain nine years of sobriety in a day, but I can lose it in a day. I am committed to working my program one day at a time for the rest of my life.

Ben D.
Sante Fe, New Mexico
Sober 4 Years

I am Ben and my life changed after thirty years of addiction, sixteen in a marriage filled with gaslighting. It all came crumbling down when I was caught in my lies of secrecy. My journey to recovery began with crushing desperation. I moved out of the house because my wife needed safety, and I was not safe anymore. Saying goodbye to my tear-filled children was the hardest thing I ever did. The reality of losing my family sank in, and it drove me to do whatever it took to get sober. I began weekly joint sessions with a marriage/CSAT counselor. I learned to talk openly about my addiction, and it helped free me from its hold. I attended regular workshops for recovery, including Mark Denison's *Life Recovery Plan* 52-week program and the 12-Steps of Sexaholics Anonymous (SA). From these programs I committed to several steps essential to my recovery:

1. Installed monitoring software on all my devices (I used accountable2you). (My wife is the monitoring person.)
2. Weekly therapy sessions with my wife.
3. Completed my 12-Steps and 52-week program.
4. Gave up alcohol.
5. Stopped watching all YouTube.
6. Set up a DNS blocker for all triggering websites in my house.
7. No more social media (twitter, Instagram, Facebook, etc.).
8. Gave up video games.
9. No more watching movies, Netflix, Amazon Prime, or movie trailers by myself. (Many of my problems were triggered because of things I did by myself, which fed my runaway imagination.)
10. Made calls and connected with others in recovery as often as possible, especially when triggered or dealing with heavy emotions.

11. Became a sponsor and helped someone else work the program.
12. Started playing a musical instrument (to replace bad mental behaviors with good ones).
13. Committed to morning daily journaling (focused on writing my emotional state, especially the things that fed my addiction).
14. Started working out regularly, especially running, which gives a healthy dose of dopamine.
15. Gave up certain foods and committed to fasting certain meals during the day. (It was amazing how food played into my addiction.)

Some would say my list is extreme, but it was what it took for me. As the years have gone by (almost four years of sobriety), many of the things I gave up I hardly miss. Lately, I find myself fascinated by monks and monastic living. While I do not believe addicts should become monks, I found much of their struggles were the same as mine (sex, food, greed, self-gratification), and we both want the same thing, connection with God. I see I cannot keep my feet in two places at one time, one in heaven and the other in the world. "If I am 90 percent in, I am 100 percent out." The challenge is to catch myself before I attempt to put my foot back into the world. For me, the key has been learning the art of surrender and admitting that I am powerless against my lust, anger, resentment, greed, self-gratification. Openly confessing my weakness to God and others and learning to give up the things that feed my compulsions has been the key to my freedom.

Hector R.
Albany, New York
Sober 5 Years

It has been a couple years since my D-Day, but I still remember the shock that I was in when I was discovered. How everything was crashing down. Many guys become desperate for recovery at that moment, and

I was no different. I dove deep into every recovery strategy that I could find: anonymous groups, therapies, workbooks, Step work, religious groups, community and connections, etc. Without even realizing it I was creating a balanced multi-faceted recovery program. Each strategy benefits me differently, and each one also builds upon the others to help me continue to grow.

A good example of this is that creating community and connections was easy for me. One of the hardest areas was learning how to ask for help. Fighting to put my ego aside, to be vulnerable about something I couldn't do or something that I didn't understand. These two overlapped because as I connected deeper with my recovery community, I was more willing to be vulnerable. As I got to know guys more and more, I learned their strengths in recovery, so when I became aware of the help that I needed, I knew who specifically to reach out to. My weakest area was strengthened by my strongest area. Practicing asking for help in my recovery community gave me the confidence to do it at work, in my marriage, and in all areas of my life. I realized it wasn't going to kill me.

My biggest breakthrough, though, was when surrender went from thought to action. When I truly decided to give God my struggles, my thoughts, my anxieties. He was always willing to take them, I just hadn't been willing enough to give them to him.

Today I am grateful for my rock bottom. I am grateful for the crushing wall God placed in front of me that turned me in a new direction. Living an honest life is a blessing, and so much better than hiding, lying, and living secret lives!

Thomas D.
Cape Town, South Africa
Sober 4 Years

I was eleven years old when I found my stepfather's hidden porn magazines. Overwhelmed by the excitement and sense of comfort looking at those images, I kept sneaking back. Over time the urge to look grew, especially when I felt alone or hurt, which happened often at a boys' boarding school where pressure to perform was tremendous.

At sixteen, I entered into a sexual relationship with an older girl. I was drawn deeper into this world of sexual secrets despite the growing shame inside me as I knew that it was a sin. At eighteen, I started medical school, wholly unprepared for the new levels of stress. Porn and masturbation became my medicine to cope. Three years into my studies I had a spiritual encounter, which changed my beliefs and circle of friends, but by then my habit was engrained and despite my best efforts, I was not able to stay away from masturbation and porn for long.

Like many other young men in church, I believed that marriage was the solution. I met a wonderful godly woman whom I married when I was a twenty-five-year-old intern. I told her about some of my struggles but was not totally honest. Almost miraculously we did not have sexual relations before marriage, and I believed that all would end well. It didn't. About six months after getting married, I went back to porn and masturbation. I was devastated by the shame and hid it from her.

Financial and relational struggles proved too much for me, and I was drawn in further than ever before and started to visit massage parlors and prostitutes, stealing money from my family and continuing the downhill path. Despite being caught multiple times, I continued until finally one day, at forty-one years of age, I received an ultimatum from my wife and realized that I was about to lose everything, including my children. I no longer had any choice, and knowing I could not do it alone, I found help online, initially not believing that it is possible to overcome sexual addiction.

After completing a 40-Days of Purity online course I was introduced to Mark Denison. Mark helped me through his 90-Day Recovery Plan, and with him and other therapists, my recovery started. I realized the value of daily accountability, learned about my triggers and past wounds and having gained some sobriety, I repeated the 90-day course. Being part of a supportive weekly men's group has further helped me on the road to victory over lust. Additionally, having a friend who knows all my struggles and whom I can pray with each week has been critical for me to overcome, which I now know is possible. While I still have a long way to go, working on character issues like anger with the help of good counselors, I now am grateful to have four years of sobriety, am still married, and I am growing in my role as a husband and father.

Rob T.
Savannah, Georgia
Sober 4 Years

I have been sober since May of 2020. How did I do it?

To be honest I never thought I could do it. I have used pornography since a very young age, and it was ingrained within me. (After four years I am still working on rewiring my brain to not objectify women.) I started to learn who (the man) and what (the husband) God wanted me to be. I started the process of going through discovery, finding a therapist, disclosure, polygraph, and the restitution letter. I think finding the right therapist is key; you are going to find out stuff about yourself that you never had thought about before (and this is hard to deal with). I think for me it was the best thing I experienced through the process.

I learned what an absentee father was. That was hard because I thought I had a perfect family growing up. When this was addressed in therapy, the light started to turn on. Then I had to deal with the shame. God does not want you to feal shame; the devil does.

During the time I was writing my disclosure, I had a slip and gaslighted it as a medical reason. That was an eye-opener. I started to see my addiction in a different way. I did have a problem and needed to fix it if I wanted to keep my wife. I had lied to her for so many years that she was looking for more answers. Then she got into the disclosure and questioned my answers. I did not understand how she could not believe me since I poured out my heart, and it was painful.

Later in recovery I understood why. I took a polygraph and passed it, but she still did not believe me. At this point I learned that I needed to do this for myself whether she believed me or not. I think this is when I changed my way of thinking. I can't go back to the person I was and self-medicate.

The road was rough up to this point, and I did not want to do it again. Then I came clean with my kids. I am still answering questions from my wife, which may go on for the rest of my life. Again, these milestones were hard—sometimes very difficult, but I did not want to do this again, which pushes me to say sober. My wife and I have been married for forty years, and I have denied her the husband and marriage she so deserved.

So, I started to look for groups to help me with tools to stay sober and continue to heal. At this point the group I got into did not work, and I was not growing and sometimes I learned what being triggered was all about. I found another group. I found out that I was not the only one going through the yoyo effect with my wife, and this was a big plus to me to stay sober. Don't be afraid to move on to another group if one does not fit. Remember this for your growth. My wife and I have done groups together, and I have done multiple men's groups. I think staying connected with guys who share your story is working for me to stay sober.

Fast-forward a couple of years and I don't want to go back and do a redo. I tell myself to keep the ball rolling forward. I still do stupid stuff that I know better than to do or say. It is all a process to be who God wants you to be. All I have control of is me. My kids see a different person than I used to be. I can have conversations with them about things I had no clue about before. To have this type of openness with them is a big plus to staying sober. I am becoming a new person through this journey, and I have a long way to go, God helping along the way. I hope it is not too late to help heal my wife. Recovery is not just for that; it applies to your whole life and other loved ones. I don't have that many years left to start again so I need to keep sober, keep learning, and give my wife a husband she can trust.

David T.
Anchorage, Alaska
Sober 4 Years

My story is a common one. I just didn't know it at the time. Born into a Catholic family in the 1960s, I was the only one I knew whose parents were divorced when I was in the second grade. I was a shy, lonely, overweight kid who was always on the outside of the popular groups. I did well in school, so I focused on that. Doing the best I could, living in a broken home, I visited my mom every other weekend.

One day, at the age of thirteen, everything changed. I discovered a porn magazine under my older brother's bed. It was like a bomb went off in my head. The images caused a flood of feelings I had never felt. I was an instant sex addict, just not knowing it. I continued with my studies and continued to live in loneliness, but now I had a place to go for comfort and excitement.

In the beginning, it was difficult to feed my addiction. As I grew older, it got easier, but I still had to search for my next fix. I didn't get married until I was twenty-nine years old, and I had had only a few girlfriends in my past. I figured that marriage would bring an end to my problem. But my addiction had other ideas.

Technology was changing, making pornography more available. I went from magazines to VHS tapes to DVDs. Then came the Internet—images at the click of a button. Soon, pictures from a slow dial-up connection were replaced by videos on high speed. Next came Wi-Fi and a tablet. Porn became available anytime, anywhere, and I began to spiral downward.

Soon, I discovered chat rooms, first just being discussion groups. But soon, I found a new thrill. I could make a fake profile and become someone else. This began what my wife calls "becoming the frat boy I always wanted to be." To me, it was all fantasy, but I was blind to the fact that I was putting my life and my family at risk.

Even when one of the young women I was talking to was able to discover my true identity, I didn't run; I continued. I was getting careless. Then came the discovery. My wife walked in during a conversation I was having, grabbed my phone, and soon everything that was in writing. She read things no wife should have to see. She was devastated, and so was I. This should have been the end of everything. I was at risk of being blackmailed, or the woman going public and ruining my life. I was on my way out, but my wife so loved her family and wasn't going to ruin all the work she had put into it all these years. She had the grace to give me another chance. I went into therapy with a marriage counselor. After weekly meetings for several months, he was convinced that I wouldn't do anything again. For many months, I was committed to putting my marriage and family back together.

My addiction had other ideas. After a year or so, I started to get back into chat rooms. I took care to stay anonymous, but it wasn't long before I became careless, and my wife found my phone. I had failed her again. She began to do the research and figured out that I was suffering from sexual addiction. I returned to my marriage counselor, and he agreed, but he couldn't really help me. He referred me to a sex addiction therapist. That's the first time I realized that my issues came from my childhood. We worked for many months, I joined his weekly group meetings with other sex addicts, and I made progress. I was committed to beating this.

But after two years of sobriety, I had forgotten how much damage I had done to my wife. I became angry with how my wife wasn't seeing my improvement. I relapsed and went on a two-week binge. I found an old tablet and began watching porn, only to be caught again. How low could I go? In discussing what happened with my friend from my group, he directed me to Mark Denison's group. Somehow, my wife had the grace to try one more time. I contacted Mark, completed his 90-Day program, and joined one of his Freedom Groups. I have just passed two years of sobriety. It took me three counselors, and six years of therapy to find success.

Several things have helped me to maintain my sobriety. I remember the pain I have caused my wife and family. I remember the life I lived in the shadows, filled with lies and deceit. I remember the damage to my wife and her self-image. I stay off social media, I bounce my eyes, and I keep no secrets from my wife. Nothing is so freeing as to live in the light.

Dale A.
Miami, Florida
Sober 7 Years

My name is Dale, and I have been sober, by the grace of God, for seven years. I have spent my entire life chasing after sobriety by just trying harder. You would think that after the first few thousand times, I would have thought that the plan just wasn't working. It took several "bottoms" and discoveries by my wife whereby I ran out of excuses and the lies were not going to cut it anymore.

I had this excuse that I had to keep my problem a secret to protect my wife from the pain of knowing the truth about me, thinking it would destroy her. My shame was mine and mine alone; I had to fix this on my own. My secrets were going to go to the grave with me. No one had this problem the way I did. I began to feel I was a lost cause. Worse yet, I was a hypocrite. I was a practicing Catholic and was actively involved in my church. I had this duplicitous life. When I acted out, I was very bad, but between those times, I was repentant and determined that this time I was on the right track, only to fall again.

After the last time I was caught, I realized the gig was up; the secret was out of the bag. I had this feeling of total helplessness and despair. Recovery circles talk about the gift of despair. I didn't know it at the time, but I was being given this gift. I was given the ultimatum to go to counseling with a Certified Sex Addiction Therapist (CSAT), and from there to Sexaholics Anonymous (SA) meetings. In those rooms and through the counseling, I knew that total and complete honesty was needed. I was told that personal recovery and possible recovery of my marriage depended on it. I was also told this was not going to be easy. Full disclosure of the extent of my acting out with the help of our therapist was the most difficult thing I ever had to do. That is, until I had to hear my wife's response letter to me after the disclosure. To this day, that letter can bring me to tears. I shattered her image of me as a loving husband and destroyed her trust.in me.

It has taken years of work and pain, but our marriage has been saved, and I am happier now than I ever was. I am not wearing this albatross around my neck anymore; a heavy weight has been lifted. My addiction is still there. I am active in two SA groups, have a sponsor and work the 12 Steps daily. My wife still gets triggered by events and circumstances, but we work through it—one day at a time. I love my sobriety and I want to keep it—also one day at a time.

Karl T.

Union City, Tennessee

Sober 4 Years

Nobody's recovery to sobriety is a straight line. My journey to recovery has not been a straight line. While recovering and maintaining sobriety hasn't been easy, it's one of the things I'm most thankful for in my life.

I was outed by a family member and then kicked out of the house by my wife in December of 2019. Within a week I was in addiction counseling and learned, to my surprise, that I was diagnosed with a dual addiction of alcohol and sex.

Thus began my long and winding road toward recovery and sobriety. What has been most helpful in my recovery process? First and foremost is a desire to change. "Do you want to get well?" was the question my first counselor asked me (which is what Jesus asked the paralytic in John 5:6). My answer to her was "Lord I believe, help my unbelief" (Mark 9:24). In short, as afraid as I was about unmasking my inner demons, I wanted to change from the inside out. Without a desire to change, I could not begin my recovery journey.

Second, and almost as important as the desire to change, it's imperative to find a God-fearing and professionally trained counselor in sex addiction. I was fortunate to be referred to a great ministry that focuses solely on sexual addiction (which is what I turned to after getting clean and sober from alcohol). Additionally, I confessed to and relied on two close friends to encourage me along the way, especially in the dark early months of my recovery process.

Third, after being in recovery for six months, I decided to double-down on my recovery. What did this involve? I joined another recovery group (nationally recognized and again focusing solely on sex addiction). I added daily accountability to my weekly accountability. And I made a conscious decision to pursue God, life, and my wife. I consciously said that while talking with a close friend during a dark time in my recovery process. "Whatever it takes" became my motto.

Fourth, and last, own your own recovery. Again, recovery is not a straight line. Don't compare yourself to others in recovery; rather, learn from them. Avoid, especially early on in recovery, the never-ending chatter of how you should do your recovery. Even if it comes from a well-meaning spouse, you must own how you navigate your recovery process. Don't let others, especially those who haven't done or aren't doing recovery, tell you how you should do your recovery.

Recovery has been a long and circuitous journey. And it is a journey, not a destination. Praise God for the wise and loving support that I found for my recovery. That same wisdom and love is available for you as well.

Steven W.
Oakland, California
Sober 3 Years

I grew up on the streets of Oakland, California. One day, I saw a pornographic magazine pinned against the bottom of a chain linked fence. My ten-year-old brain felt frozen, trying to comprehend the experience. The friend that I was with told me his older brother had a ton of books with similar photos underneath his bed at home. You can guess what happened next. We left the court and headed to my friend's house to fish through the collection. The snowball of guilt began to secretly grow as I felt unsafe to share this with anyone in my family.

Several months later, another friend showed me a video on his VHS player. For the first time, I found myself watching an X-rated video. I wasn't sure if I wanted to continue watching or not, but my eyes were glued.

As the years passed, I unknowingly developed a sexual addiction. Being raised in a dysfunctional household, positive affirmation and words of encouragement seemed to be reserved for the letters on my report card or the number of times I was able to score a touchdown or cross home plate. The message I received at home was that I wasn't good enough. I was verbally and physically abused. To cope, I turned to pornography.

Fast-forward decades later and I am now married with a family. Since dopamine serves as a "reward center," I never identified my addiction as a disease. I would tell myself things like, "I don't have an issue." "I can stop whenever I want." I dealt with sexual addiction for thirty-one years. One Sunday afternoon, I heard a soft whisper in my heart that said, "Now is the time to be free. Trust me."

This leads me to the first thing that helps me gain sobriety: complete surrender. Telling my wife what has been going on was one of the scariest things I ever experienced. I divinely came across the next milestone on my new journey of recovery. It was a website where a pastor humbly and courageously shared his battle with sexual addiction. It was the first time I heard someone describe similar battles that I faced for years. I then reached out to Dr. Mark Denison and asked for help. It took complete surrender to open up to another man and admit that I have a shameful issue I needed help with.

This leads me to the second thing that helps me gain sobriety: have a plan. Mark and his ministry have an immediate plan in place for men in my situation. His *90-Day Recovery Guide* was easy to read and manageable to maintain. Second, I got into community. I joined one of Mark's weekly Freedom Groups. Third, get into recovery. The 52-week *Life Recovery Plan* was the material we covered on a weekly basis in the group. In addition to these books, I also listen to podcasts and other audio books related to freedom and addiction.

This leads me to the third thing that helps me gain sobriety: take things one day at a time. Recovery isn't a quick fix. Recovery is something I will focus on for the rest of my life, one year, one month, and one day at a time.

Lastly, this leads me to the fourth thing that helps me gain sobriety: focus on staying sober by staying in recovery. One of the biggest shifts in my recovery happened when I focused on staying sober (by staying in recovery) rather than continuously trying to not act out. Because of the recovery guardrails structured around me, I can respond rather than react. It's no longer a matter of if something happens; it's now a matter of when something happens. *When* I have an unhealthy thought, I can *respond* with a thought replacement approach by reading Scripture. *When* I am tempted to act out because of a trigger, I can *respond* with the 20-minute miracle approach by taking a walk. When I see an attractive woman, I can *respond* with the bouncing eyes approach by looking in the opposite direction. By completely surrendering to the process, having a plan, and taking things one day at a time, this set me up for the game changer to focus on staying sober by staying in recovery.

Calvin J.
Grand Marais, Minnesota
Sober 3 Years

Hi. My name is Calvin, but you can call me Cal. I've been sober for 687 days at the time of writing this…this time. See, my story includes a nine-plus year period of sobriety. At the time, I didn't even know that I had an addiction despite realizing at one point that I was "acting like an addict."

It all started when I about twelve. I discovered fantasy and masturbation, and it quickly became a way to cope with the stress at home, church, and school. Over time, this led to my consuming more and more, eventually leading to chatrooms and an online/over the phone affair during my first marriage. A little after my first marriage ended, I finally realized I didn't want to do this anymore. I cut off my Internet and stopped...for nine-plus years.

I met my current wife during this time and admitted I had struggled with pornography, but not the depth of how bad it really was. I thought it was behind me and I was free. We agreed to be open, and I would tell her if I was struggling. I never thought I would need to tell her. About five years into our marriage, I relapsed. Remember this; I'll come back to it. We reached out for some help, and I asked a friend to be my accountability partner. That only lasted a week, and my sobriety only lasted a year. The last time it came out, I lied and tried to hide it despite knowing there was no way out. This was my final awakening that this wasn't just a struggle; it was an addiction. I knew I was caught, yet still lied; that's not even logical.

Back to that nine-plus year period of sobriety. How was I sober for so long when I wasn't in groups or going to therapy? First, I had hit rock bottom and was fed up. Then I found good community, was involved in serving others, and walking closely with God, fully surrendered. I was fully engaged with my family and others. I was open with safe men about my history. These are some of the same things that have led me to the sobriety I have now. Groups give me the community and accountability; talking and texting with men outside group keeps me from isolation. Filtering software keeps me accountable and from seeing things unintentionally. Counseling and therapy are allowing me to get to the root of the addiction itself and teaching me healthy coping skills. I work to walk closely with God. Ultimately though, what keeps me sober is this—no matter what chaos is around me or inside me, I remember there is one thing I can always control—my sobriety.

It's up to me at the end of the day to make the choice to call or text someone, find something else to do for twenty minutes, or do whatever else necessary to stay sober for one more day.

Jonathan B.
Sydney, Australia
Sober 3 Years

My name is Jonathan, and I am fifty years old as I write these words. Three years and five months ago, I reached the end of myself. I am in addiction terms "sober" today from years of porn and ultimately sex addiction.

My story may sound similar to yours. In my early life, I was a good student and had the opportunity to play many sports as I grew up in a small rural community. I was fortunate enough to attend a private school, which helped lay the foundation for academic success. During my early years I began to equate trophies, grades, and really all accomplishments with acceptance, meaningfulness, and love from my family and friends.

A good report card equaled acceptance, love, and approval. This mistaken thought process grew into other areas of my life. I was a relentless seeker of perfection, whether it was in sports or academically. I was infatuated with getting trophies at a young age. I put all these things on display in my room as a teenager. They represented tangible physical "things" that made me feel whole and worthy. Of course, I didn't realize at the time that the enemy would use this thought process against me as I navigated high school, college, and ultimately postgraduate studies and finally a specialty residency.

As time went on, I exceled academically, and I was eventually successful in most endeavors I attempted to undertake. But there were never enough accomplishments to satisfy the thought that the only way to be valued or loved was through achievement.

I had struggled all my life with low self-esteem. I never felt really "good enough" and deep in my mind I felt unlovable. This was in retrospect a lie. I was baptized when I was young, and my family attended church regularly. I know now that I had a very unhealthy relationship with God. I saw God not as a loving Father, but as an "angry" Old Testament God.

My addiction to masturbation and porn grew as the years went on. I had multiple female sexual partners during my college years; it never stopped. These experiences made me feel temporarily whole, and this only deepened my sex addiction.

To make a long story short, eventually, I met my wife and we fell in love. We raised three wonderful children together. But again, my addiction caught up with me. One fateful inevitable day, my secrets surfaced like a whale. My wife and children found out my secret. It was the worst day of my life and of my marriage.

I then was fortunate enough to get help, and I spent weeks in individual intensive therapy, couples' intensive therapy, weekly Christian group SA meetings, regular healthy worship, and daily recovery exercises.

I am today in a healthy relationship with my wife, but not only that; I enjoy a healthy relationship with my heavenly Father. It's only through his grace and mercy that my marriage and family are intact. God loves me and he loves you. He wants only the very best for us. His grace is sufficient for you. Let go of your secrets, and let God heal you and lead you to a healthy recovery.

Benjamin M.
San Diego, California
Sober 4 Years

When I found out I was a sex addict it was one of the happiest days of my life. I finally had an answer to a decade's long question, "What is wrong with me?" I knew something was wrong, but I didn't know what. I had been lonely most of my life. I never felt like I fit in. I felt more comfortable with girls than with other boys during my school years. At my core I was resentful and filled with self-pity. I began masturbating with pornography before the age of twelve. I discovered pornography in the woods behind my house and a fuse was immediately lit in my brain. In my young adult years, I was married and divorced twice within a ten-year period during which time I had sex in massage parlors and with prostitutes. In between the two marriages I had unprotected sex with anonymous women and one man.

During early sobriety and one of my stints at a treatment center, a therapist asked me about my depression. He asked the following questions: "What is behind your depression?" I said, "Anger." "What is behind your anger?" I said, "A brick wall." "And what is behind the brick wall?" I said, "A deep loneliness."

You see, I had been a loner most of my life. I liked to think of myself as a lone wolf. I was certainly a predator, preying upon women who were either divorced or separated from their husbands. I was willing to trade companionship for sex.

Recovery for me has been learning how to take down that wall I had built to keep people out. Through the 12-Step program I am continuing to learn how to take down that wall one brick at a time. The program has taught me that I need other people. I can no longer afford to isolate. I have heard it said that "The opposite of addiction is connection." I certainly believe that to be true.

From the time that fuse was lit in my brain and for the next thirty years I used sex addictively. This included compulsive masturbation with pornography, massage parlors, fetishes, dance bars and anonymous sex with both men and women. All this time that fuse continued to burn away portions of my brain. So, for me, sobriety and recovery have also involved reversing the deterioration of my brain.

With the help of my Higher Power—who for me is Jesus Christ— good sponsors, a loving wife, who works her own program and the fellowship of others with the same problem, I am able to stay sober and receive progressive victory over lust, one day at a time.

At age thirty-five I accepted Christ as my Savior. It wasn't until I had been in the program for over twenty years that I also accepted him as my Lord.

Today, I have a life I could never have dreamed possible. My wife and I have been married for over thirty years. She has been indispensable on my road to recovery. We have two surviving children and four grandchildren. I am now able to work on my emotional sobriety. I have learned such things as: "Other peoples' opinion of me is none of my business," how to "detach with love," "'No' is a complete sentence," "If I am disturbed, there is something wrong with me," and, "Acceptance is the key to all my problems today."

Art H.
Madison, Wisconsin
Sober 5 Years

The roots of my porn addiction started, like most of the fellows I have become acquainted with over the past eight to ten years, with the discovery of my dad's "men's magazines" back when I was about ten years old. This did not immediately affect me until my college years when a long-time girlfriend dumped me for another guy. This came out of the blue and really set me up to search for some kind of solace to keep me comfortable with myself.

Another series of events happened when I was in the seventh and eighth grades. I was bullied by three guys who were a couple of years older than I was. I didn't realize it at that time as my thought was that this was something normal that all guys probably went through. The impact of this was recognized later in my recovery; this had an enormous impact on my mental processes. I proceeded through college; I sought out a significant number of adult magazines to peruse to bring me to a calm place in my life. I never dated anyone in college as I didn't want to be rejected again. I ended up meeting a wonderful gal who happened to be married, and we had an affair. She was what I needed to feel good about myself. She later divorced and a year or two later, we married. I thought that I was in heaven. We struggled some, actually a lot, and when things weren't going well, I turned to my old standby of porn.

At first this was infrequent but gradually escalated to regular porn use and masturbation. I was found out about thirty-five years into my marriage. Like everyone else, I suppose, I promised to give up my porn, but to no avail. I started attending a 12-Step SAA group, and this was a revelation to me that so many guys were struggling with the same thing as I was. I had periods of sobriety, ranging from days to weeks and even months. I joined several online men's groups and found several sponsors and mentors and accountability men to help me maintain my sobriety.

I started working with a PSAP and two CSATS, one for personal growth and one that worked with me on EMDR. This EMDR was where I recognized the impact of the bullying that I had experienced early in my life. I continued to struggle with sobriety somewhat until I attended a Christian men's intensive. I currently have two years of sobriety and relish that time and the people who have helped me along this path. I follow a regular discipline of daily prayer, meditation, recovery reading, four weekly recovery meetings and lots of self-care. It is still a struggle at times to maintain sobriety, but as I look back at how far I have come, I am thankful for where I am and continue to look at a day at a time to maintain my sobriety. I still struggle with couple's recovery but that is a work in progress.

Bobby K.
Portland, Maine
Sober 4 Years

For the first fifteen years of my life, I did not follow Jesus and rarely attended church. I began to follow Jesus at age fifteen. I married my high school sweetheart at nineteen and then followed the Lord's call to ministry at twenty-two. For most of my life porn had been something I had looked at here and there. In fact, it was often years between each time of seeing it. I would stumble across it while doing some web search, it would pique my interest, I would look, but soon felt convicted and then turned away.

My wife and I agreed to help a twenty-year-old lady who was in college and struggling with family, finances, and faith. At church when I interacted with women, I had clear boundaries: don't be alone with a woman, my office had windows into the main hallway, conversation about sexual experience, etc. However, those boundaries were not kept with this lady. Because I officed from home several days a week and her schedule gave her hours of free time in the middle of the day, we would often find ourselves talking about her life struggles. Over time these conversations became more personal, involving past sexual behaviors.

My problem was that instead of recognizing how these behaviors had hurt her and seeking to help her find healing, I began fantasizing about them. Soon, I sought out porn that would demonstrate the fantasizes. Before long, that was not enough.

Eventually I discovered a way to see her while undressing. At first, it left me with a great sense of shame and guilt. However, after a few days my mind would drift back to seeing her again and I would do it again. Each time I looked at the pictures, I felt disgusted, ashamed, and guilty. I would repent day after day. This continued for several months. Finally, the Lord brought my sin to light, and I was confronted by my wife. I lost my ministry of twenty-five plus years and charges were filed, and I was given five years' probation.

Over the next six years of recovery, I learned a lot about the Lord, myself, and others. Here are just a few of the things I have learned. What you feed grows. When you feed lust, it grows to become a desire that seeks to control you! However, when you feed holiness, you desire holiness! Isolation kills us, community builds us. Guilt and shame consumed me. My sin felt visible to everyone around me. Thus, I sought to avoid others. The very thing I needed was to turn to the Lord and others. The longer I fought it the more enslaved I felt. In Christ, failure is a detour, not the end. The Lord placed this passage on my heart: *"Though a righteous man falls seven times, he will get up, but the wicked will stumble into ruin"* (Proverbs 24:16 HCSB). As the Lord has helped me find healing, restoration, and renewal in my marriage, family, and ministry, this truth has given me strength to move forward through years of sobriety.

Stan R.
Halifax, Nova Scotia
Sober 2 Years

I was eleven years old when my older brother's friend molested me. It ignited pleasure I should not have known, but that pleasure was confusing because he wasn't a girl. A short time later I found myself uncontrollably recreating that pleasure alone while looking at my neighbor's adult magazines. This heterosexual validation, however, put me on nearly a fifty-year course of exploring sexual sin and lying to hide my secret addictive life.

As a middle child I was overlooked. I did everything to be seen that was healthy: great grades, Scouts, and all the performance arts. But, as I failed to be seen, I just medicated, and tried again later. As a teen, I observed my parents seek comfort outside their marriage during the 1970s sexual revolution. That modeling helped me define how a relational man behaves. From Dad's secret book of women to Mom's constant short-term men, I was witness to it all as it reinforced avoiding lasting relationships and to seek only pleasure to avoid painful breakups.

Over the following four decades as a military and airline pilot, while traveling, I took every advantage of the countless opportunities to experiment in my risky lifestyle. Unlivable shame never left my side. Sadly, I surrendered only part of myself to Christ at forty-seven when I was born again; I liked my sin too much, but I did find the individual strength to reduce my behavior to just porn and masturbating. Yeah! No lasting victory here. Embarrassed to tell anyone who might help me break free from these bad choices, I preferred isolation.

This mocking God lasted another ten years into my second marriage, and unlike the one percent of addicts who self-reveal, I instead devastated my wife as she caught me acting out using the Internet. I couldn't gaslight or lie my way out of this one. Now, as I'm trying to triage my wife who's curled up in a ball on the floor, she wants nothing from the person who caused this. In my desperation for God to intervene, I could now really hear him. There would be no 'SHAZAM' moment; complete surrender or else was his message of truth.

My reality: addicted to dopamine since puberty, with no self-control over a drug four times stronger than morphine, I was a drug addict. As I "white-knuckled" my sobriety since discovery day I accepted and used every tool and technique offered to keep me sober. Submitting to quarterly polygraphs continues to build marital trust, and individual and group counseling helps me be fully known and out of isolation. The real breakthrough was a five-day intensive session, which educated me on brain chemistry, family of origin, and the power of prayer, but most important of all, that God determines my value, and it's precious.

Ultimately, surrendering to God and building trust in him through reforming my thinking and softening my selfish heart is where I am today and that's what keeps me sober since getting caught twenty-eight months ago.

Stephen P.
Grande Prairie, Alberta
Sober 2 Years

After struggling with lust and pornography for over forty years, I can finally say I feel free. I am so thankful for the healing I have experienced.

I won't go into all the details of my past but through recovery and therapists I had to dig it all up, explore family of origin, young life experiences, and find my "Why." Not to excuse my actions and choices, but to explain them. Some of these things included adoption, loneliness, bullying, and feeling unwanted and unseen. At a young age I came to the conclusion (subconsciously) that I needed to take care of myself.

I have always felt terrible about my acting out, but until I got serious about recovery, I just thought I could take care of it myself. Seasons of sobriety, months or years long, would convince me I was better, or cured! But I had really just pushed down all the bad memories, shame, secrets and lies, white-knuckled it and kept busy.

I told my wife about my struggle early in our marriage but kept it vague and assured her it was in the past. I thought it was, and that marriage would secure all that permanently. I coasted along the first decade or so of our marriage until I found a magazine blowing across the road late one night, which brought it all back to the surface. Sometime after that I got a smartphone and slowly got sucked back in. I figured I just needed to try harder, pray more, read my Bible more, and then I could beat this thing. But I couldn't, not alone.

I talked to a counselor, joined a Pure Desire Seven Pillars group, a Captives Free group, and read lots of recovery books. These things helped but I wasn't able to gain any real sobriety or traction until I got involved with a counselor who really pushed me and the guys in our group to get real, dig deep, and be honest.

My wife and I did a ninety-day celibacy break, and I spent five months sleeping in the basement. This was not easy for me, but during this time I hit rock bottom, scared I had lost my wife, my best friend. I also had a setting free experience with God releasing me from a childhood grip of loneliness. (This happened during a group meeting while my wife was away for the weekend.) Prior to this, whenever my wife would leave, I would feel an intense sense of loneliness, which of course was a huge trigger for me. The feeling has never returned. God is enough.

Shortly after this I did a facilitated disclosure, followed by a polygraph (which I passed). I feel this was a huge turning point in my recovery as I got all the truth out, which in turn released the shame and guilt. I've done two of them now and they have been very helpful in building trust with my wife. I will do them whenever she needs it to feel safe. I lied and kept secrets for too long; it has been a gift for both of us.

I have celebrated two years of sobriety and am very pleased to say my marriage is improving every day.

Another key for me in moving forward has been alone time with God, doing listening prayer and spontaneous journaling, adapted from and taught by Mark Virkler. Through these times God has given me many powerful personal truths through pictures and inspired thoughts. I am still learning how to share feelings better, to be honest and transparent at all times with my wife and other brothers fighting this battle. I also continue to work on developing empathy for my wife.

I currently attend one of Mark Denison's weekly online Freedom Groups and help lead one in my church using Mark's 52-Week *Life Recovery Plan* material. These groups help me to stay accountable and challenged to keep moving forward. I am thankful and grateful to God for people like Mark Denison who have taught me, encouraged me, challenged me and so many others on this journey.

Vincent W.
Crystal Lake, Illinois
Sober 4 Years

One of the best and worst days of my life was August 20, 2020—my "day of discovery." My story is like so many others—a heart wounded in childhood birthed an addiction at a young age. I fought this addiction alone and in silence for twenty-five years, until my wife could no longer ignore the occasional images being sent to her by Covenant Eyes. While I had never paid a penny for pornography, I had consumed free pornography and erotic literature by the bucketfuls. I thought I had skirted Covenant Eyes by using Twitter and other social media to feed my addiction, but I was caught. And in that moment, my world crashed around me.

Thankfully, my wife sought restoration of our sixteen-year marriage from the first moment and helped in finding support for me. Finding lasting sobriety has been the greatest challenge and reward of my life. A dear friend and brother in this journey often says, "Sobriety is not the opposite of addiction; community is." I have found this to be undeniably true in every step of my recovery journey. What I could not do alone, God has empowered in me through a community of like-minded brothers walking this road beside me. This has been the "secret sauce" of my recovery.

Do I still read Scripture and seek a deeper relationship with Christ? Absolutely. But I've realized that attempts at isolated, white-knuckled, grit-it-out recovery are doomed to failure. Only by living out James 5:16 ("... *confess your sins to one another ... that you may be healed*") was I able to achieve long-term sobriety. Finally, I have to recognize that sobriety is only as secure as the next decision I make. Weeks and months of diligence can be undone in a moment of carelessness or selfishness. It is only through God's empowering that community and diligence have allowed me to be sober these past three and a half years, and by God's grace, I will be sober today.

Trent E.
Wesley Chapel, Florida
Sober 5 Years

I first found pornography around age thirteen. As a very insecure and fearful middle schooler, I found my drug. It didn't matter whether I was happy, sad, or scared, I had a coping mechanism for my fear and pain. I tried white-knuckling days and weeks at a time. I couldn't make it more than two weeks at a time before I had to binge on pornography and masturbation. I knew I had a problem. I knew something wasn't right; however, I denied the severity and powerlessness I had over lust. Most of my formative years were spent acting out or simply trying not to act out. At times I binged almost all night before having to go to work the next day. I was desperate for something to break this addiction. Nothing I tried lasted more than a few weeks.

I thought marriage would take care of this problem. It helped at first for about a year, until the first time my wife was staying overnight with some friends away on a trip. All alone with no one around I went right back to the comfort of my drug, pornography and masturbation. This began a downward trend in my marriage of time and time again my wife finding me acting out until she had enough. It was a counselor whom she was seeing at the time who suggested I am sex addict.

Me, the problem in our marriage? No way! Denial ran deep inside me. Completely delusional, I reluctantly went to my first SA meeting. Story after story, connection after connection, the delusion began to break down, and finally I was able to admit I am a sexaholic and that my life has become unmanageable. I got a sponsor and began the journey of recovery. I began working the steps, making daily phone calls, and living one day at a time. Meetings, phone calls, steps, professional CSAT therapy, meetings, phone calls, therapy, steps and eventually I was living back home. Soon, six months passed, and then a year. Then multiple years. I am so thankful for this new life I've been given. It's still one day at a time for me. I go to meetings, and I will keep working the steps. See you there.

Nick E.
Midland, Texas
Sober 5 Years

Growing up, I always knew my parents loved me, accepted me, and were proud of me. However, like all parents, they weren't perfect. They both worked and, as a result, I had a very long leash. I was often unsupervised, even from a young age. My parents knew little that was going on in my life, and I learned most life lessons on my own. Though they faithfully took me to church, they didn't teach me how to walk out my faith.

I was introduced to pornography at age five when a magazine blew across my front lawn. I was innocently playing when I saw a picture of naked bodies mixed together in a way I didn't understand. Even at that young age, something stirred inside of me knowing it was foreign and not right. But I was curious. Two years later, I had a similar experience, but this time brought it to my parents, hoping they would explain the images I didn't understand. But instead of discussing it and warning me against it, they simply threw it away. Like many parents, they didn't know how to handle that conversation, so they decided to say nothing at all.

Curiosity, however, took root and as a teenager I became steeped in porn and masturbation. I knew it was wrong but felt powerless to its draw. As I started dating, my mind was always sexually charged. My religious background kept me from crossing the intercourse line, but I pushed the physical boundaries with each new girlfriend.

It wasn't until college that I realized I needed a way out. I decided my freshman year to start reading the Bible and praying and making my faith my own. God revealed himself to me in tangible ways. I also discovered the power of relational accountability. My faith grew exponentially through authentic community. It wasn't long before I felt called to full-time ministry. Yet, despite this spiritual progress, porn still gripped my soul.

I met my wife in college and naively thought my sexual relationship with her would solve my addiction to porn. I was wrong and early on she discovered my sinful habit. I began working at a church, growing in my leadership and joined several accountability groups, but continued to struggle. I had stints of sobriety, but relapse was never that far away. Almost five years ago, I joined a different church staff and confessed my struggle to the wrong person. In a deeply painful fashion, the pastor exposed my sin to the entire church body and asked for my resignation. I was humiliated and hit rock bottom.

You can't give up a sin until you truly hate it, and now I hated it. That betrayal and humiliation was a turning point for me, and it is when I met Mark Denison. Together we worked through his *90-Day Recovery Guide* and after ninety days I was still sober. Ninety days turned into six months, then a year, and now I have over four years of sobriety under my belt.

Rarely does a day go by that I don't have a sexually perverse thought and sometimes those thoughts turn into a battle. But I continue to choose to not give in. The longer I am sober, the easier it gets—though it will always be hard. God is good, he is able and the freedom he offers is worth the work it takes to achieve it.

Jose O.
San Juan, Puerto Rico
Sober 4 Years

I spend many years of my life escaping the worst feelings and negative situations in my life by masturbating and watching porn, I didn't have a better coping mechanism than pornography. Most of that time I wasn't even able to identify what I was feeling or needing.

At the same time, I was believing the lie that these behaviors weren't hindering my relationship with Jesus, my ministry, my marriage, and my family. I wasn't aware of the damage that I was doing to my brain, and more importantly I was in denial of the damage that I was doing to my soul. I kept my behaviors hidden from everybody until one day, several years into marriage, my wife caught me. After my sin got exposed, I touched rock bottom, I realized that my addictive behaviors, far from filling me with satisfaction, had left me empty.

God in his amazing love allowed me to see my foolishness. The Lord also blessed me with Mark's ministry, with his 90-Day program, where he showed me what was really happening in my soul and brain. He provided me with amazing tools, literature, and with a community of people that works together to recover.

I repented with all my heart from my sin and decided to walk the way of recovery, understanding that it is more a journey than a destination. This was my first real attempt to be free, and I took it seriously. I became sober and started walking one day at a time, with the guidance of Mark for 90 days and weekly group meetings where I was (and still am) able to share and listen to the experiences of other men in recovery.

After three years of attending Mark's meetings weekly and working on my recovery every day by reading and listening to information that helps me to stay sober and using the right tools and healthy coping mechanisms that I have learned, I can say that my sobriety is intact for thirty-six months. And my relationship which Jesus is stronger than ever before. In the last three years I have become closer to Jesus than in the thirty years before starting this process.

I don't rely on my own ability to do the work of recovery, even when I know it is important to do it, but I have experienced God's amazing grace, and understanding of his deep love for me and how much he has forgiven me. I really want to honor him and for me that means sobriety. The negative feelings remain, the temptations remain, the challenging situations keep coming, but now they just draw me closer and closer to God.

I have learned and trained myself on how to use the urge for sinning to get closer to God because what it reveals is that I am feeling empty and that I need to get closer to God. Instead of giving in to temptation I use the tools that Mark gave and the principles he taught me to find refuge in my relationship with God.

I am not staying sober because I am afraid of losing my wife or my family or because I am afraid of being ashamed in front of others. I am staying sober and working daily on my recovery because I don't want to be away from God anymore.

NOTES

INTRODUCTION

1. "What Percentage of Alcoholics Recover?" New Directions for Women, February 7, 2021, https://www.newdirectionsforwomen. org/what-percentage-of-alcoholics-recover/.
2. Milton Magness, *Real Hope, True Freedom* (Las Vegas: Central Recovery Press, 2017), 234.
3. Stephanie Brown, *Treating the Alcoholic: A Developmental Model of Recovery* (New York: Wilen, 1985).

CHAPTER 1

1. "Beach House Rehab Center," https://beachhouserehabcenter.com.
2. G. Alan Marlatt and William H. George, "Relapse Prevention: Introduction and Model," *British Journal of Addiction* 79 (1984): 261–275.
3. Thomas H. Brandon, Jennifer Irvin Vidrine, and Erika B. Litvin, "Relapse and Relapse Prevention," *Annual Review of Clinical Psychology* 3 (April 27, 2007):257–284, http://doi.org/10.1146/ annurev.clinpsy.3.022806.091455.
4. Milton Magness and Marsha Means, *Real Hope, True Freedom* (Las Vegas, NV: Central Recovery Press, 2017), 231.
5. T. T. Gorski and M. Miller, *Counseling for Relapse Prevention* (Independence, MO: Herald House Press, 1982).
6. Brandon, Vidrine, and Litvin, "Relapse and Relapse Prevention."
7. Steven M. Melemis, "Relapse Prevention and the Five Rules of Recovery." *The Yale Journal of Biology and Medicine* 88, no, 3

(September 3, 2015): 325–332, https://www.ncbi.nlm.nih.gov/pmc/articles/PMC4553654.‗

8. Patrick Carnes, *Out of the Shadows* (Center City, MN: Hazelden Publishers, 1983), 1.

9. Marlatt and Jones, 261.

10. Ibid.

CHAPTER 2

1. Philip Tate, "The Value of Persistence in Addiction Recovery," SMART Recovery February 27, 2018), https://smartrecovery.org/blog/value-of-persistence-in-addiction-recovery.

2. Christopher Bergland. "The Neuroscience of Perseverance," *Psychology Today,* December 26, 2011, https://www.psychologytoday.com/us/blog/the-athletes-way/201112/the-neuroscience-perseverance.

3. Michael Gietzen, "My Top 10 Perseverance Quotes," https://www.linkedin.com/pulse/my-top-10-perseverance-quotes-michael-gietzen.

4. Michelle McQuaid, "Review of *Grit: The Power of Passion and Perseverance," Psychology Today,* July 20, 2016, https://www.psychologytoday.com/us/blog/from-functioning-to-flourishing/201607/grit-the-power-of-passion-and-perseverance.

5. "Life Recovery Groups," https://LifeRecoveryGroups.com.

6. Leah Marone, "Resilience: The Power to Overcome, Adjust, and Persevere," *Psychology Today,* June 27, 2021.

7. James Haggerty, "How to Maintain Recovery by Discovering Your Passion," September 16, 2021, https://addictionfreedomnow.com/blog/recovery-discover-passion/.

8. Patrick Carnes, *Facing the Shadows* (Carefree, AZ: Gentle Path Press, 2001), 202.

9. G. J. Connors, R. Longabaugh, and W. R. Miller, "Looking Forward and Back to Relapse: Implications for Research and Practice," *Addiction* (Abingdon England) 91 Suppl (1996): S191–S196.

10. R. Magnolis, A. Kirkpatrick, and B. Mooney. "A Retrospective Look at Long-Term Recovery: Clinicians Talk to Researchers," *Journal of Psychoactive Drugs* 32, no. 1 (2000): 117–125.

11. K. Humphreys, B. E. Mavis, and B. E. Stoffelmayr. "Are Twelve-Step Programs Appropriate for Disenfranchised Groups? Evidence from a Study of Post-treatment Mutual Help Involvement." *Prevention in Human Services* (1994). 165–179.

12. R. M. Costello. "Alcoholism Treatment and Evaluation," *International Journal of Addictions* 10 (1975): 857–867.

13. "Why Volunteering Should Be a Part of Your Recovery Process," The Good Life Treatment Center, May 5, 2023, Thegoodlifetreatmentcenter.com.

14. Nathaniel M. Lambert, Frank D. Fincham, and Tyler F. Stillman, "Gratitude and Depressive Symptoms: The Role of Positive Reframing and Positive Emotion," *Cognitive and Emotion*, 26, no. 4 (September 19, 2011).

15. M. Hennecke, T. Czikmantori, and V. Brandstatter. "Doing Despite Disliking: Self-Regulating Strategies in Everyday Aversive Activities," *European Journal of Personality* 33, no. 1 (2019): 104–128.

16. Kendra Cherry, "10 Ways to Build Resilience," *Very Well Mind,* October 6, 2022, verywellmind.com.

CHAPTER 3

1. John-Manuel Andriote, "You Need Good Habit. Here Are Six to Get You Started," *Psychology Today,* August 6, 2023, psychologytoday.com.

2. Timothy Pychyl, "The Power of Habit," *Psychology Today,* April 10, 2012, psychologytoday.com.

3. B. J. Everitt, "Neural and Psychological Mechanisms Underlying Compulsive Drug Seeking Habit and Drug Memories," *European Journal of Neuroscience* 40 (2014): 2163.

4. "Habits vs. Addiction," North Star Transitions, May 11, 2022, https://www.northstartransitions.com/post/habits-vs-addiction.

5. G. Alan Marlatt and William H. George, "Relapse Prevention: Introduction and Overview of the Model" *British Journal of Addiction* 79, no. 3 (December 1984): 261.

6. Judson Brewer, "Strategies for Keeping Our Prefrontal Cortex Online," *Psychiatric Times*, August 27, 2020, psychiatrictimes.com.

7. Diana Hill, "The Neuroscience of Habits," *Psychology Today*, October 2, 2012, Psychologytoday.com.

8. Patrick Carnes, *Facing the Shadow* (Carefree, AZ: Gentle Path Press, 2001), 302–303.

9. Steve Calechman, "How to Break a Bad Habit," *Harvard Health Publishing*, May 2, 2022, health.harvard.edu.

10. Pychyl, "Do To-Do Lists Work?" *Psychology Today,* February 26, 2020, psychologytoday.com.

11. Michelle P. Maidenberg, "18 Tips to Change Your Habits for Good," *Psychology Today*, February 15, 2023, psychologytoday.com.

12. Kristi DePaul, "What Does It Really Take to Build a New Habit?" *Harvard Business Review,* February 2, 2021, hbr.org.

13. Stephanie Parker, "The Science of Habits," July 15, 2021, knowablemagazine.org.

14. Aaron T. Beck, Fred D. Wright, Cory F. Newman, and Bruce S. Liese, "Cognitive Therapy of Substance Abuse" (New York: Guilford Press, 1993).

15. Https://applications.emro.who.int.

16. Sara Berg, "Massive Study Uncovers How Much Exercise Is Needed to Live Longer," January 26, 2023, ama-assn.org.

17. Max Alberhasky, "How Much Free Time Do You Need to Be Happy?" *Psychology Today*, March 13, 2023, psychologytoday.com.

18. Natalie Proulx, "How Do You Have Fun?" *New York Times*, December 9, 2022, nytimes.com.

19. Eric Suni and Abhinav Singh, "How Much Sleep Do You Need?" September 8, 2023, sleepfoundation.org.

20. Alice G. Walton, "Seven Ways Meditation Can Actually Change the Brain," February 8, 2015, forbes.com.

21. "Five Benefits of Journaling Daily," howlifeunfolds.com.

22. "How Being Organized Can Help Life in Recovery," January 7, 2021. https://www.amethystrecovery.org/how-being-organized-can-help-life-in-recovery/.

23. "Thank Your Way Out of Addiction: How Gratitude May Be the Key to Recovery," August 26, 2023, gatewayfoundation.org.

24. The River Source, "Why Giving Back Is Important in Addiction Recovery," February 26, 2018, theriversource.org.

25. Jon Bloom, "Six Benefits of Ordinary Daily Devotions," September 20, 2013, desiringgod.org.

CHAPTER 4

1. Marian Meli, "Escape the Comparison Trap," May 27, 2022, connectedfamilyservices.com.

2. Alicia Nortje, "Social Comparison Theory & 12 Real-Life Examples," April 29, 2020, positivepsychology.com.

3. Jeff Bilbro, "Dying to the Indispensable Self," February 6, 2023, christianitytoday.com.

4. Anne Peterson, "Finding Contentment by Killing Comparisons," January 31, 2011, christianitytoday.com.

5. Juliana Breines, "The Perils of Comparing Ourselves to Others," July 31, 2016, psychologytoday.com.

6. Jim Taylor, "15 Ways to Stop Self-Comparison," July 10, 2023, psychologytoday.com.

7. Suzanne Degges-White, "Quitting Social Media May Improve Your Mental Health," August 23, 2022, psychologytoday.com.

8. Eric Owens, "How to Stop Comparing Yourself to Others," January 24, 2023, antimaximalist.com.

9. Jaclyn Margolis, "Stop Demonizing the Idea of Comparing Yourself to Others," September 22, 2021, psychologytoday.com.

10. Hannah Rose, "Why You Should Stop Comparing Yourself to Everybody Else," September 4, 2019, psychologytoday.com.

CHAPTER 5

1. Brene Brown, "What Being Sober Has Meant to Me," May 31, 2019, https://Brenebrown.com-what-being-sober-has-meant-to-me.

2. Sarah Allen Benton, "Being Sober Versus Being in Recovery," May 17, 2010, https://psychologytoday.com/being-sober-verses-being.

3. Jonathan Strum, The Recovery Village, "The Difference Between Sobriety and Recovery," June 21, 2023, therecoveryvillage.com.

4. Terence T. Gorski and Merlene Miller, *Staying Sober: A Guide for Relapse Prevention* (Independence, MO: Independence Press, 1986), 87.

5. New Hope Health Care, "Challenges of Early Recovery," 2021, https://newhopehealthcare.com.

6. The Insight Program, "Early Sobriety: What to Expect in the First Few Months of Recovery," September 12, 2022, https://theinsightprogram.com/blog/early-sobriety.

7. Randy Smith, "One Week Sober: What do Expect in the Early Days of Recovery," November 24, 2021, https://monument.com/blog.

8. The Ranch at Dove Tree, "Ten Reasons to Stay Sober," March 15, 2011, https://theranchatdovetree.com/blog-ten-reasons.

9. Joseph Skrajewski, "What's the Difference Between Sobriety and Recovery?" July 15, 2019, Hazelden Betty Ford Foundation.

10. Angela Pugh, Addiction Unlimited Podcast, 2023, myrecoverytoolbox.com.

11. Carol DerSarkissian, "What to Know About Dry Drunk Syndrome," July 8, 2023, https://webmd.com/mental-health-dry-drunk.

12. William Berry, "They Are Sober, But Why Are They Jerks?" March 31, 2011, https://psychologytoday.com/they-are-sober-but-why.

13. Ben Brafman, "Just Being Sober Isn't Enough," September 1, 2014, Destination Hope.

14. Jonathan Strum, "The Difference Between Sobriety and Recovery," June 21, 2023, https://therecoveryvillage.com/the-difference-between-sobriety.

15. Ameer M., "Sober Is Not Well," sa.org.

16. John F. Kelly, "Recovery from Addiction," December 30, 2019, https://psychologytoday.com/recovery-from-addiction.

17. Warren Phillips, "The Importance of Support Systems in Addiction Recovery," July 21, 2023, https://lantanarecovery.com/the/importance.

18. The Insight Program, "Early Sobriety: What to Expect in the First Few Months of Recovery," September 12, 2022, theinsightprogram.com.

19. Dr. Maria Baretta, "Self-Care 101," May 27, 2018, https://www.psychologytoday.com/self-care.

20. Stephanie Wright, "Tips for Dealing with Triggers in Recovery," November 12, 2021, https://psychcentral.com/addiction.

21. Ibid.

22. "Do I Need Recovery Meetings to Stay Sober?" The Cabin, https://thecabinchiangmai.com.

CHAPTER 6

1. C. Ellison, "Spiritual Well-Being: Conceptualization and Measurement," *Journal of Psychology and Theology* 11 (1983): 330–340.

2. Renewal Lodge, "Why Addiction Recovery Has a Spiritual Component," December 30, 2019, https://renewallodge.com/why-addiction-recovery-has-a-spiritual.

3. J. Scott Tonigan, Kristina N. Rynes, and Barbara S. McCrady, "Spirituality as a Change Mechanism in 12-Step Programs: A Replication, Extension, and Refinement," *Substance Use & Misuse* 48, no. 12 (September 2013): 1161–1173, doi:10.3109/10826084.2013.808540.

4. Carly Benson, "How Addiction and Spirituality Go Hand-in-Hand," Orlando Recovery Center, last modified April 26, 2024, https://www.orlandorecovery.com/resources/addiction-spirituality-go-hand-hand-backup/.

5. Brian J. Grim and Melissa E. Grim, "Belief, Behavior, and Belonging: How Faith Is Indispensable in Preventing and Recovering from Substance Abuse" (July 29, 2019), PubMed Central, doi:10.1007/s10943-019-00876-w.

6. Ibid.

7. Joseph Nowinski, "The Role of Spirituality in Addiction Recovery," January 13, 2020, https://psychologytoday.com/the-role-of-spirituality.

8. *Alcohol Anonymous*, 3rd ed. (New York: Alcoholics Anonymous World Services, 1976), 64.

9. Thomas G. Plante, "Religious Faith and Spirituality May Help People Recover from Substance Abuse," Annual Convention of APA, August 4, 2000, apa.org.

10. Megan Hull, "Five Benefits of Spirituality in Recovery," May 6, 2022, The Recovery Village, https://therecoveryvillage.com.

11. Adi Jaffe, "Seven Spiritual Elements Critical for Addiction Recovery," May 4, 2018, psychologytoday.com.

12. M. Morjaria and Jim Orford, "The Role of Religion and Spirituality in Recovery from Drink Problems: A Qualitative Study of Alcoholics Anonymous Members," *Addiction Research and Theory* 10, no. 3 (January 1, 2002): 225–256.

13. Marianne J. Brady, Amy H. Peterman, George Fitchett, May Mo, and David Cella, "A Case for Including Spirituality in Quality of Life Measurement in Oncology," *Psycho-Oncology* 8, no. 5 (September–October 1999): 417–428, doi:10.1002/(sici)1099-1611(199909/10)8:5<417:aid-pon398>3.0.co;2-4.

14. Larry Culliford, "Spirituality and Clinical Care: Spiritual Values and Skills Are Increasingly Recognized as Necessary Aspects of Clinical Care," *British Medical Journal* 325, no. 7378 (December 21, 2022): 1434–1435 (2002), bmj.com.

15. B. Riley, R. Perna, D. Tate, M. Forchheimer, C. Anderson, and G. Luera, "Types of Spiritual Well-Being," *Archives of Physical and Medical Rehabilitation* 79, no. 3 (March 1998): 258–264, doi: 10.1016/s0003-9993(98)90004-1.

16. Morjaria, et al.

17. Joseph Nowinski, "The Role of Spirituality in Addiction Recovery," January 13, 2020, www.josephnowinski.com.

18. G. Christo and C. Franey. "Drug Users' Spiritual Beliefs, Locus of Control and the Disease Concept in Relation to Narcotics Anonymous Attendance and Six-Month Outcomes," *Drug and Alcohol Dependence* 38 no. 1 (April 1, 1995): 51–56, https://doi.org/10.1016/0376-8716(95)01103-6.

19. Lance Dodes, "Spirituality and Addiction" *Psychology Today*, March 15, 2015. https://psychologytoday.com/spirituality-and-addiction.

20. Dustin A. Pardini, Thomas G. Plante, Allen Sherman, and Jamie E. Stump, "Religious Faith and Spirituality in Substance Abuse Recovery: Determining the Mental Health Benefits," *Journal of Substance Abuse Treatment* 19, no. 4 (December 2000): 347–354.

CHAPTER 7

1. *Alcoholics Anonymous*, AA "Big Book" (New York: Alcohol Anonymous World Services, 1939), 106. https://www.aa.org.en_step12.

2. Renee W., "A Secret Weapon in Helping Others," November 11, 2020, Camino Recovery, UK: 441282953399, caminorecovery.com.

3. Marianna Pogosyan, "In Helping Others, You Help Yourself," May 30, 2018, psychologytoday.com.

4. "The Benefits of Addicts Helping Addicts," March 4, 2019, reviewed by Isaac Alexis, https://www.rehabcenter.net/addicts-helping-addicts/.

5. Maria E. Pagano, William L. White, John F. Kelly, Robert L. Stout, Rebecca R. Carter, and J. Scott Tonigan, "The 10-Year Course of AA Participation and Long-Term Outcomes: A Follow-up Study of Outpatient Subjects in Project MATCH," January 1, 2014, doi:10.1080/08897077.2012.691450.

6. "The Benefits of Addicts Helping Addicts."

7. Soyoung Q. Park, Thorsten Kahnt, Azade Dogan, Sabrina Strang, Ernst Fehr, and Philippe N. Tabler, "A Neural Link between Generosity and Happiness, *Nature Communications* 8, no. 15964 (July 11, 2017), https://www.nature.com/articles/ncomms15964.

8. N. Weinstein, and R. M. Ryan, "When Helping Helps: Autonomous Motivation for Prosocial Behavior and Its Influence on Well-being for the Helper and Recipient." *Journal of Personality and Social Psychology* 98, no. 2 (2010): 222.

9. Mark Rowland, "What Are the Health Benefits of Kindness?" Mental Health Foundation, https://mentalhealth.org.uk.

10. "The Benefits of Addicts Helping Addicts."

11. Mark Rowland, "What Are the Health Benefits of Kindness?"

12. N. Weinstein and R. M. Ryan, "When Helping Helps."

13. Emily Ansell, "Helping Others Dampens the Effects of Everyday Stress," *Journal of the Association for Psychological Science*, December 14, 2015, psychologicalscience.org.

14. "The Benefits of Addicts Helping Addicts."

15. Tasha Cain, "Study Says the Average American Hasn't Made a New Friend in Half a Decade," May 12, 2019, https://www.wtsp.com.

16. "The Benefits of Addicts Helping Addicts."

17. David Susman, "A Dozen Ways You Can Support Someone in Recovery," June 1, 2017, psychologytoday.com.

18. Ibid.

19. "The Benefits of Addicts Helping Addicts."

20. Anne Frank, https://www.brainyquotes.com.annefrank.

21. Jill Suttie, "Can Helping Others Keep You Sober?" *Greater Good Magazine*, April 14, 2016, https://greatergood.berkely.edu/can-helping-others-keep-you-sober.

CHAPTER 8

1. Steve Sussman, Nadra Lisha, and Mark Griffiths. "Prevalence of the Addictions: A Problem of the Majority of the Minority?" *Evaluation & the Health Professions* 34, no. 1 (September 27, 2010): 3–56, https://doi.org/10.1177/0163278710380124.

2. Sussman, Lisha, and Griffiths, "Prevalence of the Addictions."

3. David Hodgins, "Increase and Decrease of Other Substance Use During Recovery," *Psychology of Addictive Behaviors* 31, no. 6 (September 2017): 727–734, https://www.researchgate.net/publication/.

4. Carlos Blanco, Mayumi Okuda, Shuai Wang, Shang-Min Liu, and Mark Olfson, "Testing the Drug Substitution-Switching Addictions Hypothesis. *JAMA Psychiatry* 71, no. 11 (November 7, 2014): 1246–1253, https://www.ncbi.nlm.nih.gov/pubmed/25208305.

5. Trey Dyer, "Cross Addiction" (February 26, 2020), https://www.drugrehab.com/addiction/cross-addictions/.

6. Steve Sussman and David Black, "Substitute Addiction: A Concern for Researchers and Practitioners," *Journal of Drug Education* 38, no. 2 (February 2008): 167–180. 10.2190/DE.38.2.e.

7. "Ten Most Common Addictions," Addiction Center, htttps://www.addictioncenter.com/addiction/10-most-common-addictions/.

8. "Substituting One Addiction for Another," Gateway Foundation, https://www.gatewayfoundation.org/addiction-blog/substitute-addictions.

9. Shehan Karunaratne, "Are You Substituting One Addiction for Another?" Eudaimonia Recovery Homes, September 13, 2017, https://eudaimoniahomes.com/substituting-one-addiction-another/.

10. Brittany Oliver, "Substituting One Addiction for Another: Cross Addictions in Recovery," Nexus Recovery, July 17, 2019, https://nexusrecoveryservices.com/blog/cross-addictions-in-recovery/.

11. Shahram Heshmat, "10 Patterns of Addictive Behavior," February 22, 2017, psychologytoday.com.

12. Lance Dodes, "The Psychology of Addiction," October 31, 2010, psychologytoday.com.

13. "Addictive Personalities: When One Addiction Is Replaced by Another," Present Moments Recovery, May 16, 2022, https://www.presentmomentsrecovery.com/addictive-personalities.

14. Richard J. Herrnstein and Drazen Prelec, "Melioration: A Theory of Distributed Choice" *The Journal of Economic Perspectives* 5, no. 3 (Summer 1991): 137–156, http://links.jstor.org/sici?sici=0895-3309%28199122%295%3A3%3C137%.

15. "Ways to Not Trade One Addiction for Another," Cliffside Malibu, https://www.cliffsidemalibu.com/blog/4-ways-to-not-trade.

16. Ibid.

17. Brittany Oliver, "Preventing Cross Addictions," Nexus Recovery, July 17, 2019, https://nexusrecoveryservices.com/blog/cross-addictions-in-recovery/.

18. "How to Prevent Cross-Addiction," in *Principles of Drug Addiction Treatment: A Research-Based Guide,* 3rd ed., https://www.drugabuse.gov/publications/principles.

19. Ibid.

20. "What Is Sex Addiction?" https://psychcentral.com/lib/what-is-sexual-addiction/.

21. Randi J. Heisler, "Promote Lasting Recovery by Replacing Addiction with Meaningful and Relaxing Activities," St. Gregory Recovery Center, October 15, 2019, https://stgregoryctr.com/replacing-addiction-with-meaningful-activities/.

CHAPTER 9

1. C. S. Lewis, *Mere Christianity* (San Francisco: Harper Press, 1980), 121–122.
2. Steven M. Melemis, "Relapse Prevention and the Five Rules of Recovery."
3. Shernide Delva, "The Dangers of Overconfidence in Addiction Recovery," Palm Partners Recovery Center, https://palmpartners.com/the-dangers-of-overconfidence/.
4. Randi Gunther, "How Self-Centered Pride Destroys Intimacy," January 31, 2020, https://www.psychologytoday.com/intl/blog/how-self-centered-pride/.
5. Shernide Delva, "The Dangers of Overconfidence."
6. John Amodeo, "Why Pride Is Nothing to Be Proud Of," June 6, 2015, psychologytoday.com.
7. Andrew Murray, "Why Humility Matters," Moment by Moment, momentbymoment.com.
8. "The Dangers of Pride in Recovery" American Addiction Centers, May 31, 2022, alcoholrehab.com.
9. Shernide Delva, "The Dangers of Overconfidence."
10. St. Augustine, brainyquote.com.
11. Dimitrios Tsatiris, "The Underappreciated Power of Humility," February 4, 2023, pshchologytoday.com.
12. J. Crocker and L. E. Park, "The Costly Pursuit of Self-Esteem," *Psychological Bulletin*, 130, no. 3, (2004): 392–414.
13. Alcoholics Anonymous, https://alcohol.org/step-7/.
14. John Amondeo, "Why Pride Is Nothing to Be Proud Of," June 6, 2015, psychologytoday.com.

15. "Overcoming the Dangers of Pride in Addiction Recovery Through Step 7," 12Step.com.

16. Patrick Carnes, *Facing the Shadows* (Carefree, AZ: Gentle Path Press, 2015), 125.

17. Henry Ford, "ForbesQuotes," https://www.forbes.com/quotes/4089/.

18. Randi Gunther, "How Self-Centered Pride Destroys Intimacy," January 31, 2020, psychologytoday.com.

CHAPTER 10

1. Terry Hurley, "The Importance of the 12 Steps in Addiction Recovery," English Mountain Recovery, September 19, 2021, http://englishmountain.com/importance-12-steps-addiction.

2. Alcoholics Anonymous, "5 Benefits to Gain from 12-Step AA Meetings," September 11, 2023, alcoholicsanonymous.com.

3. Mandy Erickson, "Alcoholics Anonymous Most Effective Path to Alcohol Abstinence," March 11, 2020, med.stanford.edu.

4. Lyle R. Fried, "What Is Success in Recovery?" The Shores Treatment and Recovery, March 30, 2018, http://theshoresrecovery.com/measuring-success-in-recovery/.

5. April Smith, "To Count or Not to Count? The Pros and Cons of Counting Sobriety Days," May 31, 2022, americanaddictioncenters.com.

6. Friendly House, Los Angeles, CA, https://friendlyhousela.org/sobriety-milestones/.

7. April Smith, "Count or Not to Count."

8. Egon Hagen, "One-Year Sobriety Improves Satisfaction with Life," *Journal of Substance Abuse Treatment* 76 (May 2017): 81–87, 10.1016/j.jsat.2017.01.016.

9. Fried, "What Is Success in Recovery?"

10. Sherry Gaba, "Financial Responsibility for Addicts and Their Partners," December 12, 2019, psychologytoday.com.

11. Fried, "What Is Success in Recovery?"

12. Karen Dodge, Barbara Krantz, and Paul J. Kenny, "How Can We Begin to Measure Recovery?" *Substance Abuse Treatment, Prevention, and Policy* 5, no. 31 (December 7, 2010), https://pubmed.ncbi.nlm.nih.gov/how-can-we-begin-to-measure-recovery/.

13. "Adding Exercise into Treatment May Reduce Substance Use," CNN, April 26, 2023, https://www.cnn.com/health/physical/.

14. Lantie Jorandby, "The 'Aha!' Moment in Addiction Treatment," June 7, 2022, *Psychology Today*, www.psychologytoday.com/us/blog/use-your-brain/202206/the-aha-moment-in-addiction-treatment.

15. Mark A. Smith and Wendy J. Lynch, "Exercise as a Potential Treatment for Drug Abuse," *Frontiers in Psychiatry* 2 (January 11, 2012), https://doi.org/10.3389/fpsyt.2011.00082.

16. Martin Preston, "The 5 Benefits of Exercise in Addiction Recovery," Delamere.com.

17. Fried "What Is Success in Recovery?"Peg O'Connor, "Addiction and Friendship," February 14, 2014, psychologytoday.com.

18. Kelly E. Green, "Relationship Recovery Is Critical for Addiction Recovery," June 30, 2021, psychologytoday.com.

19. Kristen Fuller, "Why Do We Need Friends? Six Benefits of Healthy Friendships," October 2, 2017, psychologytoday.com.

20. Johann Hari, "The Science Behind the Importance of Love and Connection in Recovery," October 19, 2017, https://www.beachhouserehabcenter.com/the-science-behind/.

21. "The Importance of Family Support During Recovery," Ashley Recovery, https://www.ashleytreatment.org/rehab-blog/family-support-during-recovery/.

22. Thomas G. Plante, "Religious Faith and Spirituality May Help People Recover from Substance Abuse." (2000), American Psychological Association, https://apa.org/news/press/releases/2000/08/faith.

23. Ibid.

24. Olivia Gillespie, "Christ Values that Support Recovery" (October 11, 2023), St. Gregory Recovery Center, stgregoryctr.com.

25. Friendly House, https://friendlyhousela.org/sobriety-milestones/.

26. Jo Neale, Daria Panebianco, Emily Finch, John Marsden, et al, "Emerging Consensus on Measuring Addiction Recovery: Findings from a Multi-stakeholder Consultation Exercise. *Drugs: Education, Prevention and Policy,* 23, no. 1 (November 2015): 1–10, 10.3109/09687637.2015.1100587.

CHAPTER 11

1. Robert Weiss, "The Opposite of Addiction Is Connection," September 30, 2015, *Psychology Today*, https://www.psychologytoday.com/us/blog/love-and-sex-in-the-digital-age/201509/the-opposite-addiction-is-connection.

2. Glenn C. Altschuler, "The Surprising Benefits of Social Connections," January 27, 2020, *Psychology Today*, https://www.psychologytoday.com/us/blog/is-america/202001/the-surprising-benefits-social-connections.

3. Dennis Swanberg, *The Man Code* (Nashville: Hatchett Books, 2009).

4. David Mathis, "Time Alone for God," August 6, 2020, desiringgod.org.

5. Bobby Jamieson, "The Man of God You Could Become," February 5, 2022, desiringgod.org.

6. Charlie Riggs, "Four Ways to Connect with God," August 18, 2020, https://billygraham.org.stories/.

7. "Seven Ways to Pray," Navigators, navigators.org.

8. P. J. Howland, "Personal Growth," August 31, 2022, leaders.com.

9. "The Importance of Accountability," Cedarville University, September 12, 2022, https://www.cedarville.edu/-/media/Files/PDF/Student-Life-Programs/CU-Lead-301/.

10. Michael Hyatt, "The Leadership Strategy of Jesus," May 27, 2020, www.https://michaelhyatt.com/the-leadership-strategy-of-Jesus.

11. Peter Bregman, "The Right Way to Hold People Accountable," January 20, 2016, *Psychology Today*, https://www.psychologytoday. com/us/blog/how-we-work/201601/the-right-way-to-hold-people-accountable.

12. Philip J. Spener, *Pia Desideria*, trans. Theodore G. Tappert (Philadelphia: Fortress Press, 1964).

13. Bruce Hindmarsh, "History of Small Groups," February 11, 2022, desiringgod.org.

14. "14 Benefits of Addiction Support Groups," Addictions.com, June 25, 2021, https://www.addictions.com/blog/14-benefits-of-addiction-support-groups/.

15. Rick Warren, "Why Are Small Groups So Important?" October 5, 2021, pastors.com.

16. Kelly E. Green, "Relationship Recovery Is Critical for Addiction Recovery," June 30, 2021, https://www.psychologytoday.com/us/blog/addiction-and-relationships/202106/relationship-recovery-is-critical-addiction-recovery.

17. Harold Koenig, "The Health Benefits of Congregational Life," *Psychology Today*, April 26, 2019, https://www.psychologytoday. com/us/blog/the-power-community/201904/the-health-benefits-congregational-life.

18. Kevin Makins, "11 Incredible Benefits of Going to Church," https://hebrews12endurance.com/benefits-of-going-to-church/.

19. Rick Warren, "Why Having a Church Family Matters," September 2, 2022, pastorrick.com.

20. Bill Bright, "Creating a Personal Strategy to Fulfill Great Commission," https://www.cru.org/train-and-grow/.

CHAPTER 12

1. Steven Melemis, "Relapse Prevention and the Five Rules of Recovery."

2. Jay Westbrook, "The Top 5 Reasons You Should Keep Going to 12-Step Meetings," June 8, 2022, recovery.org.

3. Tim Stoddart, "The Importance of Meetings," April 16, 2013, sobernation.com.

4. Milton Magness and Marsha Means, *Real Hope, True Freedom* (Carefree, AZ: Gentle Path Press 2017), 76.

5. Dillon McClernon, "The Benefits and Limitations of 12-Step Programs for Addiction," Recoverycentersofamerica.com.

6. Brandon Duncan, "Benefits of Structure in Addiction Recovery," September 7, 2017, https://stepworks.com.3-big-benefits/.

7. Rhett Power, "Accountability Groups: The Support You need to Succeed," https://forbes.com/accountability-groups/.

8. Sean Galla, "Accountability Group: Everything You Need to Know," https://www.mensgroups.com/accountability-group/.

9. Dillon McClernon. "The Benefits and Limitations."

10. Hanley Center, "What Are the Advantages of 12-Step Programs?" February 28, 2019, hanleycenter.org.

11. Alcoholics Anonymous, alcoholicsanonymous.com.

12. Michael Formica, "Addiction's Blind Spot," May 15, 2012, psychologytoday.com.

13. Granite Recovery Centers, Salem, NH, April 23, 2011, graniterecoverycenters.com.

14. Shernide Delva, "The Dangers of Overconfidence."

15. Tyler Woods, "Why Holding onto Secrets Can Be So Harmful," September 17, 2021, psychologytoday.com.

16. Ruben Castaneda, "How Your Secrets Can Damage and Maybe Even Kill You," June 26, 2017, health.usnews.com.

17. Josh Gressel, "Truth and Addiction Cannot Coexist," April 4, 2021, psychologytoday.com.

18. Carnes, *Facing the Shadows*, 13.

19. M. L. Slepian, J. S. Chun, and M. F. Mason, "The Experience of Secrecy" *Journal of Personality and Social Psychology*, 113, no. 1, (2017): 1–33.

20. Darlene Lancer, "How Secrets and Lies Destroy Relationships," January 31, 2018, psychologytoday.com.

21. Rachel Miller, "Defeating Defensiveness," May 7, 2021, psychologytoday.com.

22. Seth Meyers, "Why Some People Are So Defensive," September 28, 2021, psychologytoday.com.

23. "Gaslighting," *Psychology Today*, https://www.psychologytoday.com/us/basics/gaslighting.

24. Bruce Tulgan, "Attitude Matters, a Lot," March 10, 2021, psychologytoday.com.

25. Steven Stosny, "What's Wrong with Criticism?" April 18, 2014, psychologytoday.com.

26. Steven Berglas, "Why Are Some People So Critical?" March 6, 2014, *Harvard Business Review*, hbr.org.

27. Lauren Edwards-Fowle, "Four Truths about People Who Are Overly Critical of Others," *Learning Mind*, 2021, learningmind.com.

28. John Piper, "How Can I Resist a Critical Spirit?" December 6, 2021, desiringGod.org.

CONCLUSION

1.   Patrick Carnes, *Out of the Shadows*, 195.
2.   Tal Ben-Shahar, verywellmind.com.
3.   Brainyquote.com.

RESOURCES FROM THERE'S STILL HOPE

Books

Porn in the Pew

Jesus & the 12 Steps

Recovery Rules

90-Day Recovery Guide

12-Week Partner Recovery Workbook

Broken Vessels

365 Days to Sexual Purity

Life Recovery Plan

Couples Recovery Guide

Porn-Free in 40 Days

52 Exercises

Other Resources

Weekly Freedom Groups for Men

Weekly Recovery Groups for Women

Weekly Couples Groups

Daily Recovery Minute Devotional (email)

Daily Recovery Rule (text)

Speaking at Churches and Conferences

Contact Information

Mark@TheresStillHope.org

Beth@TheresStillHope.org

www.ingramcontent.com/pod-product-compliance
Lightning Source LLC
Chambersburg PA
CBHW060011100426
42740CB00010B/1455